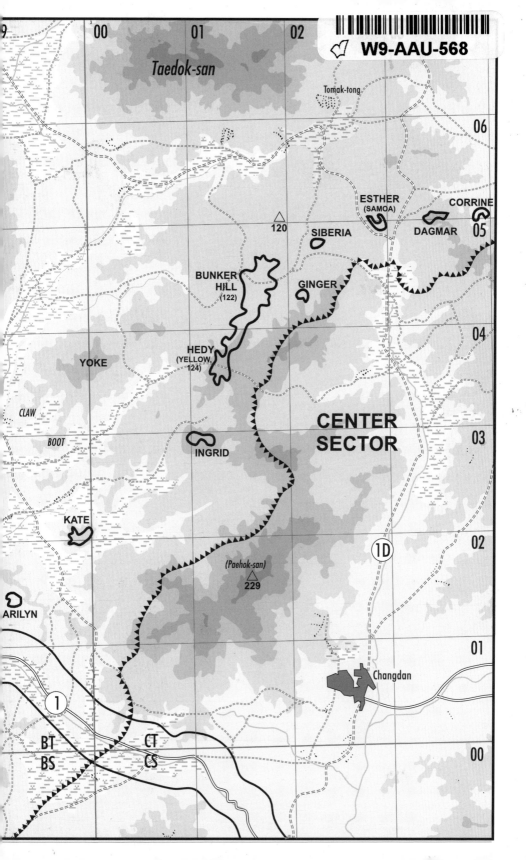

Taedok-san

Tomak-tong

ESTHER
(SAMOA)

CORRINE

SIBERIA

DAGMAR

120

BUNKER
HILL
(122)

GINGER

HEDY
(YELLOW,
124)

YOKE

CENTER
SECTOR

CLAW

BOOT

INGRID

1D

KATE

(Paehok-san)
229

ARILYN

Changdan

1

BT
BS

CT
CS

THE
OUTPOST
WAR

SELECTED KOREAN WAR TITLES
FROM BRASSEY'S

The Korean War: The Story and Photographs
by Donald M. Goldstein and Harry J. Maihafer

Odd Man Out: Truman, Stalin, Mao, and the Origins
of the Korean War
by Richard C. Thornton

From Pusan to Panmunjom: Wartime Memoirs
of the Republic of Korea's First Four-Star General
by Gen. Paik Sun Yup

This Kind of War: The Classic Korean War
History—50th Anniversary Edition
by T. R. Fehrenbach

THE OUTPOST WAR

U.S. MARINES IN KOREA
VOLUME I: 1952

BY LEE BALLENGER
FOREWORD BY ALLAN R. MILLETT

BRASSEY'S
WASHINGTON, D.C.

Library of Congress Cataloging-in-Publication Data

Lee, Ballenger.
    The outpost war : the U.S. Marines in Korea, 1952 / Lee Ballenger.—1st ed.
      p. cm.
    Includes bibliographical references and index.
    ISBN 1-57488-241-4 (alk. paper)
    1. Korean War, 1950–1953—Regimental histories—United
States. 2. United States. Marine Corps. Division, 1st—History. I. Title.

DS919 .L44 2000
951.904'242—dc21

                                      99-086415

ISBN 1-57488-241-4 (alk. paper)

Printed in the United States of America on acid-free paper that meets the American National Standards Institute Z39-48 Standard.

Brassey's
22841 Quicksilver Drive
Dulles, Virginia 20166

First Edition

10 9 8 7 6 5 4 3 2 1

THE OLD MAN

The old man knelt and bowed his head.
Beside the torn and silent dead,
While battle smoke still lingered where
He touched the bloody matted hair.
A shattered helmet lay beside
The fallen fighter where he'd died
And on that littered battlefield
The old man's senses churned and reeled.
So many times he'd seen before
This senseless legacy of war
Where pain and blood and lonely death
Were common as a sudden breath.
He prayed that he might live to see
His native land where men were free
So he could tell the brutal story
Of men who died in pride and glory.
He did not pray for endless years
To calm his heart or dry his tears,
Just long enough for him to note
When he'd be old enough to vote.

—R. A. Gannon

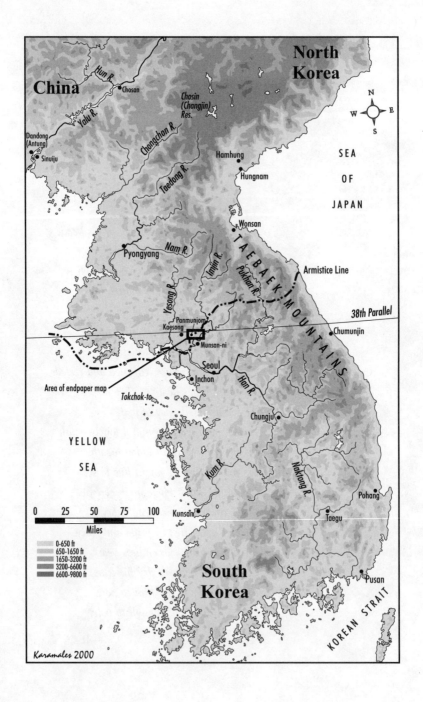

China

North
Korea

Hun R.

• Chosan

Chosin
(Changjin)
Res.

Yalu R.

Chongchon R.

Dandong
(Antung)

• Sinuiju

Taedong R.

Hamhung •

Hungnam •

SEA

OF

JAPAN

Wonsan •

Pyongyang •

Nam R.

Yesong R.

Imjin R.

Pukhan R.

T A E B A E K   M O U N T A I N S

Armistice Line

38th Parallel

Panmunjom •
Kaesong •

• Munsan-ni

Chumunjin •

Area of endpaper map

Seoul •

• Inchon

Han R.

Tokchok-to

Chungju •

YELLOW

SEA

Kum R.

Naktong R.

0   25   50   75   100

Miles

Pohang •

Kunsan •

Taegu •

0-650 ft
650-1650 ft
1650-3200 ft
3200-6600 ft
6600-9800 ft

South
Korea

Pusan •

K O R E A N   S T R A I T

Karamales 2000

CONTENTS

MAPS

FOREWORD

In March 1952, the 1st Marine Division received orders from Lt. Gen. James A. Van Fleet, commander of the U.S. Eighth Army, to leave the division's fortified perches along the western extension of the Taebaek Mountain range in east-central Korea. It would occupy another divisional sector in western Korea. Having won a well-deserved reputation for combat effectiveness during the first eighteen months of the Korean War, the Marines now paid the penalty for that reputation by moving to a critical part of the Jamestown Line, the Eighth Army's Main Line of Resistance (MLR). The 1st Marine Division assumed responsibility for a 35-mile stretch of the MLR that started on the north bank of the Imjin River and ran through a series of ridges and small streams until it reached the western bank of the Samichon River, a tributary of the Imjin-gang. The 1st Marine Division's move to western Korea was only part of Operation Mixmaster, Van Fleet's plan to shift units before he—or the Chinese generals who commanded the Chinese People's Volunteers Force (Renmin Zhiyuanjun)—could take advantage of the improving weather and start offensive operations.

Van Fleet had done the Marines no favors, although the immediate impression held by the Marines was that the new sector would be a better sector to defend than the rugged, cold Korean mountains they had left. The announced reason for the exchange of sectors was that Van Fleet and his superior, Gen. Matthew B. Ridgway, commanding general of United Nations Command (UNC) and all American armed forces in the Far East Command (FECOM), wanted the Republic of South Korea (ROK) Army to hold the mountain areas where its lighter supply requirements would relieve some of Eighth Army's logistical problems. The ROK Army would also assume the mission of fighting its Communist counterpart, the Korean People's Army (Chosun Inmingun). There was more to the shift of divisions than ensuring more Korean fratricide. Van Fleet and Ridgway had little confidence that the

UNC–Communist armistice negotiations, started in July 1951, would produce any sort of final agreement unless UNC increased its military pressure on the Communists. The 1st Marine Division had been selected to play a big role in any future UNC offensive operations, and it would ensure that the Chinese would not succeed if they started an offensive of equal magnitude.

The most obvious reason to place the 1st Marine Division in the Imjin-Samichon sector of the Jamestown Line was to defend Seoul and the administrative areas around the city of Munsan-ni. The UNC delegation sortieed from Munsan-ni to the armistice talks then going on at Panmunjom, an obscure village roughly 1–2 miles from the most advanced UNC positions and five miles from the MLR. Should any incident occur at Panmunjom or the should Communists block the road into the negotiating site, the Marines would be a perfect fast-reaction force. They had their own helicopters and close air support fighter-bombers. Marine fixed-wing aircraft fell under the operational control of the U.S. Fifth Air Force, commanded by an Air Force general and committed to an interdiction bombing campaign on North Korea, but the 1st Marine Aircraft Wing's observation squadron (VMO-1) and one transport helicopter squadron (HMR-161) moved into an expeditionary airfield designated X-83 and located southeast of Munsan-ni. Although most of the 1st Marine Aircraft Wing remained at the K-3 airfield near Pohang on the east coast, Marine Aircraft Group 12 (two squadrons of fighter-bombers and service units) set up operations at the K-6 airfield near Pyongtaek on the west coast. The group could reach the front in minutes, if necessary, guided and controlled by the Marine air-ground close air support system that was envied by the Army and condemned by the U.S. Air Force.

Another factor in the change of sector involved interallied relations. During the fighting in 1950 and 1951, Great Britain had sent two independent brigade groups (three infantry battalions each with reinforcing armor, artillery, and service units) to Korea where they had performed with great professionalism and courage. When a third brigade from Canada arrived in mid-1951, the British argued that all their units ("their" including an Australian infantry battalion, a New Zealand artillery battalion, an Indian hospital and ambulance unit, and the Canadian infantry battalion already in Korea) be reconstituted as the British Commonwealth Division, formally established in August 1951. In October 1951, the Commonwealth Division fought its way to the Jamestown Line during Operation Commando. As the best division in the U.S. I Corps, the Commonwealth Division still held its advanced positions, both flanks tenuously anchored on the Imjin-gang, in the spring of 1952. Maj. Gen. A. J. H. Cassels, a stubborn Scot, was very particular about what units he had on his flanks if his division was to defend the Jamestown Line. He had little confidence in the soldierly practices of the U.S. Army, from its generalship to its lax practices of fortifications, security, and intelligence gathering and assessment. Cassels actually preferred to have the 1st ROK Division on his flank rather than a U.S. Army division. Under British pressure, Van Fleet retained the 1st ROK Division in the I Corps, but shifted it to a sector on the right of the Commonwealth Division. The 1st Marine Division went into the sector of the 1st ROK Division when the Marines went west in 1952. For the remainder of the war, the Commonwealth Division and the 1st Marine Division operated with mutual respect to hold their portion of the Jamestown Line. Both divisions believed they were much better off without Army divisions on their flanks, and both worked well with the ROK units within the U.S. I Corps.

In addition to their defensive mission—to control the key terrain north of the Imjin-gang—the 1st Marine Division and the Commonwealth Division played a key role in General Van Fleet's Operation (Op) Plan 8-52 (October 1952) after Gen. Mark W. Clark replaced Ridgway. This plan assumed that the Truman administration would become convinced that the armistice negotiations were simply a Communist stalling tactic and would approve a strategic initiative with an amphibious landing at Wonsan and an overland offensive by the Eighth Army in the east-central and eastern corridors that led to Wonsan. The 1st Marine Division played an essential role in Op Plan 8-52 in two ways. First, as part of I Corps, it had to ensure that any Chinese preemptive attack toward Seoul would be stopped well north of the Imjin-gang. Second, the division had to be prepared for a hasty embarkation through the Seoul-Inchon port and logistics center in order to be the spearhead of the UNC landing force, just as it had been at Inchon in September 1950. The move to the western front reunited the Marine division with two of its essential amphibious units that it had not needed in central Korea's mountains, the 1st Armored Amphibian Battalion and the 1st Amphibian Tractor Battalion, as well as service and shore party elements stationed in the Seoul-Inchon area. Even if Op Plan 8-52 did not materialize, the Marine division would be available for more limited landings on the Onjin peninsula and the coast of Hwanghae Province, where a nasty little guer-rilla war had been raging between the Communists and anti-Communist Korean partisans.

Much of this big picture did not reach the Marines in 1952, and many of them still do not realize that the 1st Marine Division had changed sectors for sound reasons. In addition to the contingency plan-ning that influenced the change of sector, the 1st Marine Division held irresistible attractions to Army corps and field army commanders. Unlike its Army counterparts, the 1st Marine Division stayed up to strength and did so with well-trained, ardent young junior officers and enlisted men sent to Korea from Marine bases in the United States. The Marines had no units in Germany or mobilized National Guard divi-sions to draw off quality personnel. A full-strength Marine division, structured for air-ground operations and amphibious assaults, numbered around twenty-five thousand officers and men, compared with an Army infantry division whose strength was around nineteen thousand.

For reasons that mystified even President-elect and retired general Dwight D. Eisenhower, the Army could not keep its combat divisions at full strength, and it adopted the expedient of using South Korean con-scripts as infantrymen in its organic units. These Koreans, known as KATUSAs (from "Korean Augmentation to the U.S. Army") proved a mixed blessing; many of them served useful purposes, but few became first-rate fighters. In 1952, every Army division still had as many as 2,500 KATUSAs, who made its infantry a little less effective than it might have been. (Even today, the *real* soldiers of the South Korean army regard KATUSAs as slackers who take American rations and other material rewards while they enjoy relaxed American discipline and easy training.) The 1st Marine Division included South Koreans, but they were the tough men of the 1st Regiment of the Korean Marine Corps (Hae Pyong Dae), well supported by U.S. Marine Corps advisory teams. Since 1950, the 1st Regiment of the Korean Marine Corps had been a fourth infantry regiment for the 1st Marine Division.

What the Marines did know in 1952 was that the new sector was a bad deal for the nine Marine infantry battalions that manned the MLR. The sector was even more dangerous for the Marines in the combat outposts (COPs) and observation posts (OPs), required by the Eighth Army, out to a distance of more than 2 miles, depending on the terrain, from the MLR. From the time that UNC shifted to the strategic defen-sive (October 1951) until the signing of the Armistice (July 1953), the American contingent within UNC lost one third of its total dead, missing, and wounded for the entire war, or 140,200, of whom 33,667 died or were missing in action. For the Marine Corps, losses after the division shifted to the western sector amounted to 40 percent of its total wartime casualties of 29,529 officers and men.

Although this part of the war—the "stagnation phase," as it is characterized by many superficial commentators—held little promise of a World War II–style victory, the Marines still fought with admirable ardor and fair skill. (Even Marines admit that tactical expertise declined in 1952–1953.) The best Marines did not worry about "dying for a tie," as 1952 military wags put the issue. Certainly, the rules of engagement and defensive posture of the I Corps did not help, and senior Marine officers liked their situation no better than did their men. The concept of an extended and distant "line"—a euphemism for a loose chain of small defended hills—of combat outposts did not make Marine and British officers very happy, nor did the concept of the counterattacks and combat patrols invariably required at night. The Commonwealth Division leaders demanded a reduction of their patrolling requirements and more autonomy on deciding which outposts to maintain and which to abandon. The Marine Corps did not seek such relief with much ardor, for which the troops have a justified complaint.

Of course, the Marines had the Chinese to blame as well. They did not know much then about their enemy (nor do they now) except that there were too many Chinese (the *horde syndrome*), that they fought at night, and that they seemed to have plenty of artillery and mortars. The last insight requires some explanation because Communist indirect fire caused a larger proportion of the Marine casualties in 1952 than it had in 1950 and 1951. By 1952, the Chinese People's Volunteers Force (CPVF) had completed the rearmament program that gave its divisions a complete family of Russian ordnance and munitions. The 65th Army (three infantry divisions and an artillery division) that faced the 1st Marine Division entered the new campaign with well-trained and well-armed troops. Moreover, the CPVF had a new and aggressive commander, Deng Hua, who replaced de facto the nominal Chinese commander, Peng Tehuai, when Mao Zedong recalled the exhausted and discredited Peng to Beijing in 1952. Deng Hua had been the senior Chinese armistice negotiator for more than a year. He knew the UNC's sensitivity to casualties, especially those inflicted in the I Corps area, which crawled with war correspondents from many nations.

Deng Hua agreed completely with Mao's latest strategic concept, *niupitang,* a term that took its name from a sticky candy popular in

Mao's home province of Hunan. In *niupitang* operations, as Deng Hua refined them, the Chinese mounted sudden nighttime attacks against the UNC combat outposts, then held the position in order to draw the inevitable UNC counterattack. The Chinese greeted the enemy in the open with sudden artillery and mortar barrages and showers of hand grenades. As long as the Chinese were able to kill and wound UNC soldiers, they held a position, but they withdrew if UNC artillery and air strikes became too devastating. As an adjunct to these attacks, the Chinese mounted ambushes on UNC patrols and troops moving to and from the outposts.

The zone of action of the Chinese 63d and 65th Armies, roughly the sector of the 1st Marine Division, held two special attractions for such operations. First, the Kaesong neutral zone rules of engagement still applied, which meant that the Chinese forces could mass there without fear of American artillery or air strikes. Second, the weather in 1952 conspired to present inordinate logistical problems for the Marines. The Marines learned that *pi* (rain) and *mul* (water) have special meaning in Korea when there is too much of each—as there was in 1952. The snow runoff into the Imjin could be managed, but the heavy 1952 monsoon rains (which start with regularity during the last week of June in the Imjin-Han river valleys) endangered or wiped away every bridge along the Imjin-gang and washed out Marine bunkers, trench lines, ammunition and ammunition storage emplacements, and roads. Thus, the Marine division's earliest battles with the Chinese were conducted in conditions comparable to those of the other Western Front in 1916 and 1917, all of which makes the Marines' fighting spirit even more admirable.

The largest outpost battles of 1952, however, occurred after the monsoon rains halted in August. Although the Marines did not know all of the details, Deng Hua's staff decided that Clark and Van Fleet might put Op Plan 8-52 into effect, and the Chinese reinforced their armies held in counterinvasion reserve in Hwanghae Province (west coast) and around Wonsan (east coast). Attacking the 1st Marine Division played a part in these calculations because an elite American division, taking casualties and deep in combat, could not be easily pulled out of the line and placed on board amphibious shipping. To be sure, the attacks on the Marines were only part of a more general offensive plan adopted by Deng Hua, but the Marines who fought for the Hook and Outposts Reno, Carson, and Vegas could hardly worry about anyone else.

But fight the Marines did, and the Chinese found no special advantage in throwing their best troops into a battle with the 1st Marine

Division. The battles along the combat outpost line in 1952 had nothing of the postcombat aura of Iwo Jima or the fighting withdrawal from the Changjin (Chosin) Reservoir. For the men of the 1st Marine Division, however, the Korean war of 1952 again proved just how much young Americans can do on the battlefield in the name of Corps and comrades. This book is a fitting tribute to those who fought the most truly unknown part of "the unknown war."

–Allan R. Millett
Mason Professor of Military History

PREFACE

> *It was very easy to start a war in Korea.*
> *It was not so easy to stop it.*
> —Nikita Khruschev, 1894–1971,
> speech before the Bulgarian
> Party leadership

The last half of the war in Korea is often referred to as the *stalemate*. Compared with the first half, little has been written about it. Peruse the shelves of a library or a bookstore. Thumb through the few books found there looking for information on the years 1952–1953. One will find very little, perhaps an analysis of the truce negotiations or possibly a narration on the Communist prisoner riots on Koje-do Island. A few authors might mention the heavy Marine fighting for Bunker Hill; the Reno, Carson, or Vegas Outposts; or the U.S. Army's bloody battle for Pork Chop Hill, but then what? Were the last eighteen months of warfare—the stalemate—limited to two or three battles? Of course not. Men continued to die while they waited for the armistice to be negotiated. The difference was that they died by ones, twos, and fours or by squads and platoons, rather than by battalions.

Statistics reveal that nearly 40 percent of all Marine Corps casualties in Korea occurred after April 1952 during the last sixteen months of war. On average, there were twenty-seven casualties each day, or more than one per hour. Seventeen hundred Marines died, and fourteen Medals of Honor were awarded. This was the stalemate, the part that was too insignificant to report and almost ignored altogether.

The purpose of this book is to illuminate that latter portion of war. I have chosen to write about the 1st Marine Division in western Korea, not because it fought more or with greater valor or because it accomplished greater achievements, but because that is where my interest lies. I am a former Marine. I was there.

Military history does not always have to be about tactics, politics, weapons, and generals. War can be a story of people, predominantly young men in their teens or barely out of them. War is teenage privates and twenty-one-year-old lieutenants led by field grade officers and staff noncommissioned officers who are not much older. War is living in the dirt and rain, not bathing for weeks, keeping weapons cleaner than one's teeth, pissing into a tube frozen in the ground, eating cold beans from a can, crapping into the empty container, and throwing the contents out of a fighting hole. It's sleeping in the dirt, a tent, a tank, or a bunker and sharing clothes, farts, dreams, food, and fears.

Combat consists of a few minutes of total and complete confusion. Eventually, the brain kicks in, as do training and leadership, and the young men begin to perform well—in some cases, even heroically. Despite what Hollywood has tried to portray, young men do not fight for the flag, motherhood, or the American way. Like a team, they fight because their buddies are fighting. They fight for each other, for their squad, for their fire team or platoon. They fight because the alternative—not fighting—is unacceptable while their buddies are there beside them.

Between battles, when the "war work" is done, the young men play. They engage in practical jokes, and sports, as well as other, less wholesome activities—of which their mothers might not approve. In reserve or when otherwise off the battlefront, they can enjoy horseplay, sports, drinking, gambling, and whoring, almost a summer camp atmosphere. In between, they train, retrain, and train some more, as they prepare for the next stint on line and for the next battle. Disciplinary problems arise proportionately in reserve. Too soon, however, relaxation is over and the men return to the fighting, where they are exposed to death—but safe from sin.

In war, many people are heroic. Some of them are observed and awarded medals, while others just die. A greater number of people perform heroic acts that are never witnessed or acknowledged by anyone except a few companions. Many more do their jobs without heroics at all. They simply follow their training, their leaders, and their orders. These men are our warriors.

INTRODUCTION

*There has never been a protracted war
from which a country has benefited.*
Sun Tzu, 400–320 B.C.,
The Art of War, ii

As 1952 began, the Korean War had run a course of twenty-one months. Fighting had continued along the length and breadth of the peninsula. Seoul, the capital city of South Korea, had changed hands four times. Finally, the war evolved into a defensive military effort stalled by political considerations. For both sides, it was siegelike with no significant movement or conquest, a positional war.

This was the era of the Cold War in Europe, an offshoot of World War II. The Soviet Union had not disarmed after the war and was overtly acquisitive of former Axis-occupied nations. The Red Bear kept Europe in a turmoil by creating the Iron Curtain. In Asia, it supported Mao Zedong's Communist revolution in China, armed North Korea, and covertly supported its invasion of the South. Communist Chinese Forces (CCF) had driven Chiang Kai-shek's Chinese Nationalists off the Asian continent to the island of Formosa. Communist China had entered the Korean War in opposition to the United Nations (UN) forces and was seeking to establish itself as a world power.

The United States was concerned about the expansion of Communism. With Korea, President Harry S. Truman believed that he was treading a thin line between peace and an emerging new world war. With Communist China actively engaged in the war, the United Nations feared that excessive military efforts in Asia would tempt Russia to become more aggressive in Europe. By 1952, President-elect Gen. Dwight D. Eisenhower was under enormous pressure at home to negotiate an end to the war in Korea while simultaneously seeking to defend Europe from Communism.

The Chinese were also eager to extract themselves from Korea. The war was becoming expensive. Their supply lines were long and increasingly difficult to maintain. They were losing large numbers of troops to the fighting and gaining little in return. The Korean War became a political hot potato, a "limited war," in which both sides desired to extricate themselves without losing prestige or granting concessions. China, the UN, and the United States were all unwilling to spend the resources, financial or human, to pursue a final decisive campaign and risk a greater, worldwide conflict.

INVENTING THE LIMITED WAR

A limitation on military offense was one of the defining aspects of the Korean War. For the first time in modern history, total victory over an enemy was rejected. It was replaced by a policy of containment—of warfare that extended only as far as politically defined limits and no farther. Referring to the initiation of peace talks in 1951, military historian and author D. Clayton James wrote, "According to an official source now, 'the objective was an end to the fighting and a return to the status quo; the mission of the Eighth Army was to inflict enough attrition on the foe to induce him to settle on these terms.'"[1]

Under political constraints, UN military forces could not attempt to win the war on the battlefield. Aircraft could not bomb airfields or other military targets in China. They were not allowed to chase opposing pilots across the border in hot pursuit. Naval vessels off the Chinese coast could not shell targets on the mainland or blockade China's harbors. On land, there would be no amphibious landing behind the Chinese lines. Land forces were not permitted to advance or capture any significant new territory on the Korean peninsula or elsewhere. Introduction into Korea of additional divisions for reinforcement was also rejected. Most important, for the times, the atom and hydrogen bombs in possession of the United States and deployed to Okinawa and to an aircraft carrier in the Pacific were not used. This was most remarkable in view of the fact that, based on post–World War II political and military thought, the atom bomb was America's primary weapon of offense.

To appreciate just how remarkable these limitations were, one must consider that both China and the Soviet Union also took steps to limit their responses to the Korean threat. Much of the possible escalation to war that could have happened did not occur. The Soviet Far East Fleet stationed in Vladivostok, for example, made no pretense of confronting the U.S. Seventh Fleet in the Sea of Japan. No Soviet submarine presence was detected, nor were there any belligerent Soviet maneuvers or routine naval exercises to worry UN naval forces.

In the air, Communist limits were equally apparent. Russian MiG-15 fighters, with Soviet pilots, provided to the Chinese were never sufficient in number to threaten UN air superiority over the peninsula. UN targets in South Korea, though highly vulnerable to interdiction by Communist air forces, were never threatened.

The UN decision not to employ Nationalist Chinese forces in Korea was met with a Communist quid pro quo: Formosa was never threatened with invasion. China also ignored Japan, the site of UN Headquarters and a major staging and supply area for the war. In Korea, Chinese Army manpower, tactics, and strategy were consistently maintained at levels that continued the belligerency without significant escalation.

Thus, without formal agreement and without a word being exchanged, both sides of the Korean War confined their fighting solely to the land peninsula of Korea. It remained a limited war. Whether these limitations caused the avoidance of a larger war is pure speculation. If that was the measure, however, the limited war was a success.

It is purely rhetorical but nonetheless must be asked. Would a shorter war, a quicker but more extensive war, have been cheaper in terms of lives and treasure? Would the Soviet Union have entered the war? Would China have sued for peace? History has no answers to rhetoric, only facts and statistics. It is a fact that truce negotiations clearly favored the Communists. It is also a fact that, during the period of stalemate (March 1952–July 1953) while negotiations were in progress, more than thirteen thousand U.S. Marines were killed, wounded, or captured.

The tragedy of those last months of war in Korea was that they were so futile. Adm. C. Turner Joy, the chief UN negotiator, revealed later in his book, *How Communists Negotiate,* that the final agreement of 27 July 1953 was substantially the same as that submitted on 28 April 1952.

More than two thousand years ago, in *The Art of War,* Sun Tzu wrote, "When, without a previous understanding, the enemy asks for a truce, he is plotting." It was clear to the Chinese, why not to the UN policymakers?

Nearly a year and a half of war transpired with nothing whatever to show for it except death and suffering. That was the Outpost War.

THE OUTPOST WAR

On 12 November 1951, Gen. Matthew B. Ridgway, Commander in Chief, United Nations Command (CINCUNC), ordered Lt. Gen.

James A. Van Fleet, Commander, Eighth Army, to cease offensive action and begin active defense of the front line, the Main Line of Resistance (MLR). UN troops were prohibited from attacking the enemy with anything over a battalion of men without first securing CINCUNC's permission. Van Fleet's operations "were limited to: strengthening the MLR, resisting enemy attacks, and establishing an outpost line up to 5,000 yards ahead of the main positions."[2]

By late 1951, UN naval forces had blockaded the peninsula on all sides and UN air forces had full control of the air over North Korea and South Korea. Opposing armies faced one another on a line roughly corresponding to the 38th Parallel. Land forces had dug in to provide trench lines, known as the MLR, across the breadth of Korea. In the no-man's-land between opposing MLRs, both sides had established isolated combat outposts, strongpoints often referred to as OPs, or combat outposts (COPs), that commanded hills of high ground from which enemy activity could be observed, controlled, and raided. Outposts were used defensively to protect weak spots in the line created by low ground or other terrain features. These outposts ranged from squad- to company-sized salients. Some were constantly occupied, others were manned only at night, and a few were only daylight positions. Much of the ground combat at this time involved fighting for control of outposts, which, because of their tactical position, caused a domino effect on the MLR when one changed hands.

The war slowed, yet, as history has shown, it was far from over. Rather, its nature had changed. It was a different war, a defensive war, a fight for the high ground. For the next eighteen months, while negotiators debated, soldiers and Marines fought. They bled and died for possession of outposts that, as frequently as not, were later abandoned within weeks or months.

The Korean War was an infantryman's war. There were planes, tanks, and artillery, but the burden of war rested disproportionately on the back and feet of the foot soldier. On both sides, the infantrymen carried the battles and lived in the dirt as they fought with rifles, hand grenades, mortars, machine guns, and, in many cases, fists and shovels.

It was a sergeant's and a lieutenant's war; generals were nearly irrelevant. Brig. Gen. S. L. A. Marshall, the U.S. Army historian, wrote, "Troops in a death grapple can be helped or hurt by the behavior of subalterns and sergeants. But generals can do little more than regulate the support and advance the reserves."[3] This axiom was never better demonstrated than in Korea.

To the men on the line, it was a personal war filled with individual fighting and loss. All too often, they fought close to the enemy in contests of individual strength—face to face and toe to toe. Soldiers of the Chinese Communist forces were numerous, brave, strong, and intelligently led. Fighting hard and tenaciously, Chinese troops were opponents with which to be reckoned.

By 1952, the truce talks had halted over an impasse on the issue of what to do with large numbers of Communist prisoners of war who had refused repatriation. Politically, there was much optimism about resumption of the talks, but, thus far, they had failed to materialize. Neither side was willing to initiate a major offensive. Rather, each side preferred to fight for small bits of critical real estate and adjust its MLR to improve its bargaining position at the negotiating table in Panmunjom.

In the United States, the situation appeared to be different. The Korean War became old news. To some people, it was even boring—not, by any means, to the troops fighting the war but certainly to members of the press, the politicians, and the citizens at home. It was all going to be over soon anyway, they thought. War news was relegated to the back pages of newspapers. Interest had waned. Yet, the troops who were in Korea saw no peace. Their war was real and happening then. Soldiers were still shooting at one another, artillery and mortars were still exploding, troops were dying, and the weather was miserable.

In March 1952, the U.S. Eighth Army in Korea undertook a massive redeployment of units called Operation Mixmaster. The movement amounted to a complicated rearrangement of fighting units across the entire Korean front. It shuffled nearly 200,000 men with all of their supplies and equipment over distances of 25 to 180 miles. Mixmaster was a tactical realignment of UN forces designed to put more South Korean Army units on the MLR and to strengthen the entire line with five corps sectors rather than four.

The 1st Marine Division was relieved in position amid the eastern mountains of central Korea and redeployed to the Jamestown Line in western Korea. There, they fell under the command of I Corps (often referred to as Eye Corps). It was a ponderous exercise of musical chairs without the music.

Amid the fighting, several divisions of U.S. and Republic of Korea (ROK) troops were pulled out of the fight, moved more than a day's march away, and reestablished in a new and strange terrain.

The Marine outpost defense in western Korea was not a planned tactic. Rather, it was one that evolved by trial and error. In March they moved into existing positions of the ROK army, which apparently had not vigorously pursued the war. The Marines changed all that. They brought the war to the enemy using familiar tactics, a line of defense guarded with a few temporary outposts in front. Cumulatively these small outposts soon became known as the Outpost Line of Resistance (OPLR).

This term, OPLR, was misleading, as the hilltop positions were not fortified to resist an attack. Most were too far forward of the MLR to receive fire support or reinforcement. Forming a weak chain in front of the main line, the outposts more accurately served an early warning function. Faced with an enemy attack of any strength, the men on an outpost were instructed to retire to the MLR rather than defend the ground.

By May this tactic had proven unsatisfactory. The outposts weren't useful, did not deter attacks on the MLR, and resulted in too many casualties with too little gained. Something needed to change.

For the remainder of 1952, the Marines continued their search to find the right outposts and to hold on to them. All the while, hills were gained and hills were lost but always with the cost of lives.

CHAPTER 1
THE MOVE WEST

*Everything that is shot or dropped on you
in war is most unpleasant but of all the horrible
devices, the most terrifying is the land mine.*
—Sir William Slim,
Unofficial History, 1959

It was brass-monkey cold in the back of the open truck. Snow had begun falling early that morning, and now the vehicles were having trouble negotiating the slick, muddy road. Seated on the wooden slat benches in back of a six-by-six truck, the men hunched over and stared at the floor. They tried to keep the snow out of their clothing, but it was useless. The wet slushy snow splotched their boots and trousers, everywhere their ponchos failed to cover. Soon they were soaked to the skin. Their full packs, lying on the floor, grew soggy. Many of the men had stretched condoms over their rifle muzzles in an effort to keep them dry. The trucks were equipped with canvas covers over the back, but they were furled to facilitate escape in the event that enemy aircraft approached. The men simply got wet.

The vehicles ground on, downshifting as a hill steepened, slowly grinding to the top, and then, just as slowly, moving down the other side. The long convoy of trucks, jeeps, trailers, and artillery pieces, winding its way west through the hills and valleys of central Korea, passed through poor villages of even poorer people. Each village looked like the last one, with houses made of mud plastered white and thatched roofs. A flue running up one side of each building constituted a primitive but efficient heating system. A fire was built in a pit beneath the house, and the heat and smoke traveled under the house to emerge up the flue on the other side. It worked well. Korean houses stayed toasty warm during the winter, provided that wood could be scavenged.

Often the roads were lined with people, like the old man with a wispy white beard who was carrying an A frame of firewood taller than he was. A more prosperous individual might have a wooden cart pulled by an emaciated ox and piled high with goods for sale or for personal use. Lining the roadside were dirty, cold Korean children, with dripping noses and red cheeks, wearing dirty padded jackets and rubber shoes, often without socks. Some were peeking from behind their mothers' skirts while others, bolder perhaps, ran alongside the road and shouted with their hands outstretched, "Alo Joe, chocolato, chocolato." At first, the Marines threw them candy or other unwanted items from their small supply of C rations. Soon the "presentos" ran out, as did their concern.

After a few hours of bouncing on hard benches, of being cold, of wet snow turned to rivulets running down their backs, the Marines lost interest. They didn't care about the problems of others. Heads nodded as the men tried to sleep, but cold, potholes, bumps, gear shifts, noise, and odors combined to defeat any attempts at rest. Like cargo, they just rode.

The 140-mile trip to the new position took about ten hours to travel. Every two or three hours, the convoy stopped for a break. The men made a bee line for a tree or the side of the road to relieve themselves. Many just walked, stretched their legs, and worked out kinks until they had to reload and continue west. Breakfast, lunch, and dinner were cold C rations eaten on the truck.

For nearly two weeks, vehicles shuttled back and forth over the dirt roads and hills of Korea as they carried Marines and their supplies west and returned east with ROK Army troops. The weather was no help. On 18 March, it began to rain and then snow again. Temperatures dropped into the low 20s. The roads turned first to slime and then to mush as truck tires churned and slued in trying to find traction in the reddish-brown chowder that once was a road.

Some of the trucks were so full that the men were jammed into the rear almost as an afterthought. One battalion had so few vehicles that it loaded each truck with "eighteen men, sleeping bags, seabags, tents, stoves, cots and nine cases of C Ration."[1] Other trucks were less crowded, and gear was replaced by more bodies. Many units had just come off-line. The men had not had a hot meal, a shower, or a change of clothing in weeks, and it would be a while before they would encounter any of them. In that respect, the open trucks and cold weather were probably a blessing to the senses.

This was Operation Mixmaster. Although not intended to be an exercise in torment, it worked out that way for some Marines. Each day for a week, the scenario was repeated despite the rain, the snow, the cold, and the ever-present Murphy's Law—"anything that can go wrong will go wrong."

One battalion of 5th Marines had only eighty trucks to move one thousand men and their equipment. Later, a battalion of 1st Marines had to relieve positions on the MLR with one map to share among all the officers. Planning had not been perfect. Some men with the 1st Marines suffered the ultimate of indignities—riding on top of a loaded truck trussed up like a chicken en route to market. One of them recalled that the men from his small headquarters unit had loaded all their weapons, personal gear, field desks, files, and supplies on the back of a truck until there was no room for people. Then, because the men still had to go, room or no room, they climbed to the top of the pile and got into their sleeping bags for warmth. Atop the trucks, they were lashed to the load and covered with canvas to ward off the wind and snow. Their only relief during the trip consisted of head calls and chow. Uncomfortable as they were, they preferred riding to walking, the more traditional mode of moving infantry.

The sole exceptions to the tedious migration were amphibious tractors, tanks, and engineering equipment. They were too heavy to cross the small bridges, and their continued operation on the ungraded dirt roads of Korea would have destroyed the road for subsequent use by wheeled vehicles. As a consequence, tracked vehicles traveled by sea on board Navy ships.

Before dawn on 18 March, elements of Able, Charlie, and the Korean Marine Corps (KMC) tank companies lined up on the dirt road. The tanks, accompanied by heavily loaded trucks, trailers, and jeeps full of equipment, formed one of the largest and most deadly convoys seen by anyone in years. At first light, the lead unit received the word to move. In perfect order, the tracked behemoths, belching two feet of flame from their twin exhausts, snaked down the road toward the rising sun.

The following morning, 19 March, the send-off was repeated with a second convoy, this time with elements of Baker and Dog Companies accompanied by five tanks from the 5th Marine's Anti-Tank Platoon. On 20 March, there was another convoy and again on 21 March, until finally the entire battalion had displaced to the east.

The first convoy that left on the eighteenth, Able, Charlie, and the KMCs, was typical of the twenty-four-hour trek experienced by the tankers. They traveled all that day and into the night. Inside the tanks the men slept and ate as best they could. By midnight, it began to snow and then to storm. Falling snow obscured vision, dropped inside their hatches and stuck to their faces. They couldn't button up and most of the heaters had long ago ceased to function. Still, the convoy traveled east, slower now and more cautiously, but moving nevertheless. During the fifty-mile trip on narrow Korean roads the column paused only for gas and relief stops, to rotate drivers, and to try and thaw out exposed skin.

As the sun rose the next morning, each convoy reached the east coast village of Sokcho-ri. Looking to sea, the Marines watched as the Navy came in to pick them up. LSTs (landing ship, tank), escorted by destroyers and cruisers, fourteen ships in all, were steaming toward shore. The LSTs beached. Opening their enormous doors, they dropped loading ramps that invited the Marine tanks inside. Like the maws of some mythical monsters, they absorbed the men and vehicles into the guts of the ships. The loading went quickly. The ships soon returned to the sea, leaving Sokcho-ri as they had found it, a sleepy Korean fishing village. The villagers would be able to pass on stories to their children of the day that a hundred steel monsters clanked into town and were swallowed by great ships that took them out to sea, hardly a normal day in the life of a poor fisherman.

The ocean trip to the west coast took five days. For the Marines, it was a welcome respite, a chance to get dry, eat hot food, take showers, and change into clean clothes. They also used the time for maintenance, to clean and service vehicles and weapons. The war was not over, and they knew that they would be back in it soon enough.

When the ships arrived at Inchon harbor the Marines off-loaded their equipment and bid farewell to the Navy. On the road, they drove forty miles northeast to the village of Munsan-ni, the battalion's new home in west Korea.

MOVING IN

Battalions of the 1st and 5th Marine Regiments replaced elements of the ROK 1st Army Division on the Jamestown Line, the current MLR. During that relief, the first Marine casualties on the western front occurred. At 1315 on 24 March, a man from Item Company, 3/1 (3d Battalion, First Marines), tripped a land mine. One Marine was killed in action (KIA) and another wounded. The following day, six men from Charlie, 1/1, were wounded and evacuated; they too had met up with land mines.

The waning days of March saw more Marines become casualties as they explored their new surroundings to get a feel for the area and learn danger spots. Each night, squad-sized units of Chinese probed and poked at positions on the MLR and various outposts. The probes were small, usually unsupported by heavy weapons, just a few soldiers with small arms and grenades. During the day, mortarmen and snipers on either side plied their trade, also taking a toll. Each side was looking for weak spots as it sized up its new opponent.

In all, more than thirty Marine casualties occurred during the relief. Although not a heavy loss, the casualties were all the more tragic because so many resulted from snipers and land mines, which indicated an unfamiliarity with the terrain and enemy positions. Mixmaster had happened too rapidly and without sufficient reconnaissance. The Marines found, for example, that many of the ROK minefields near their positions were poorly marked or, in some cases, not marked at all. Too frequently, they discovered the minefields the hard way.

On 24 March, 2d Lt. Bernard Trainor, platoon leader in Charlie Company, 1/1, was taking his platoon out to Hill 159 (later named Outpost Yoke) to relieve the ROK troops there. He tells how that relief was accomplished:

> We were silently wending our way up a narrow trail on the back side of the hill when I spotted figures hurrying down the hill on either side of the column. Suspecting they were the Koreans we were to replace, I hissed at the Korean interpreter on loan to me for the relief of lines, "Find out who they are!" No sooner was that said, when the familiar sound of burp guns [PPsh guns, called burp guns, were fast firing sub-machine guns of Russian design. The name is derived from the very rapid staccato sound it made when firing.] broke the silence from the crest of the hill, followed by the bellow of a Marine behind me who was hit. In a nano-second it was clear what happened. The Chinese had become suspicious and sent out a reconnaissance patrol to see what was going on. The ROK's saw them coming, we were late, and they had no interest in a firefight just when they were being relieved. So, they simply headed down the hill for the rear. The Chinese were now on the position and firing at whatever was coming or going on the slope below them. At that point I issued the shortest "five paragraph combat order" of my career . . . "LET'S GO!" As if by magic the squads and fire teams dropped their heavy packs, spread out and assaulted, the BARs gaining fire superiority as we went. It was just like the endless assault drills we practiced at Camp Tripoli while in reserve. Like the working of the human hand, each finger is different and moves independently, but all work in harmony to do what the hand needs to do. A well trained unit, with perfect trust in one

another, operates the same way. It wasn't much of a fight. The Chinese were firing high. They had found out what they came for and were faced with a platoon of pissed-off Marines coming at them—they scurried down the far side of the hill.

Taking only the one casualty caught in the initial fire, we had the abandoned hill under our control in short order. It was well after midnight when the platoon took up a hasty defense in the ROK trenches. The "relief of lines" was late and inelegant, but complete. Not sure if the Chinese would be back, we had one man per fire team go back down the hill to bring up the packs without regard to squad ownership. We would sort them out when it got light. It was not long, however, before the outraged working party came panting up the hill with the news that most of the packs had been grabbed by the ROK soldiers on their way to the rear. "Those bastards were in too much of a hurry to stay and fight, but they had plenty of time to loot," summed up our feelings. The loss of our gear was no small thing. Everything we owned was jammed into a "Willie peter" bag and tied to a packboard. Goodbye to parkas, sleeping bags, rations, spare ammunition, personal effects, and in my case, binoculars. As the division was still on the move across the peninsula, we knew there would be little in the way of resupply and replacement in the days to come. We were in for some cold and hungry days.[2]

The enemy was well aware that U.S. Marines had traded places with regular ROK Army troops and needed to take their measure. Conversely, the Marines were now facing battle-hardened soldiers of the Communist Chinese Forces (CCF), instead of the war-weary North Koreans. Most assuredly, the war situation had significantly altered.

THE NEW HOME
The new sector of responsibility was little improved from where the Marines had been and, in terms of defense, worse. Extending east from the Kimpo Peninsula on the Yellow Sea, the Jamestown Line included the Imjin River Basin at the confluence of the Han and Imjin Rivers. Composed of low hills and broad valleys, the Imjin River Basin was the traditional invasion route into Seoul and the agricultural lands beyond. For centuries incursions from the north had used this broad plain to move south. Unlike the mountainous east, this terrain could support tanks and vehicular troop movements.

Anchored at the sea, the Jamestown Line extended northeast across the peninsula crossing over the 38th Parallel a short distance from the coast. The 1st Marine Division, reinforced with a KMC regiment, was

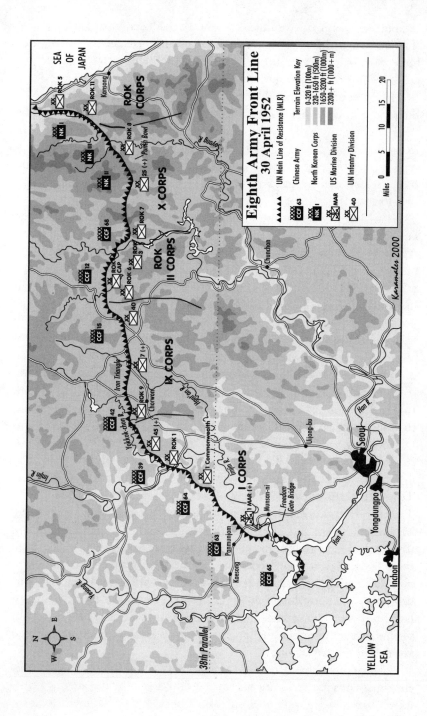

Eighth Army Front Line
30 April 1952

responsible for thirty-five miles of front. Backed against the Imjin River, the division had little room to maneuver and was dependent on four bridges for supply and support. Three of the bridges were temporary creations subject to the capricious whims of flooding and weather.

The chief problem faced by the Marines on the Jamestown Line was the ratio of men to miles. Even with the additional numbers provided by the KMC regiment, thirty-five miles meant an extremely thin spread of manpower. Just how thin is best illustrated by comparing this deployment with the doctrine of the U.S. Army, which was responsible for deploying the First Division. Typical Army policy at the time called for an infantry division to defend approximately eight to nine thousand yards of line. The 1st Marine Division was called on to defend more than sixty thousand yards of line,[3] six times the recommended amount of real estate. After the division established itself on the Jamestown Line, the reality of this weakness became so apparent that it was necessary to redeploy the 5th Marine Regiment, originally slated to be used as a reserve regiment in the Kimpo area.

The defense strategy that evolved, therefore, depended on a thinly manned MLR protected by forward outpost positions and mobile reserves to the rear. In the event of invasion, the outposts would serve as early warning alarms. Troops on the MLR were expected to hold until reserves could be moved forward.

The hills and valleys of western Korea were not unlike the inland coastal area of Southern California, particularly Camp Pendleton in San Diego County where the Marines had trained. Western Korea was much colder, of course, and wetter in the summer, but the hills were low and the valleys broad. Vegetation was low scrub pine with shrubs of an indeterminate genus growing on the hillsides. In the valleys, rice paddies with dirt berms, or dikes, terraced the plots and created dams for standing water.

The Jamestown Line, a meandering trench line across the high ground, faced north. Incorporated into the trenches were machine-gun positions, fighting holes, and tank slots, along with sandbagged log bunkers serving as command posts, first-aid stations, and living quarters. Depending on the terrain, a trench might be five or six feet deep, or maybe a mere eighteen inches, requiring one to crawl on his belly to avoid enemy sharpshooters.

A few feet in front of the trenches was concertina—barbed-wire entanglements meant to discourage and slow an advancing enemy. Makeshift alarms, often ration cans filled with pebbles that clattered when the cans moved, hung from the wire. Occasionally, in particularly trouble-some spots, the Marines set booby traps, typically white-phosphorus grenades rigged to explode when disturbed.

There was no foliage around the MLR. It had all been cut away to create fields of fire, or it had been burned away by explosives. Piles of dirt, holes, and stumps of vegetation were the residue of countless rounds of artillery and mortar shells—the MLR's "incoming mail."

In front of the MLR was the OPLR, the Outpost Line of Resistance. The OPLR was the first line of defense and, in fact, where the bulk of the fighting occurred. It consisted of a series of hilltops, roughly paralleling the MLR but well forward of it. Like a picket line during the American Civil War, the OPLR was created to give early warning of an attacking enemy to the troops in the MLR. Nightly, squads or platoons of men left the MLR and trekked to a designated outpost to spend the night. They might remain on duty at the OPLR anywhere from a few hours to twenty-four hours.

During darkness, the outpost was on full alert. The men watched for the enemy and listened for movement or, worse, for bugles, whistles, and flares signaling an attack. They also manned listening posts, small fox-holes in front of the wire where one or two men listened for movement, voices, the smell of garlic, or anything to indicate that enemy soldiers were nearby. Communications on the outposts were usually by landline, telephones connected by thin communication wire. The men spoke qui-etly, communicating in whispers or, better still, by clicking a transmis-sion switch and not speaking at all. As the purpose of the outpost was to delay the enemy and alarm the MLR, its occupants were expected to fall back to the MLR when it was attacked.

Not surprisingly, reality turned the book of war topsy-turvy. As the war developed, outposts themselves became military objectives, whereas the MLR was merely a place from which to support them. The line of weakly manned temporary outposts faded into obscurity, to be replaced by fewer, more heavily fortified and strategically placed positions. Rather like medieval forts, they often came under siege.

Restricted by orders to avoid advancing any farther into North Korea and limited to offensive actions of less than battalion strength, the Ma-rines, like all UN troops in Korea, were confined to a defensive war. Hurt the enemy, but not enough to win the war. Outposts, because of their for-ward positions, became the common focal points for aggressive actions.

The disposition of the Marines that began in March 1952 remained unchanged throughout the entire seventeen months of war, except for the months of May and June 1953. The left sector on the west was held by men of the KMC.[4] The center and right sectors were each allocated to one of the three regular U.S. Marine regiments, which allowed for a third regiment to be in reserve at all times. Often, units from the reserve regiment were deployed on special operations against enemy positions, thus leaving the assigned defenses unchanged.

Supporting arms of tanks tended to follow a similar pattern of rotating units. The 1st Marine Armored Amphibian Battalion, semipermanently situated with the KMC regiment on the banks of the Han and Imjin Rivers, used its amphibious capabilities for patrolling, crossing, and defending the water line. The U.S. 11th Marines, an artillery regiment, positioned its four battalions behind the lines to support the infantry. The tank battalion split its four companies, with one company assigned to each infantry regiment and one to the KMCs. A reserve company was maintained at Munsan-ni for mechanical maintenance of the vehicles.

Thus, as spring progressed, the Marine Division settled in to fight a new war with a different enemy, in a new place, and with different tactics.

On the last day of March a new major unit was organized and deployed. The Kimpo Provisional Regiment (KPR) was the most heterogeneous UN military unit of the war. Composed of elements of U.S. Marines, Navy, and Army, the Korean Marine Corps, and civilian National Police, this unique multinational, interservice unit, under control of the 1st Marine Division, was formed for the sole purpose of defending the Kimpo Peninsula—a verdant and fertile piece of land north of Seoul. It was, as the name implies, surrounded on three sides by water. On the left side was the Yom River, a tributary of the Han that flowed into the sea. On the north and right was the Han, where it was joined by the Imjin. Across the Han River, in front of the peninsula, were the Chinese Communists.

The KPR was formed to consolidate command of a variety of units that formerly had acted independently. The regiment was charged with defense of the approaches to vital UN command facilities: the Kimpo airport, the supply center at Ascom City, the port of Inchon, and the ROK capital city of Seoul. Among the units assigned to the KPR were the 1st Marine Armored Amphibian Battalion, acting as supporting artillery; the 5th KMC Battalion; the 13th ROK Security Battalion; two platoons from the 1st Marine Reconnaissance Company; and one battalion of infantry from the division reserve.

The Kimpo Peninsula, although a vital link in the MLR, was fortunately not one of frequent enemy activity. Fighting in other sectors, however, managed to compensate for that lack.

A PROBLEM WITH MINES

One of the major problems facing Marines on the Jamestown Line was land mines. 2d Lt. Howard Matthias, a platoon leader with Dog Company, 2/5, recalled one of his early encounters with land mines:

> A sergeant in my platoon was killed less than a hundred yards from my bunker. He was new to our outfit and either missed the path or tried to take a shortcut. He was evidently moving quickly. He set off a mine of the "bouncing Betty" type. This type mine is designed to bounce in the air and explode about waist high. The damage caused to the human body at this height is beyond description. My sergeant was killed by a piece of shrapnel that pierced his throat and cut his jugular vein.[5]

ROK troops, the former occupants of these positions, had made extensive use of land mines and placed them liberally throughout the network of trails and roads between the MLR and the OPLR. Unfortunately for the Marines, they had often failed to mark these minefields or map their whereabouts (leading some to conclude that perhaps the ROK Army did not send many patrols out in front of the MLR). Worse yet, the ROK soldiers apparently did not, or could not, warn the relieving Marines of their existence. As a consequence, during the first few months of the year, land mines became the cause of more casualties than did Chinese bullets.

The Marines sent out patrols daily and manned outposts nightly. They spent a great deal of time in front of the MLR looking for the enemy. With tragic frequency, mines were tripped and Americans were killed or maimed. According to Meid and Yingling, during the first weeks in I Corps sector, mines of all types caused 50 percent of all Marine casualties.[6]

Land mines in Korea originated from two predominant sources, the United States and those of Soviet manufacture. Both sources produced antitank mines and antipersonnel mines. The most commonly found Soviet mine was the Schu mine, consisting of a crudely constructed wooden box, about half the size of a cigar box, with a hinged lid. The explosive charge was a three-eighth–pound block of TNT. It was fused with a standard Soviet pull-type fuse projecting through the front wall of the hinged lid. This weapon required only two pounds of weight to detonate and contained no metal to register on a mine detector. Buried in a path or road edge, it instantly ended the war for an unsuspecting infantryman.

The American antipersonnel mine, called Bouncing Betty, was particularly insidious. When triggered, often by trip wire, it sprang from the ground and exploded at waist height of a walking man. Instead of taking a foot or a leg, as did the Schu, the Bouncing Betty targeted bigger body parts, such as the abdomen, and was most effective in taking the victim out of action, usually forever.

As might be expected, antitank mines were far more powerful than their personnel counterparts, but they were often adjusted for antipersonnel purposes. The most common antitank mine in Korea was the Soviet box mine, a larger version of the Schu. Greater quantities of TNT were packed into the box mine, and the device was adjusted to require greater pressure for activation. For this reason, foot troops leading a tank on a road might pass over the mine only to have it activated by the tank. Box mines were found stacked one on the other or resting atop a 55-gallon drum of explosives. Detonation of these mines could raise a 50-ton M-46 tank into the air and leave a crater the size of the vehicle itself.

A cousin to the land mine and equally prevalent was the booby trap. This was any explosive charge, usually a mine, a mortar bomb, or a hand grenade, ingeniously rigged with trip wire or pressure release to detonate when the trap was sprung. Tripping a fine wire, stretched across a trail and unseen at night, triggered the device. A trip wire was one of the most frightening situations that a point man could experience. It is difficult to imagine what thoughts pass through the mind during that split second after a wire is felt pulling on one's boot. Second Lt. Stan Rauh of Able, 1/7, wrote of such an incident:

> At dusk I took a small patrol out to set up an ambush not very far forward of the MLR. The squad leader, a respected and seasoned corporal, was soon to rotate stateside. Suddenly he froze. He indicated that he had stepped on a trip wire. Believing it to be a pressure release type device, I held the wire down and told him to back off. He was indeed frozen and couldn't move. I had another Marine move up and replace me holding the wire down. It was necessary for me to "cold cock" the corporal. Another Marine and I caught him as he fell, then we placed a rock on the wire to keep pressure on. The corporal—a fine Marine who had had enough—was moved to the rear.[7]

The following excerpt from the 3/5 Command Diary for April 1952 illustrates some of the unique efforts devoted to clearing mines and booby traps:

> Lieutenant Horner and Technical Sergeant Wolfe of How Company developed a wire device made from the wire on "Charlie" Ration boxes to help detect the almost invisible trip wires. This consisted of making a bend at one end of a three (3) to four (4) length of wire and slowly pushing this along the ground ahead of the lead man in a clearing detail. The heavier wire bend would pick up the trip wire enough for detection but would not give enough disturbance to detonate the mine or grenade.[8]

Slowly and methodically, the Marines created fighting room. As trails and paths were cleared, more and more patrols were sent out to greater distances. So much energy and manpower were necessarily spent in clearing mines that opportunities for aggressive action on the ground were limited. In this situation, much of the offensive action of carrying the fight to the enemy was left to artillery, a few air strikes, and tanks. The tanks, firing their 90-mm rifles and heavy machine guns from the safety of the MLR destroyed countless positions, bunkers, buildings, and gun positions, not to mention enemy soldiers.

LEARNING THE NEIGHBORHOOD

Initially, the 7th Marine Regiment saw little action. It was in the division reserve, where the men trained and maintained security patrols of the rear area. With the KMC regiment on the left, the 5th Marines were in place in the center sector and flanked by the 1st Marines on their right.

Communist activity confined itself to spasmodic artillery and mortar demonstrations. Chinese soldiers also occupied much of their time digging and improving fortifications. The Marines, too, spent their days with home improvement projects, such as construction of trenches and bunkers. Division Headquarters ordered that all units rebuild their positions sturdy enough to withstand a direct hit from shells as large as 105-mm. They also were to combine living bunkers with fighting positions so as not to get caught in the open while running from one to the other. The men learned that, for an infantryman, the shovel can be as important as a rifle.

The first week in April saw little significant action, routine but not boring. When sixteen enemy soldiers were seen carrying ammunition into tunnels near Outpost One, they were dispersed by mortar fire. A platoon of Able Company tanks destroyed several buildings and killed or wounded twenty-eight Communists. On 2 April, when Marines with Able Company, 2/1, observed what appeared to be a Chinese officer studying their lines with field glasses, they called in more mortar fire and believed they hit him. Later that afternoon, a Marine sniper picked off a Chinese soldier who failed to keep his head down.

As dawn broke on 2 April, tanks from Able Company, 1st Tank Battalion, which was supporting the KMCs, crawled atop a hill. The Marines blew up seventeen buildings and four gun emplacements and killed or wounded eight Chinese soldiers. On another day, a tank gunner spotted an enemy tank well north of the MLR. The marksman quickly aimed his 90-mm and scored a hit. The enemy tank, obviously damaged, limped away.

RAID AT TOMAK-TONG

Trained for offensive assault rather than static defense, Marine infantry could not long sit idle. Companies on line chafed at a role that called for so little aggressive action and that allowed the initiative to remain with the enemy.

In the center sector of the MLR, Item Company, 3/5, initiated a raid on Chinese positions in early April. The raid was planned to capture prisoners and destroy enemy mortar sites in the vicinity of an abandoned village identified on the map as Tomak-tong. It was only a dozen isolated houses in a small north-south valley surrounded by rice paddies on three sides. A dirt road, equally poor and abandoned, meandered its way north from the MLR and turned east at the southern edge of the village. It was situated at the base of Taedok-san, an imposing mountain that stood at 236 meters (775 feet) and was the undisputed high ground for miles around. Taedok-san was a major Chinese strong point facing the Marine MLR, heavily fortified, and well dug in.

The raiding force was built on the 1st Platoon of Item Company, augmented with mortar and machine-gun squads. The reinforced platoon was divided into four units. The assault group consisted of four fire teams (sixteen men), supported by a second group, a light machine-gun squad, and two more fire teams to provide covering fire. The third group was a forward base of fire that consisted of two 60-mm mortar squads, two fire teams, and a .50-caliber machine-gun squad. Behind the forward firebase was the fourth group, a rear base of fire identical in composition to the third group.

At 2230 on 8 April, the raiding force slipped from the trenches. The point consisted of a fire team followed by the platoon leader, a runner, a radioman, and the remainder of the assault group. The various fire support groups followed in the order in which they would drop off to set up their firebase. The men tried hard to be quiet. No one spoke, and metal gear was taped or tied down. Still, one could hear the swish of cotton clothing, belts, and straps. It was impossible for that many men to be absolutely silent.

Walking in single file, the men maintained a five-to-ten–pace interval between them as permitted by the terrain and darkness. They held formation throughout their approach as they followed a barely discernible path through minefields. Reaching the OPLR at 2255, they continued down the nose of a hill to the valley floor and thence to the road. Dropping off the rear firebase at the road edge, the column continued across the rice paddies to a site where the forward firebase could set up on a hillside to the left of the village. Moving through the village and out the other side, the assault group dropped off its covering group on the high ground to the left and continued on the trail as it turned left (west) to climb the hill toward Taedok-san.

At 0130, six enemy mortar rounds exploded south of the covering group. Five minutes later, still in column, the assault group reached the enemy trench line and attracted the fire of a burp gun. The point fire team returned the fire and silenced the gun. Almost immediately, Chinese soldiers began throwing hand grenades and firing burp guns at the Marines. The Marines returned fire and scattered into a wedge formation on either side of the point. At the same time, two enemy machine guns opened up in a deadly cross fire and mortar rounds began to fall. Two members of the point fire team jumped into the Chinese trench and fired weapons up and down the line.

By now, the assault squad had suffered numerous casualties. With his men wounded, outnumbered, and outgunned, the platoon leader ordered a withdrawal. No sooner had the order been given when a hand grenade exploded and killed him instantly. Pfc. Robert Beatty and another Marine saw their lieutenant fall and rushed to his aid. Observing that he was dead and unwilling to leave him, the two men began carrying, pulling, and dragging him down the hill. The task was made the more difficult because of their own injuries, and they were still under considerable hostile fire.

The assault group managed to join its base of fire, and both groups fell back toward the forward firebase. Sporadic machine-gun and mortar fire from enemy positions continued to follow their progress. About 0210, they rendezvoused with the forward firebase and began to reorganize for a head count. Noting the missing men (Beatty, his companion, and the platoon leader), they tried to request help from the command post, but their radio had been disabled during the firefight.

Meanwhile, at approximately 0220, Beatty and his companion appeared at the rear firebase position. Inadvertently, they had bypassed the forward firebase. The men related that they had carried their platoon leader's body away from the scene of initial contact until they finally grew too weak to continue. Hiding the body under a clump of bushes, they tried to locate other members of their squad. Unsuccessful, the two Marines made their way to the rear base.

During the first platoon's withdrawal, friendly artillery fired on enemy mortar and machine-gun positions, but incoming fire continued to fall in the vicinity of the rear firebase. Simultaneously, the Item Company commander moved forward from the MLR to the rear firebase and established a forward command post (CP). Item Company's 3d Platoon moved from the MLR and reported to the forward CP to stand by for possible rescue operations. Item Company's platoon was replaced on the MLR by George Company's 2d Platoon, which moved forward from battalion reserve.

At the forward CP, a muster revealed that the platoon leader was the only Marine unaccounted for. 2d Lt. George W. Alexander, Jr., the battalion intelligence officer, volunteered to take out a detail of men to recover the body. Private First Class Beatty, concealing his wounds, offered to guide the group back to where he had hidden the body. A hastily assembled squad of eight men left for the village. They crossed the paddies and continued to the south side of the village, where three men were dropped to set up a base of covering fire. Beatty led the remainder of the rescue party through the town to the thicket where he had concealed the lieutenant's body.

Placing the dead officer on a stretcher, the group made its way back over a different route. The men became separated by 20 yards as they paralleled a small stream east of the village. At 0552, they came under enemy cross fire from three directions. The initial burst of fire killed one Marine and wounded another. The others, who were across the stream, were not hit, but they were immediately pinned down. As enemy troops closed on the survivors, the Marines returned fire and wounded two of them. Lieutenant Alexander shot two more enemy soldiers as the patrol worked its way back. One of the men from the recovery party hid near a stream as the enemy soldiers passed him. Later, he worked his way back and rejoined his companions.

By 0600, the recovery detail was reformed. Using flashlight signals, Alexander called for artillery to silence the enemy machine guns, but the Marines were still pinned down. As they husbanded their ammunition in anticipation of an imminent assault, artillery came in to cover the Chinese with smoke. As it commingled with the morning mist and drifted across the paddies, the Marines lost all visual and fire contact. Taking the opportunity of light from the rising sun to search for the missing men, two members of the recovery detail relocated the body of the 1st Platoon's lieutenant and returned to the base of fire for help.

At this time, a Marine from the forward CP ran across the paddies and joined the men at the firebase. He was sent back as a runner to call for more smoke and for help with carrying bodies. The bodies of the platoon leader and of another Marine, as well as a wounded member of the detail who had been pinned down in a nearby bunker, were all recovered and assembled at the firebase. The detail awaited more smoke to cover its withdrawal to the forward CP.

In the meantime, things were not going smoothly at the forward CP. A section of 81-mm and 4.2-inch mortars had been called from the MLR to augment the artillery and supplement the application of smoke. During their movement forward, the Marines entered an unmarked minefield. Someone activated a trip wire, and three men were wounded.

By 0730, with a screen of smoke masking their movements, the recovery detail began its withdrawal to the forward CP and arrived there at 0815. Thirty minutes later, a withdrawal from the forward CP commenced and all hands returned to the MLR by 1000.

Overall casualties resulting from the operation were eight Chinese killed and eleven wounded (determined by a count and an estimate) and two Marines killed and seventeen wounded. Among the wounded was Private First Class Beatty, who had taken two more hits as he returned to the MLR after guiding the recovery detail to his platoon leader's body. Tactically, one could not say that Marine objectives were attained. No prisoners were taken, and no mention is made of destroying Chinese mortar emplacements.

This action, however, was the first raid by the Marines on Chinese forces in west Korea, and they gained important intelligence. An intelligence summary accompanying the 3/5 Special Action Report indicated that the enemy, "had well camouflaged firing ports and positions along trench line . . . apparently had no knowledge of patrol's presence until they were almost up the trench line . . . was aggressive but seemed over-anxious which permitted friendly recovery patrol to close with enemy and work back to base of fire . . . talked and yelled to each other consistently during fire fight which gave friendly patrol advantage in spotting them."[9]

Lieutenant Alexander and Private First Class Beatty were each awarded a Navy Cross for their heroism during this action.

FOG OF WAR

Elsewhere on the line, men of the 1st Marine Regiment were also getting serious about the war. The 2d and 3d Battalions, on the right sector, were defending the line between the British on the east and the 5th Marines on the west.

At 0900 on 9 April, men from Charlie Company (temporarily attached to 2/1) and Easy Company were ordered to abandon their respective outpost defenses temporarily while an air strike was called to destroy nearby enemy positions. Simultaneously, a platoon of five tanks from Charlie Company, Tank Battalion, drove to the MLR to join in. Marine air struck the reverse slopes with bombs and bullets as the tanks fired nearly 250 rounds of 90-mm at various Chinese positions on the forward slope. During the air strike, Marine observers on line noted the position of an enemy machine gun firing at the diving planes. Calling in the map coordinates enabled fire controllers to direct tank fire accurately into the machine-gunner's position and destroy it.

On 10 April, Charlie Company, 1/1, personnel were relieved from the OPLR and returned to their parent battalion. They were replaced by Dog Company. No sooner had the relief been effected when the men began receiving mortar fire. Spotting the source, artillery was called in to saturate the area with VT.* Watching from atop the hill, the Marines cheered as Chinese troops fell into mass confusion, threw hand grenades among themselves, and fired burp guns everywhere. From the outpost, it appeared that the Chinese soldiers did more damage to each other than was caused by the artillery.

The Chinese, however, had no corner on the market when it came to confusion. On that same day, the Division Reconnaissance Company, deployed on the east side of the Han and Imjin Rivers, reported that two of its company's positions were attacked by friendly aircraft. The incident, observed by officers and men of the 1st and 2d Platoons, was reported in irate detail to Division Headquarters.

---

*Variable Time artillery fuses that can be adjusted to cause air bursts over the target.

At 1925, eight planes, identified as American F-80s or F-84s, passed over the company area and headed south at an estimated altitude of 1,500 feet. Four of the planes flying in column went into a shallow dive toward the Marine position. Sgt. Leroy Modrow, following the action through field glasses, watched in horror as muzzle flashes from the diving aircraft spit a stream of bullets at a group of ten Marines in the open. The rounds missed the Marines but impacted the dirt in front of them.

Completing the strafing run, the jets continued south along the Imjin River still at 1,500 feet. The lead plane then turned and made another pass, this time firing at Cpl. James Mayberry and Pfc. Samuel Bayless, who were manning an outpost. As the planes dived, the Marines immediately took cover. The aircraft fired two distinct bursts that missed the Marines by 15–20 yards but drilled holes through their shelter halves erected nearby. After killing the tent, our heroes flew off into the wild blue yonder.

As might be expected, the men were first frightened, then relieved, and finally very, very angry. Both platoon leaders, Lt. William Whitney and Lt. Robert Smith, witnessed the incident and wrote complete reports. The outcome, if documented, is not available to the author. A few days later, however, a shiny blue jeep drove up to the platoon CP and stopped. Two U.S. Air Force pilots dismounted and, meeting with Lieutenants Whitney and Smith, apologized for the error.

On the night of 15 April, Item Company, 3/1, received an enemy probe on one of its outpost positions (Hill 27). Fifteen minutes later, Easy Company, on a small hill to the south, was likewise probed by five or six enemy soldiers. The Marines returned fire, and the enemy withdrew under cover of increasing artillery fire. Suddenly, both outposts were hit with 76-mm artillery fire, accompanied by 82-mm and 120-mm mortar rounds. Within ten minutes, communications from George Company personnel related that Hill 27 was thought to be overrun. At midnight, all companies were reporting that they were receiving incessant artillery and mortar fire.

The fighting on the outpost that night is most accurately related by quoting from 3/1's Command Diary for 16 April 1952:

> At 0015, three men from Item Company's outpost came into the MLR, and at 0020 one more came into the MLR. All four men had suffered wounds and reported that their outpost had been over-run by 75 to 100 enemy. They believed that the remainder of the outpost were KIA. At 0030 all companies reported still receiving incoming rounds of all types. At 0130 one man from Item Company outpost reported into the Easy Company sector of the MLR. This man was

badly wounded and was evacuated. At 0130 artillery and mortar fire had decreased and only sporadic fire was being received by all companies on the OPLR. At this time the enemy was forced to withdraw by friendly mortar fire. During the attack the enemy fired approximately 765 rounds of mortar and artillery. This battalion suffered a total of 14 WIA's [wounded in action] and 5 MIA's [missing in action]. The 5 MIA's were believed to be KIA's. At 1401 a reinforced patrol from Item Company was sent to investigate results of the enemy probe. At 1425 the patrol reached the objective. 4 bodies of friendly KIA, previously listed as MIA, were recovered, leaving one MIA. A thorough search was made for this remaining MIA but no trace of him was found. Medical treatment was administered and the enemy WIA was evacuated but died while in transit to the MLR.[10]

MAKING A STAND

OP-3 was a 400-foot hill, well forward of the MLR, near Panmunjom. On the hill were eighty Marines, a reinforced platoon of Easy Company, 2/5. During the day, the men worked at improving defenses and digging trenches and fighting holes. At night, they stood watch.

During the late afternoon of 15 April, the outpost received two rounds of enemy 76-mm artillery that exploded without harm. Later, at dusk, it received four rounds of 122-mm mortar that injured one Marine. Unknown to the Marines on the hill, Chinese artillerymen were registering their pieces in preparation for an assault.

A half hour before midnight, a single green flare arched through the sky from Hill 67, an enemy strong point about 1,900 yards to the southwest. As the flare descended, Chinese artillery began to fire. Marines on the outpost were subjected to an intense artillery bombardment as 120-mm mortars and 76-mm artillery rounds fell around them. Twenty minutes later, another green flare, fired from the same place, signaled cessation to the shelling. Following an eerie five-minute silence, a third green flare appeared from Hill 67 and shelling resumed, this time impacting west of the outpost. Simultaneously, with the shift in artillery, waves of Chinese infantry began to attack.

The assault initially struck the front of the outpost but soon enveloped the hill on three sides. Drawing into a tight perimeter at one corner of the hill, the Marines fought back with small arms and hand grenades. The fighting raged, and the defenders were soon completely surrounded. They lost all communication with the MLR but they held. The first assault failed to dislodge the Marines.

There was a lull in the fighting as the Chinese pulled back to regroup, but they soon resumed the attack. The second attempt also failed, and they lost three of their number, who were captured by the defenders. For three hours, the fighting continued with wave after wave of enemy troops assaulting the small group of Marines. At one point, the momentum of attack carried Chinese soldiers into the defense perimeter among the Marines. The battle went hand to hand as the men used fists, bayonets, feet, and rifle butts to drive off the attackers. Still, the outpost held.

At 0315, the Communist forces withdrew from the battle of OP-3. It was estimated that they had thrown six to eight hundred troops into the assault and failed to drive the eighty Marines from the hill. Their casualties numbered ninety-five known and estimated killed or wounded. They also lost three men as prisoners of war. Marine casualties were six killed, five missing, and thirty-six wounded.

Although not a famous battle, the firefight on OP-3 was equal in courage to any of the last stands recorded in military history. There was one exception, however—this stand was successful. Greatly outnumbering the Marines, enemy troops failed in their objective, and most of the defenders survived.

Easy Company's Cpl. Duane Dewey, a machine gunner, was twice wounded. He contracted his second wound when an enemy hand grenade landed nearby as he was being treated for his original injury. Seeing the grenade, Dewey pulled the attending corpsman to the ground, called a warning to those around him, and rolled over onto the weapon as it exploded. Miraculously, he survived. A year later, Corporal Dewey reported to the White House in Washington, D.C., where President Eisenhower awarded him the Medal of Honor.

By mid-April, it became evident that some adjustments on the east side of the MLR were in order. On the far right, the line dividing the U.S. Marine division from the British Commonwealth division needed to be extended east, not that the Marines needed more area to defend but rather because they wanted to take better advantage of the natural terrain. The dividing line became the Samichon River, situated in a narrow north-south–oriented valley with defensible high ground on either side.

The change was effected on 14 April when the 1st and 3d Battalions of the 1st Marines were pulled from regimental reserve to relieve two Canadian regiments, the Royal Canadian Rifles and the Princess Patricia Light Infantry. The Canadians, displaced to the right, accepted responsibility for the heights on the east side of the valley. The new Marine sector would later become the site of some of the most lethal fighting of the war—at a place called the Hook.

BEHIND THE LINES

While the 1st and 5th Marine Regiments were on line during April, the 7th Marines functioned as the division reserve. The 2d Battalion was deployed on the Kimpo Peninsula with the Kimpo Provisional Regiment. The 1st and 3d Battalions were located south of the Imjin River behind the Jamestown Line. Although the men were away from the rigors and dangers of combat, reserve duty was not an opportunity for rest and relaxation. The troops followed a heavy training regimen and maintained a constant state of readiness while they awaited the call to move forward.

Between attending various schools, such as Noncommissioned Officers (NCO) School and Mine Warfare School, and performing training exercises, the troops improved rear blocking positions and patrolled for infiltrators. A typical day consisted of six hours of training, with much of the tactical work accomplished during hours of darkness. Squad- and platoon-sized patrols went out daily. In reserve, the term *patrols* was often a euphemism for long conditioning marches and twenty-four–hour hikes to maintain physical strength and unit cohesion.

It is a soldier's axiom that combat is endurable when compared with training. Without the adrenaline rush that fear inspires in combat, training can be tedious and boring. Despite the obvious drawbacks, most young Marines prefer life on line to the drudgery of training while in reserve.

Korean civilians presented an added difficulty to the Marines in reserve as they began to occupy former ROK army positions. Months earlier, in accordance with I Corps orders, a "stayback line" seven miles south of the Imjin River had been established to limit the movement of unauthorized civilians into forward areas. It was soon discovered that the ROK Army had been lax in enforcing this policy. Even in front of the MLR, there were occasional populated villages. Farmers were observed cultivating fields. Commerce across the river was brisk. One officer reported that there "was even a school operating in one area ahead of the Marine lines."[11]

Civilians who lived or worked forward of the stayback line were removed by Marine patrols augmented by the Korean National Police. Military police set up roving patrols and checkpoints to keep unauthorized civilians out of the stayback area and away from military installations.

Military police (MP) patrols working out of Division Headquarters spent much of their time enforcing the stayback rule. The concern was not only with spies, saboteurs, and Communist infiltrators but also with prostitution. Daily, MPs arrested suspected prostitutes; when they raided makeshift brothels and cribs, they arrested both civilians and military personnel. The randy men were usually Marines and occasionally American soldiers. Once, they even found five British soldiers poaching on the American side. In all cases, they turned the prostitutes over to civilian authorities and returned military personnel to their respective units for disposition. For the MPs, it was an endless project. There was no stopping the world's oldest profession. Although training in reserve might be arduous for some of the men, others took advantage of their time off line to sample offerings of the ladies. As might be expected, the incidence of venereal disease rose as units rotated into reserve.

ABANDONING THE OPLR

Meanwhile, changes were being made on the MLR. The extension of the line eastward that occurred on 14 April, when elements of the 1st Marines replaced Canadian units at the Samichon River, created a manpower problem. The Marine division was now responsible for 35½ miles of resistance, and the thinly held line was stretched well beyond capacity. Considering his options, Maj. Gen. John T. Selden, 1st Division commander, decided that manning the OPLR would be discontinued. While providing an additional line of resistance in front of the MLR, it also constituted a heavy drain on manpower. He chose instead to strengthen the MLR and to provide a stronger, more maneuverable reserve force behind the line. The OPLR was to be abandoned.

Frontline battalions were required to position all of their companies on line, thus doing away with reserve companies at the battalion level that had been manning the OPLR. Instead, a few permanent combat outposts were established that could be supplied and supported from the MLR. These outposts became permanent fixtures for the remainder of the war and, over time, witnessed the bulk of the fighting.

On 28 April, Sgt. Robert McNesky was a squad leader in the 2d Platoon of George Company, 3/1. His reinforced squad had been defending Hill 190.5 for the past week or two. When he received orders to abandon the outpost, the men were not pleased. McNesky remembers how he and his men felt:

> The orders were to abandon the outpost; we were quite let down as we felt we had earned every foot of it. Although we had suffered no casualties, we had been without food and sleep and we were in a high state of anxiety and anger; it was a perfect atmosphere for someone to get shot.

The relief squad left about noon. We policed the area, and I booby trapped the entire top of the hill, all the bunkers and the trench line. In the early afternoon we left 190.5 and as we backed out, I armed all the mines and put the pins in my shirt pocket.[12]

Sergeant McNesky's squad reached the MLR about 1600, and the exhausted Marines turned in for some long missed sleep. But it wasn't to last. Hearing an explosion on Hill 190.5 early the next morning, the squad was roused and told to investigate. The suspicion was that the enemy was planning to attack the Marine MLR but was first occupying the recently abandoned outpost in preparation for the assault. The third squad, led by Sergeant McNesky, was ordered to find out. McNesky tells of his squad's return to the hill on April 30:

. . . I picked five men out of the squad who were still eager to do some exploring. In order not to attract any attention, we crossed the saddle just below the ridge line, and on the way to Hill 190.5 I disarmed several mines.

We entered the deep trench on 190.5, being careful not to utter a sound. The trench leading into the bunkers was very deep and narrow; it went straight in and then encircled the outer perimeter of the hill.

The Chinks had been there all right; there were many signs and I could make out some blood and parts of clothing. The light was good at this time. I placed the men and gave orders not to move because it appeared to me that some of the mines had been moved.

All of a sudden, mortar shells were coming down like rain. We had no where to go! I had previously mined the entire area, and for all I knew the Chinese could have added mines of their own. Moving forward, I called for the rest to follow me to the open bunkers on the back side of the hill. We would have to take the chance that these had not been mined.

Carrying my carbine in my right hand, I turned to give the order to follow while running down the trench. After but a few steps, I detonated a mine; it could have been one of ours or it could have been one of theirs.

A flash of fire, with no noise. I went straight up in the air with my legs over my head. While flipping in the air, I saw that my right foot was gone and that my heel was hanging by the Achilles tendon. I hit the ground on my back, just a little back from where I had detonated the mine. My right finger and a small part of my hand was gone. I could only see out of my left eye, and a large piece of shrapnel was buried in my right cheek, sticking out so far I could see it with my good eye. My right hand and arm were full of shrapnel and my flak jacket was shredded on the right side.

Mortar shells were still coming down like rain. Lying on my back, I crawled up the trench, disarming the booby traps as I came to them. At each one, I had to turn over on my stomach and get a pin out of my pocket and insert it into the hole. Oddly enough, I was in no pain and my hand was steady. After each mine I prayed that the Chinese hadn't moved any more or placed some of their own. Soon the rest of the squad arrived and helped us into the bunkers. We had to get back to Hill 190, so Cpl. Melvin Weiss picked me up, putting me across his shoulders in a fireman carry, and made his way across the saddle, running most of the way.[13]

Sergeant McNesky was evacuated by helicopter from Hill 190 to a forward aid station where his condition was stabilized. He was subsequently flown to a hospital ship lying offshore in Inchon Harbor for more intensive treatment. Though severely wounded, had he not made the effort to disarm the remaining mines in that trench, the rest of his squad, no doubt, would have suffered a similar fate. He was later awarded a Silver Star for his action that morning.

CHAPTER 2

OUTPOST DEFENSE

*The most arduous, while at the same time the
most important duties that devolve upon soldiers
in the field are those of outposts.*
—Sir Garnet Wolseley

On 3 June 1952, Gen. Mark W. Clark, USA, Commander-in-Chief, Far
East; Lt. Gen. James A. Van Fleet, USA, Commander, Eighth Army; and
Maj. Gen. John W. O'Daniel, USA, Commander, I Corps, visited the 1st
Marine Division command post to attend a morning briefing presented
by the 1st Marine Division Commander, Maj. Gen. John Taylor Selden,
USMC. General Selden's address summarized the past four months of
progress in western Korea, known as the Outpost War. Excerpts from the
text of that summary constitute an informative and useful recap of the
war to that date:

> . . . The 1st Marine Division is opposed by two, top flight Chinese
> Communist Armies; namely, the 63rd and 65th, for a combined T/O
> strength of some eighty-odd thousands. Each army is composed of
> three divisions—all well trained, well equipped, and well supplied,
> and whose combat efficiency we can attest to.
>
> Since our arrival on the western front, the enemy has tightened
> and improved his defense considerably, evidencing a good deal of
> apprehension at our being here. His main concern seems to be to
> defend his command, communication, and supply center in the so
> called neutral city of Kaesong. He has demonstrated to a considerable
> degree, an ability to conduct well coordinated small unit probes and
> to place heavy concentrations of artillery and mortar fire accurately
> and in a short space of time. He retains a substantial attack and/or
> reinforcement capacity which he could execute at a moment's notice.

Recent indications are not sufficient, however, to make this his most likely course of action at this time.

The enemy's most probable course of action is to continue to defend with 24 battalions, supported by 12 battalions of artillery. This will give him a local reserve of 30 infantry battalions, plus one armored battalion, all of which he could commit within eight hours.

On the 12th of March, this division was holding a section of the main line of resistance on the eastern front. On that date, General Van Fleet visited my CP and announced his decision to detach the division from the Tenth Corps and to move it into the left sector of the I Corps, the move to be made by truck, (heavy equipment and tracked vehicles by sea) and to be accomplished prior to 1 April. On 16 March, Tenth Corps published the relief order. On 17 March, the First Korean Marine Regiment, at that time occupying the left of the division sector, entrucked and moved into position on the left of the new sector on 20 March. By the night of 24–25 March, the division had three of its four infantry regiments in the new sector and at 0400, the 25th, I assumed sector responsibility of Line Jamestown.

It was readily apparent that the relieved ROK Division had not been conducting an aggressive defense. Well populated villages existed between opposing lines. Farmers were cultivating their fields in full view of both forces. Traffic across the river was brisk. The ROK Division was in no position to hold Line Jamestown and, in fact, only expected to delay on it.

The sector of the main line of resistance assigned this division falls on unfavorable terrain, as it offers the enemy several main avenues of approach. Abnormal frontage precludes any appreciable depth and the position has the additional handicap of having a formidable obstacle, the Imjin River, at its back.

In actual frontage, from its right boundary to the First Korean Marine Regiment's left boundary, we have 19 and 2/10 miles of MLR. To the south, an additional area held by the LVT Battalion and Reconnaissance Company, totals 8 and 1/10 miles and on the KIMPO Peninsula, where I have a Provisional Regiment, we have 8 and 2/10 miles of frontage; making a total of 35 and 1/2 miles of actual frontage.

During its occupancy of this sector, the division has endeavored to conduct as active and aggressive a defense as possible. This is being accomplished by vigorous patrolling and full employment of supporting weapons, despite the handicaps imposed by the neutrality zone, the no-fire lines, the no-fly line and ammunition restrictions. An additional and very severe handicap has been the tremendous number of mines found in this sector—both enemy and unmarked friendly. The casualties caused by mines from 23 March to 10 April, amounted to 58 per cent of the total battle casualties, and from 10 April to 1 June, 17 per cent; or an average, since we have been in this area, of mine casualties, totaling 35 per cent.

In addition to active operations, the division begins, this month, refresher training in amphibious operations. It is planned that one battalion every two weeks will participate in landing exercises on one of the islands off Inchon. One CVE, one APA, an LSD, and two LST's will be employed in these operations.

One of the questions you asked, General Clark on your last visit, was whether or not I had my air with me. You may remember that, while I answered in the affirmative, I qualified it with the statement that they were not under my control, but under the control of the 5th Air Force. This has resulted in being required to submit requests for close air support through JOC. Eighty-seven such requests have been made (in compliance with existing directives) since our arrival in this sector, of this number, 42 requests were answered; 19 of the requests being furnished by Marine planes. The remaining 45 requests brought forth no aircraft.

The average time lag between origin of request and planes on target has been three hours and 39 minutes. The present system, from a Marine's point of view, is most unsatisfactory as too often the planes, even when they report, are not properly armed for the assigned mission. The scarcity of planes being furnished this Division has materially affected the proper coordination and training of both forward air controllers and pilots. This division has at all times, complied with orders issued by the Commanding General, 8th Army, which were published in November 1951, and on many occasions where close air support was desirable, requests were not submitted because they were not one hundred per cent in conformity with existing policies. The policy that I speak of is that aircraft will be available for close air support only to attack targets of opportunity which cannot be effectively engaged by artillery, such as troops in the open and definitely located artillery or tanks.

In all fairness to the Commanding General, 5th Air Force, I wish to bring to the attention of the Commander-in-Chief that, as of two weeks ago last Saturday, the Commanding General, 1st Marine Air Wing, obtained the approval of employing three divisions (four planes per division) daily over the 1st Marine Division sector for a period of thirty working days. This was done in order that the pilots and forward air controllers could once again become proficient in this most difficult and important technique of attack. While this token offering is appreciated, it is definitely not sufficient for this division, or, in my opinion, what is required for any other division on the 8th Army front. It is my earnest recommendation that the 1st Marine Air Wing be relieved of all deep support missions and this highly trained unit be assigned the mission of furnishing close air support across the 8th Army front. During the period 21 May to 1 June, 12 days, the First Air Wing flew 131 close support sorties. During the period the following damage was inflicted on the enemy:

Sixty-six bunkers destroyed, 49 personnel shelters, 6 observation posts, 53 counted killed in action, 27 mortar positions, one command post, 10 supply shelters, 5 artillery positions, 2 mortars, 4 artillery pieces and numerous other smaller installations, plus 7 secondary explosions were observed.

This division is fortunate in having a squadron of large helicopters temporarily attached. Headquarters Marine Corps sent this squadron to the Division for the purpose of developing helicopter tactics. Since its arrival, the squadron has been employed in two different operations in the presence of the enemy. Both proved highly successful. In addition, on the eastern sector, front line battalions were supplied and rotated by these helicopters. Since arrival on this coast, the Marine Reserve Battalion and the Korean Marine Battalion on Kimpo were rotated by the use of helicopters and one battalion of the Division Reserve was moved across the Imjin River. It is contemplated utilizing the squadron during amphibious training. They will move one company from the CVE to the beach.

While the defensive attitude dictated by the situation is foreign to this division, we are maintaining the offensive spirit by taking as much offensive action as permissible. We have control of the tactical situation and we expect to retain it.

Our supply plan is simple and flexible. In general, supplies arrive at the division railhead at Munsan-ni or Ascom City where distribution to the unit is made by utilizing the organic means of the division. In addition to supporting a reinforced Marine division, we are also responsible for the support of the First Korean Regiment, totaling 192 officers and 4,274 enlisted, and some 7,309 U.S. Army and Korean units; making a total of 38,986 individuals. This support does not mean that we furnish them with all classes of supply. There are certain units that only receive class one, others one and three, still others one, three and five.

We maintain 110 miles of road in this sector, plus 40 miles of the Kimpo Peninsula. Due to the scarcity of lumber for engineering missions, we are now operating a logging camp in rear of the First ROK Division. All organization and field maintenance is performed on vehicles in the Division by organic maintenance units. Laundry, bath, shoe repair, textile, typewriter repair facilities and fresh bread are handled by our Service Battalion. It is therefore quite obvious that we relieve, and reduce to the minimum, the cost on army service units not so completely equipped. However, the Army has been most helpful when our facilities were taxed to the maximum.

This division has a Medical Battalion consisting of a Headquarters Company, three Medical Companies and a Clearance Company. Our wounded and sick are usually evacuated, either by rail or helicopter, to the Naval Hospital Ship off Inchon. This procedure reduces the burden on MASH Hospitals.

In summation, I think it is safe to say that the morale of the First Division is excellent. The 1st Marine Division is ready and willing to move forward on order. We have written orders to defend Line Jamestown and it will be defended. We would likewise be happy to have the enemy attack down the Samichon Valley. That historical corridor is closed to Chinese traffic.[1]

That summarized the current situation of the First Marine Division in western Korea, a circumstance that was not destined to change until war's end: a static defense war for which the division was neither prepared nor equipped. The reinforced division was stretched thinly across a front that more properly should have been held by a corps. Backed up to a major river, deprived of nearly half their air support, and outnumbered nearly two to one by enemy troops, the Marines were expected to hold a determined enemy with little more than courage and audacity.

EVOLUTION OF THE OUTPOST DEFENSE
U.S. Marine Corps doctrine, as based on the successes of World War II campaigns, encourages maneuver and attack. Offensive combat experienced first on Guadalcanal and evolving through the island fighting of that war stressed one simple objective—destroy the enemy or drive him into the sea. During the first few months of the Korean War, that doctrine remained unchanged.

The Marines were organized and trained as light infantry to hit hard and to maneuver swiftly. The idea of digging in and fighting defensively for any great length of time was foreign to Marine thinking and training. Siege warfare was the antithesis of Marine Corps philosophy. Creation of a military stalemate during the last half of the Korean war, however, found the Marines in precisely that position. Consequently, they had to improvise, to create tactics, and to improve methods with which they had had little experience. Outpost warfare was not a planned tactic; it just evolved, lubricated by the blood of some thirteen thousand young men. Painfully and slowly, the Marines learned from trial and error that a static war could be as deadly as one of maneuver. It simply took longer. Functioning in slow motion, it was a war of attrition against the largest army in the world.

In 1952, the Marine division on the Jamestown Line was truly a round peg in a square hole, despite the fact that it was still the best fighting unit available in Korea. Providing the greatest bang for the buck, the 1st Marine Division remained deployed for defense when it should have been withdrawn for assault elsewhere. Yet, there were to be no more amphibious assaults. In Korea, the Marines had to learn to fight defensively, to dig in and await an attack, to fortify a position and hold it—and, worse yet, to let it go.

Throughout history, armies have posted security details in front of the main body of troops to provide early warning of enemy threat. The practice is neither new nor unique. Known by many names—picket line, listening post, or outpost—a forward security detail is regularly accepted as an essential element of military tactics. During the maneuver phase of the war in Korea (1950–1951), an outpost often consisted of fewer than a dozen men, a squad or fire team posted around or in front of a company perimeter while the company paused for the night. The following morning, the outpost was abandoned and the men rejoined their unit. Everyone moved out. An outpost was temporary security lasting a night, maybe two.

Because the use of outposts was an accepted and necessary practice while the Marines were on the move, it became a simple matter to continue it when the situation evolved into static defense. Later, the Marines realized that temporary outposts were not a satisfactory tactic. No one was going anywhere. They were now dug in and facing the enemy. The siege had begun.

Earlier in 1952, the OPLR had been one of the initial efforts of defense building. Established when the Marines moved onto the Jamestown Line in March, the OPLR consisted of a series of strong points built around commanding terrain features that screened the MLR. On average, the OPLR was about 2,500 yards forward of the MLR.

The flaw with the OPLR defense was its application. Originally a temporary tactic, it was not functioning on a permanent basis. In most cases, outposts were established in the same place each night by different units as if they were going to move elsewhere the following day and never return, such as in a war of maneuver.

Commonly manned by a fire team or squad, or occasionally a platoon, the job of the outpost was to give warning. The men were not charged to defend a hill. The following evening, the cycle repeated itself as a different unit left the MLR to man the outpost for another night. Thus, each unit went out as though the outpost was being manned for the first time. Food, ammunition, weapons, and supplies were carried out, and the trails were checked for mines. En route, the men were wary of ambushes. When they arrived, because the location had been abandoned, even briefly, they reexamined each position for booby traps. Daily, the Marines took casualties as squads and fire teams went out and returned from positions on the OPLR. S/Sgt. Dave Evans of George Company, 3/1, described his recollections of the OPLR:

A lot of the smaller outposts were only manned or checked during the daytime and were abandoned at night. Sometimes an assortment of mines and booby traps were left behind because the Chinese had these outposts during the night hours. As the summer wore on the Chinese became good at finding our little surprises and occasionally either moved or stole our booby traps.

At daybreak Marines from larger outposts would now engage in an exercise called "Recovery." This would usually be a squad with a machine gun that would go out to check these smaller outposts to see if we still owned them. Most of the time this was a routine affair, but sometimes the surprise would be on the recovery group. Frequently the Chinese would add their own booby traps, and a number of Marines lost feet and legs to these surprises.[2]

On 2 June 1952, Pfc. Carl Winterwerp, a machine gunner with George Company, 3/1, described one of the surprises that the Chinese troops left on an outpost for the returning Marines:

...We quickly moved toward the listening post at the base of Hill 190 [later Outpost Elmer]. I remember setting my gun to cover the patrol which checked positions as it moved into the listening post.

After a while they called me in. After setting the gun up in an existing gun emplacement, I began heating a can of C ration hamburgers for breakfast. I heard an explosion on my right. At the same instant that I turned toward the explosion, I was blown into the air out of the gun emplacement. Everyone was hollering, "Incoming, incoming, take cover!"

When I hit the ground, I found I could not stand. I found my buddies in my position were both wounded pretty bad; one had lost his leg below the knee, the other was blinded by the flash and his face was peppered with fine pieces of shrapnel.

I crawled on my belly to the patrol leader's position, telling him that the area had been mined. Apparently the Chinese had slipped into the listening post the previous night and had placed "shoe [Schu] box mines" in our positions. These anti-personnel mines were not meant to kill, just to inflict serious wounds. Three eighteen year old Marines lost their right legs below the knee. Even though my legs were injured severely, the Navy surgeons were able to save them.[3]

A second flaw with the OPLR defense was manpower. Battalions on the Jamestown Line were spread so thin that they could ill afford to degrade defenses further in order to man outposts. By default, the reserve battalions furnished troops to man outposts. This practice severely encroached on the purpose of having a reserve. Not only were training, resupply, and recovery curtailed, but, as it turned out, the men from reserve who went out to the outposts each night were doing more fighting than units on the MLR. The manpower situation had become topsy-turvy.

In April 1952, the OPLR was abandoned in favor of a series of strong points located closer to the MLR. Although many of the new positions were manned only at night, they were closer in and the routes to them could be better and more consistently observed. Their proximity also had the effect of reducing, but not eliminating, enemy opportunities for ambush and the mining of trails. These positions could be manned by personnel from line battalions on line rather than by those from reserve.

To maintain an aggressive defense, MLR units employed snipers all along the Jamestown Line and sent out daily patrols to seek out Chinese activity and to probe defenses. Battalions routinely reported as many as 300 to 400 men deployed daily in front of the MLR to patrol or to man various outposts. With four battalions on line, this amounted to a total of approximately 1,500 men. It was here that the bulk of the ground fighting occurred—frequent small skirmishes between patrols in no-man's-land or probes, raids, and assaults on enemy positions. During later months, some of the outpost fighting became particularly intense, but rarely was the MLR seriously attacked, which perhaps supported the validity of the outpost defense as a tactic.

When the OPLR was pulled back, new outposts began to gain varying degrees of permanence. Closer to the MLR, they were more defensible and more easily supplied. Typically, an outpost was within eyesight, or even earshot, of the MLR. Units from a single company on the MLR rotated posting to an outpost for a night, a week, and in rare cases a month or more. As 1952 progressed, the Marines dug permanent trenches, fighting holes, and bunkers. They emplaced guns, laid communication lines, and strung defensive wire. Outposts took on the appearance of defendable fighting positions, which in fact they had become. In some cases the outposts even had outposts—listening posts in front of the wire that one or two Marines manned at night to warn of enemy activity.

Although surrounded by no-man's-land, an outpost was generally most secure to its rear where it was protected by observation and fire from the MLR. This was not always the case, however, as terrain features could sometimes obscure enemy approaches. Also, darkness brought with it the opportunity for an unseen enemy approach, the furtive mining of trails, or a silent ambush. Nearly all of the combat in Korea occurred at night.

A rifle company supporting an outpost to its near front was relatively secure from serious enemy probes, but the reality of a sniper's bullet or incoming artillery was a constant reminder that the troops were not on a field exercise. On the other hand, if the outposts were farther away, both the outpost and the MLR had even greater vulnerability to enemy attack.

During the day, outposts were valuable places for observation. Overlooking, or at least in sight of, Chinese positions, the Marines could often spot enemy weapon, mortar, and machine-gun emplacements. During an air strike, observers might locate antiaircraft fire as forward air controllers direct the bombing. When the Marines saw Chinese soldiers moving in the open, they could direct artillery and mortars to blast them.

After dark, the outpost became a checkpoint for patrols, a gateway to enter hostile territory and patrol, set up ambushes, and initiate raids on enemy outposts. It served as a safe haven for withdrawal under fire and for the evacuation of wounded, as well as a position for directing fire and gaining intelligence. Frequently, a fire team or small group of Marines from the Reconnaissance Company left an outpost during darkness to conduct a layout. Two to four men entered no-man's-land to lay out for the night or, in many cases, for a complete twenty-four–hour cycle. Moving only when necessary, the layout team, having preselected a likely site, could observe and note enemy movements and activity. If the location proved unproductive, the team might quietly move to another site.

Traveling light, the recon men carried their own food and depended upon stealth and camouflage to survive. On rare occasions, when radio communication was adequate, a layout team might direct mortar fire or a sniper to an opportune target. After returning to the outpost and then to the MLR, the patrol leader submitted a detailed intelligence report describing enemy trenches and positions of activity, new areas of digging, or the lack thereof. Layouts were the next best thing to capturing a prisoner.

MANNING THE OUTPOST

Over passing months, many outposts became stabilized, whereas others were lost altogether. As new positions were established, former outposts were written off as too expensive in men and material to retain. Across the four-battalion Marine Corps front, excluding the Korean Marine sector, there were anywhere from ten to twenty outposts. As a general pattern, the number of outposts slowly diminished from June 1952 through the end of the fighting in July 1953.

The size of outposts varied considerably. The oldest was Combat Outpost Two. Located near the Panmunjom neutral corridor, it was the most heavily fortified outpost on the Jamestown Line. The hill was manned by a rifle company reinforced with heavy machine guns and mortars and later with tanks. Smaller outposts had to manage with much less, a platoon or squad; some had only a six-man reinforced fire team commanded by a sergeant.

The complement of a typical platoon outpost might be a lieutenant, platoon sergeant, radioman, corpsman, mortar forward observer, rifle squad, and machine-gun squad. Defense of the hill depended more on supporting arms from the MLR than on outpost weapons. Moreover, because nearly all attacks took place at night, hand grenades were usually the weapon of choice. Barrages of friendly mortars from the MLR zeroed in on approaches to protect the defenders. The Marines learned that it was most efficient to garrison an outpost with as few men as possible. If a hill was overcrowded, sudden doses of incoming enemy fire resulted in too many casualties.

Because the Chinese were able to observe most outposts, the Marines were careful to minimize movement and exposure during daylight. They had learned that Chinese snipers could shoot accurately and that sporadic incoming fire frequently resulted from a careless display of a head or an arm. Most of the men remained under cover in their holes and bunkers while they slept, cleaned weapons, and waited for the night.

As darkness fell, the men prepared for an attack that they knew would come, either on their position or on another outpost. Nights were eerie. The men could see flares and lines of tracers off in the distance as one or another position was attacked. Artillery flashes lit the horizon. To the rear, the fire was friendly; in front, it was Chinese. Men in fighting holes were alert. Rifles were unlocked and ready, rounds were in the chambers of machine guns, and grenades were stacked like rows of eggs on a shelf, within arm's reach. They waited.

Each night supply trains, columns of Korean Service Corps (KSC) laborers, brought in supplies of food, ammunition, wire, sandbags, and mail from the MLR. Everything the outpost needed was carried on the backs of Marines and KSCs. By October 1952, each Marine regiment had as many as eight hundred Korean laborers. Usually, a supply train was escorted by a patrol of Marines that protected the Koreans and carried some of the less cumbersome supplies. As soon as a supply train left the protection of the MLR, it was subject to ambush or enemy mortars zeroing in on the trail. The Chinese were as aware of the routine as were the Marines.

On many occasions, civilian KSC laborers acted as stretcher bearers on return trips to the MLR. Seriously wounded men on an outpost had to be carried or walked back to the MLR to receive medical attention. Corpsmen on an outpost could only stop the bleeding, administer morphine, and dress a wound, all temporary measures. Airlift or motorized transport for the wounded was impossible. Using healthy Marines to carry the wounded diminished the outpost defense by that many rifles, usually four. Korean laborers were the bearers of choice. A large number of Marines owe their lives to old, unarmed Korean men, unfit for military service, who frequently put their own lives at risk to carry supplies to and wounded from outpost strongholds.

Nighttime was the only opportunity to repair and reinforce barbed-wire entanglements surrounding the hill. The Marines placed booby-trapped grenades near the wire and hung empty C-ration cans containing a few pebbles on the wire to rattle when disturbed. They dug deeper trenches and built storage bunkers and heads on the reverse slope. Outpost maintenance never ended.

Listening posts were established a dozen yards or more in front of the wire. Armed with a bag full of grenades so as not to give away his position, the man on a listening post watched and waited. He strained his eyes and ears in the darkness as he looked for enemy troops. If he saw them coming, he might give two clicks on his sound-powered phone and try to make it back under the wire. He might even throw a few hand grenades to slow them, but they seldom did. When the Chinese attacked, they charged right over the top of their dead and wounded companions, not to mention a Marine listening post that might be in the way. As Staff Sergeant Evans said:

> Every night, immediately after nightfall, which someone always took great pains to identify as 2200, every rifle platoon would have each squad send out men to man a listening post. This fun activity

involved a fire team with one man carrying a hand receiver which would be hooked up by a wire that was connected to the platoon or company CP receiver. The fire team leader would then lead this group well in front of all company positions. Normally this was a 4 hour watch with a very minimum of moving around unless circumstances dictated you move out; this circumstance was supposed to be approved by a voice on the end of the receiver. Trying to whisper in a hand receiver that 10 enemy soldiers were 20 yards on your right flank made for a lot of wet pants or worse.[4]

Responsibility for manning, supplying, and fortifying a combat outpost was delegated to the frontline company commander, usually a captain but often a first lieutenant. He had to weigh its demands against those of his portion of the MLR as he tried to obtain maximum use of resources in both efforts. Simultaneously, he was expected to fulfill the battalion's requirements for nightly patrols in front of the MLR.

Where an outpost was close to the MLR and relatively safe from enemy fire, the strain on the rifle company was less severe. But when the advanced position was 800–1,000 yards distant, under persistent enemy bombardment, and subject to encirclement or assault each night, the company commander was forced to employ every trick he had to prevent the exhaustion of his men or the success of enemy tactics. It was not unusual to find two thirds of a company forward of the MLR during darkness, either manning outposts or protecting them.

Direct-fire weapons on the MLR were sighted in to furnish long-range support in case of attack. The company commander coordinated his mortar fire with those of higher units as further support for this forward echelon.

DEFENDING THE HILLTOPS

With manpower as their greatest asset, Chinese army commanders were content to suffer daily artillery shelling while awaiting an opportune moment to attack. For days, Chinese retaliation might be weak to non-existent, but the Chinese soldier was not idle, merely patient.

Each night, when darkness masked their movements from the air, the Chinese were digging. Industriously creeping toward an outpost, enemy soldiers constructed approach trenches and bunkers in which to place supporting machine guns, mortars, and rocket launchers. On the chosen night, they massed several companies and, with a concerted effort, attempted to rush and overwhelm the position. The rush was usually preceded by mortar and artillery fire that began as much as a day before the attack. It was not abnormal for barrages to reach concentrations of more than a thousand rounds per hour as they fell on one small, platoon-sized area. It was a wonderment that anyone lived through such a shelling. Many Marines did not.

When the attack came, Chinese soldiers charged up a hill under and often inside their own falling artillery. They came in overwhelming numbers, waves of men armed with burp guns, satchel charges, machine guns, and hand grenades. An outpost defended by a squad might be attacked by a company or a platoon by three companies. In some of the major outpost battles, Chinese battalions attacked Marine positions defended by fewer than forty men.

During an attack, the Marines made every effort to isolate the outpost with artillery and mortar fire. Their objective was to create a curtain of exploding shells between the defenders and the attackers. When possible, a squad or fire team held a blocking position between the outpost and the MLR to observe and guard against envelopment.

When an outpost was surrounded, targeted with enormous artillery and mortar concentrations, and then hit by overwhelming numbers of enemy troops, the Marine defenders might have had little chance of survival except for previously prepared concentrations of friendly supporting arms, tanks, artillery, and mortars firing from the MLR and beyond. Prearranged "box-me-in" barrages (friendly artillery or mortar patterns that surround the target) from Marine lines had a devastating effect on the mass of enemy troops advancing toward an outpost. Fire from the outpost itself, mostly from automatic weapons with overlapping fields of fire, created a wall of death. This tactic was especially effective as the assault slowed to breach barbed-wire entanglements strung generously around the position.

When the enemy penetrated the outpost defenses (a frequent occurrence, given the fact that Chinese generals did not seem concerned about the death rate of their men), the last resort was to call in VT. Facing VT-fused artillery was a step short of suicide. When overrun, outnumbered, and low on ammunition, an outpost garrison might withdraw into the deepest and strongest bunkers on the hill and the leader call for artillery on his position. The VT-fused shells resulted in repeated aerial bursts falling like rain over the outpost. The effect was devastating. Swathes of exploding hot shrapnel rained over the position. Nothing exposed was able to survive. Enemy soldiers on the hillsides and in the trenches were destroyed. Virtually nothing of flesh remained intact after a VT barrage. To troops in the open, the effect was gruesome.

Unfortunately for the Marines, Chinese soldiers who found bunkers for themselves also survived. Upon cessation of the barrage, it was an easy matter for a surviving enemy soldier to throw a grenade or demolitions charge into a bunker full of Marines, thus proving that for every defense there can be a superior offense.

Sooner or later, the Chinese ran out of manpower, ammunition, or enthusiasm and withdrew from the hill. The defenders were left to patch up, clean up, reinforce, and prepare for the next assault that was certain to come.

NAMING THE HILLS

Over the months, outposts received the ultimate symbol of permanence—a name. Formerly, in keeping with the temporary aspects of maneuver war, outposts were unnamed. Why bother? There was no need to name a place that would be briefly held.

As the year progressed, it was becoming apparent to even the most aggressive Marine that his outfit was not likely to be moving forward soon. Permanent defensive positions were in place. The large-scale assaults were prohibited. Outposts, like the MLR, began to take on permanent functions.

At first, outposts, like all the hills, were simply referred to by their map elevation in meters, such as Hill 190 and Hill 124. Ultimately, this created identification problems because not all the hilltops were numbered on the topographical maps. Moreover, many hills that were numbered had identical elevations, hence there were duplicate numbers. Outposts were later assigned individual identifying numbers, sometimes sequential (e.g., OP-1, COP-2, OP-3).

The naming of hills and places became a more practical way to identify various locations. The names can be very confusing to the historian, however, because the names did not remain consistent throughout the war. Irregularly, for reasons of security, it became necessary to change names. Hill 190, for example, became Outpost Chicago for a time and was later changed to Outpost Elmer. Finally, after being lost to the Chinese, it remained unnamed and was thereafter referred to only by grid coordinates on the map. Outposts One and Two, near Panmunjom and the neutral corridor, remained unchanged throughout the war. Other outposts changed names three or four times. Outpost Yoke, for example, was lost to the Chinese in June 1952 but continued to be referred to as Yoke for the remainder of the war, even after it became a Chinese outpost.

A Chinese strong point named Taedok-san on the map was always referred to by its proper Korean name, never by its elevation of 236 meters. Paradoxically, a few thousand yards south of Taedok-san was the Marine command post on Paehok, known universally by its elevation, Hill 229.

Other places assumed names based on their identifying character-istics on a topographical map—Boot, Hook, Arrowhead, and Three Fingers. Some outposts carried men's names, including Clarence, Bruce, and Allen, whereas others were named after women: Marilyn, Ingrid, and Hedy. (Rumor has it that Outpost Dagmar, because of its two pro-nounced peaks, was named after a large-busted actress popular at the time.) Later, many of the names were changed to reflect the names of cities, such as Reno, Warsaw, Frisco, Detroit, and Berlin.

Among outposts, Combat Outpost Two (COP-2) was different. Most outposts were relatively small and less than a mile in front of the lines. By contrast, COP-2 was six miles in front of the MLR, deep in hostile land. Sited on a large hill, there was enough room to position a heavily reinforced company. At that extreme distance, it could not have existed except for the strange rules of warfare in Korea. The enabling factor for survival of COP-2 was the Panmunjom neutral corridor. Like a huge umbilical cord, the secure neutral corridor extending from the MLR safely provided the means to sustain the men perched in no-man's-land, but the corridor also created a barrier to adequate defense of the posi-tion. The vulnerability of COP-2 was described in a letter written by Capt. Bernard W. Peterson, a Marine forward air controller at COP-2:

> The goonies consider OP2 a thorn in their side, and it is anticipated they will try to recover it by any means possible. They could actually encircle us and wouldn't be in violation of the corridor because the corridor only extends 500 meters on either side [of the road]. If we should become encircled we would, by sheer necessity, be required to call in aircraft to aid in getting us out. And, if my request was granted, the aircraft would have to violate the air corridor and Panmunjom in order to get in close enough to give me close air support, and we would then be in violation of the peace talk arrangements—and Boom WWIII!! . . . I'm frankly quite shook, especially after having studied the enemy situation map.[5]

EFFECTIVENESS OF THE OUTPOST DEFENSE

In October 1952, following several costly battles for outpost positions, the division commander ordered a survey of the tactical requirements for existing outpost positions and an analysis of all Jamestown Line defenses. The report pointed out that certain outposts could be defended successfully against determined attacks, whereas others could be readily neutralized and overrun whenever the enemy was willing to sacrifice the manpower. It was also noted that occupation of terrain did not necessarily control an area.

Marine combat outposts in western Korea evolved into platoon or squad defense areas, rather than into security and delaying positions. They added depth to the entire defense in that they were actively defended, but many were still too far forward of the MLR to be strongly supported. By December, most of the combat outposts had been moved back to a more practical supporting distance from the MLR.

As the year progressed, a number of Marine infantry unit commanders concluded that the main line of resistance concept had been too literally interpreted on the Jamestown Line. Rather, they felt that a concept of a main area of resistance with depth should be introduced. It was argued that a wide-fronted linear defense dissipated strength and made strong, mutually supporting fire difficult. The lack of depth did not provide for receiving the shock of an enemy attack or for weakening the attackers before their ejection by counterattack.

Instead of a long, thin trench line, it was felt that a defense in depth, using a series of strong points, was desirable. This was the tactic used by the British Commonwealth Division in the sector on the 1st Marine Division's right. Using a series of strong points, which insofar as possible were mutually supporting, the British did not attempt to hold a main line of resistance. Neither did they hold outposts. The British felt that if a piece of ground was worth fighting for, it should be included in the main defenses. Outposts or not, their sector was effectively defended, but it was also a good deal smaller. One Scottish officer, in discussing the Marine organization of defense, stated, "You dissipate your strength trying to make your basketball courts in the rear safe."[6]

Lt. Col. Norman W. Hicks, in writing his master's thesis, quoted the opinion of a Marine officer concerning his experience with the outpost war:

> With regard to the outpost warfare in general, frankly, our defense at that time was not sound. The MLR was a continuous line—and a damned thin one with scattered outposts out in front of it. The outposts were not strong points, and any time the enemy put pressure on one, it had to be reinforced. While a far greater area had to be defended than was considered conventional, I am convinced we could have done it with much more effectiveness by a series of strong points in lieu of the line we maintained. I found the best way of coping with

this situation was by active and energetic patrols which kept the pressure of the creeping enemy back. This activity was also great for morale because it kept the men physically engaged rather than sitting in holes worrying about incoming.[7]

Before one completely embraces the British system, one must accept the reality of a thirty-five–mile sector—three times greater, for example, than any sector held by a single division during World War I—defended by a single division. The line was so thin that it was nearly transparent.

As a consequence, a defense in depth also would have been considerably more shallow than was desirable. Writing for the *Marine Corps Gazette,* Lt. Col. R. J. Batterton, Jr., made the point that the method of defense depended more heavily on terrain and the enemy. In some areas, the Marines maintained mutually supporting strong points like those of the British. In others, it was impractical, if not impossible. Faced with the ever-present "economy of manpower," the Marines based deployment of their defenses on the terrain situation at hand.[8]

Contributing to that decision was the fact that the predominant tactic of the Chinese Army was one of infiltration and envelopment, rather than a blitzkrieg through the line. Neither the outposts nor the MLR would have been sufficient to stop, or even slow, a Rommel-like push south across the Jamestown Line.

The Chinese Army was not equipped to sustain or maintain such a push. The Chinese built their tactics on their strength, rather than their weakness. They continued to use infantry and artillery without support of tanks and air, hence the effort to infiltrate, surround, and conquer. Recognizing that tactic as a fact, Batterton supported the Marine outpost/MLR defense when he wrote, "The enemy simply cannot be permitted the opportunity to threaten infiltration, envelopment of a flank, or isolation of a position where cover and concealment prevent our supporting fires from locating and stopping him."[9]

DEFENDING THE MLR

The whole point of outposts, aggressive patrolling, and other tactics was to defend the MLR, that thinly held trench line meandering along and over the hilltops of Korea. Behind its outposts, minefields, and barbed wire, the Marine MLR defense was a single continuous trench linking bunkers, fighting holes, and weapons emplacements. Built as a line, rather than as a series of unit perimeters, the forward-slope MLR effectively stopped enemy units from infiltrating to the rear.

Where Marine outposts in no-man's-land shielded the MLR from surprise attack, the line was manned with relative impunity. Where no such buffers existed, the MLR was subjected to small unit probes, daily harassing fire, and the threat of an all-out attack. Like the men on an outpost, line companies on the MLR had to be prepared to deal with an enemy attack. Unlike the men on the outpost, however, those on the MLR had to hold until reinforced because they had no place to go. Consequently, the MLR became heavily fortified bastions. A rifle company on line was heavily beefed up with attached weapons. Freed from the burden of backpacking their ammunition, mortarmen and machine gunners often manned double their allocation of weapons. Frequently, the battalion weapons company distributed extra men and machine guns to the line. Crews for up to four heavy .30-caliber and a brace of .50-caliber machine guns to provide long-distance support augmented a company's normal complement. Where terrain permitted, a company might have 75-mm recoilless rifles and tanks firing from revetments dug into the hilltops.

A company also had mortar, air, and artillery forward observer teams; mine-clearance teams; and cooks and clerks all capable of being pressed into use as riflemen. Additionally, in times of need, platoons of men from battalion headquarters were rushed forward to the MLR. The Marine practice of training every man to be a rifleman had frequently proved to be valid. There was little rest for men in a line company, regardless of their job. Everyone managed to share the misery and danger of life on the MLR.

Platoon frontage on the MLR varied between 400 and 700 yards, depending on the number, strength, and location of the company outposts. In numbers of men, a typical line platoon was quite large. It often consisted of a lieutenant, a platoon sergeant, two corpsmen, three rifle squads, a light machine-gun section, a heavy machine-gun squad, wiremen, and company rocketeers and engineers, for a total of seventy to one hundred men.

Reinforcement of the line was the primary function of reserve units. Frequently, components of the reserve battalion were moved forward to augment a company that found itself engaged and fully committed. To allow the enemy to break through the MLR was unthinkable.

Maintenance and improvement of fighting positions were constant preoccupations on line. As the war progressed into 1953, the Chinese became increasingly well equipped with artillery and mortars. Likewise, they improved their accuracy and accumulation of ammunition. As a result, supply routes, outposts, and the MLR received more incoming fire, more frequently and in greater and more severe concentrations, than ever before. It was essential that the line be well dug in if the men were to survive the daily allocation of severe incoming barrages that accompanied the Chinese attempts to break through the MLR.

Ideally, trenches were dug 6–8 feet deep. Bunkers were constructed from timbers 6–12 inches thick. The completed framework was covered with roofing felt and multiple layers of sandbags. The finished bunker was designed to withstand direct hits from 105-mm or 120-mm shells.

Construction on line was facilitated by KSC laborers, who hauled timbers, dug holes, and built bunkers. Often, as much as 60 cubic feet of earth and rock would have to be moved with pick and shovel to excavate a single four-man bunker.

After the war, Batterton wrote that, in his opinion, bunkers on the MLR were often overbuilt. Twelve-by-twelve timbers, he noted, were nearly impossible to carry, especially up the steep paths leading to positions atop the Korean hills. Observing that a direct hit was relatively rare, he recommended bunkers of lighter construction, with 8-inch or even 6-inch beams, built lower to the ground.[10]

Batterton was probably right. Accidental deaths from rain-soaked collapsing bunkers appeared to be far more prevalent than those caused by direct hits. Prefabricated bunkers were also devised, but in the long run, they proved to be unsatisfactory for installation on the MLR.

Barbed Wire

Barbed wire was an essential but labor-intensive asset on the MLR and at the outposts. Suffering the ravages of frequent incoming fire, its replacement and repair were nightly chores. Carried to the MLR by KSC laborers in bulky 100-pound rolls, barbed wire was used to fashion thick double belts of concertina in front of the trenches. In areas of light enemy activity, the Marines were often able to "persuade" (read: bribe with cigarettes, food, or warm clothing) the KSC men to unroll and string wire across the forward slope. In areas of greater activity, where the Chinese were more aggressive, no persuasion was possible. The Marines did it themselves under cover of darkness.

The wire had to be strung quickly and quietly without using light. If the Chinese detected that a wire party was working, they shelled the location with mortars. John J. O'Hagan, a sergeant with the 7th Marines, reminisced about wire details in a letter:

After a period of time the outpost would lose its barbed wire. Wire would be blown up and cut by shrapnel. The stakes especially would be knocked over and required regular repair.

One night I was involved in laying additional wire on the right front of OP Dagmar. With a fire team of Marines and six KSC's, we proceeded down the forward slope. It was winter and bitterly cold. I had just made sergeant and was second in command of the outpost.

Try and imagine driving a five foot steel stake in frozen clay, quietly. One or two KSC's would hold the stake while another would hold a folded sand bag over the top to muffle the sound. The guy with the sledge hammer swung, trying to hit the stake. Believe me, the poor guys holding the stake would end up with a pair of sore, swollen hands from the times the sledge missed.

This night our fire team was down side from the wire with three KSC's. We drew some mortar fire and two of the KSC's were hit. They received minor shrapnel wounds in both legs. I sent both of them back to the trenchline. We tried driving more stakes but couldn't get them deep enough to support the wire. I had to cancel that detail and spread the single roll of barbed wire on top of what was already there. The slope definitely needed more but would have to wait for warmer weather when the ground thawed out.[11]

Reflecting on working with barbed wire, O'Hagan recalled, "Wire gloves and cutters were always in short supply, apparently considered necessary in only small numbers by logisticians. When more were requested the answer received was that we had our allowance, we just lost them or didn't take care of them."[12] Some aspects of war never seem to change.

PSYCHOLOGICAL WARFARE

Bullets and bombs were not the only weapons used in Korea. There was also the battle of words—psychological warfare. The Marines found it amusing.

The EUSAK (Eighth U.S. Army Korea) Psychological Warfare Unit was a small group of U.S. soldiers who traveled about the MLR and broadcast propaganda over huge loudspeakers directed toward Chinese units. They also left leaflets for the enemy to pick up and read. The Chinese, too, had their psychological tactics and directed the same sort of rhetoric toward the Americans. The objective of both endeavors, of course, was to persuade members of opposing sides to lay down their arms and surrender. Because it had little visible effect on the troops of either side, psychological warfare, as practiced in Korea, appeared to be a small, if not quaint, waste of effort.

During May, the EUSAK Psychological Warfare Unit was in the area occupied by the 1st Marines, the far right sector of the MLR. The unit broadcast five or six brief Chinese lectures every night. To induce a feeling of nostalgia, the lectures were preceded by the unit interpreter playing Chinese music on a harmonica. The lectures carried assorted appeals based on the futility of further resistance and gave detailed instructions on how to surrender. They offered evidence of the good treatment given to UN prisoners of war and emphasized fair treatment, good food, adequate shelter and clothing, and medical assistance. Timely news items injected into the lectures countered Communist fabrications.

Typical of the Chinese response were personal letters written in Chinese that the Marines found in front of the MLR one morning. The letters had been left in front of Hill 229, a place seldom patrolled by the Chinese. Obviously, they were intended for the Marines. One letter read:

> To all American Soldiers:
> Since you came to Korean battlefield you don't have the chance to sleep during the night or day. You are forced to work very hard. You don't get enough to eat. We can give you powdered eggs. They give you little cans of food. We give you powdered eggs; we guarantee there are no germs in the eggs. Any time you want the eggs, you come to us. Chinese are kind to prisoners of war. When you get these eggs and letter your interpreter will explain this to you. I can't talk anymore.[13]

It was signed "Someone." Who could possibly resist such a warm appeal? As no Marine was ever known to desert for his share of powdered eggs, it might be fair to assume that the invitation was not very effective. It did help the Marines to begin their day on a lighter note, however.

COMMUNICATIONS
Communications was a major problem on outposts. It was critical for the OP commander to maintain contact with his parent unit on the MLR. Requests for supporting fires originated from the OPs, as did reports of the coming and goings of patrols, both friendly and enemy. During an attack, it was essential that targets for artillery and tank fire be communicated, as were requests for illumination or reinforcements. An outpost without effective communication was not useful to the MLR and was quite vulnerable.

Mobile radio equipment was subject to the vagaries of age, weather, abuse, battery condition, and other gremlins of war. In short, it was not reliable. The preferred mode of communication was telephone, a simple but reliable device connected to the MLR by the communication (comm) wire that was occasionally buried in the ground but more often simply strung along its surface.

Sergeant O'Hagan mentioned some of the communications problems on his outpost:

> Communications were a joke. For the most part we used sound power units with comm wire that was brittle, outdated, and easily broken. As it was usually lying exposed on the ground the wire was frequently severed by incoming shells or cut by infiltrators prior to an assault. When that happened new wire had to be restrung.
>
> We had the new version of the "Walkie Talkie," the PRC-6. We also had the back pack PRC-9. Both radios worked fine, under ideal conditions. The batteries had to be up and the weather and distance satisfactory. A lot of care had to be given these radios, they couldn't be banged around. Now isn't that a helluva note. Shells coming in and you have to hit the deck. Who is going to worry, or be careful with a damn radio.[14]

When land lines were intact, wire communications were secure and clear. *Intact,* however, was the operative word. Exposed comm wire lying on the ground surface across no-man's-land was vulnerable to weather, incoming rounds, tank tracks, and enemy sabotage. One of the unsung heroes of war is the wireman, a private or corporal whose job it was to lay and repair communications. Behind the line, the job was nearly as safe as "Ma Bell," but it was a different story in front of the MLR. While riflemen remained in the relative protection of trenches, bunkers, and fighting holes, the wireman was exposed to snipers, incoming artillery, land mines, and booby traps. More than once, a wireman, while troubleshooting or relaying a length of wire, found himself in the middle of an unmarked minefield. During the summer fighting on Bunker Hill, Pfc. Don McClure, a wireman with How Company, 3/7, recalled:

> As darkness fell the incoming increased. Our lines were constantly being blown up and of course our job was to maintain communication between all three platoons and the line to the MLR. The darkness eliminated our sniper problem, but we had to be careful around our own troops. Some of our guys were a little jumpy, which was understandable, so we devised unique signals as we were trouble shooting our lines. In another area a wireman had been killed at night by friendly troops.[15]

The need to "make do" was seen repeatedly on line, and nowhere was there more evidence of it than in the age-old military art of "midnight requisition." Illustrating one illicit solution to communications needs that was applied to the requirements of a platoon spread too thin, a platoon leader described his own introduction to the MLR:

The company was authorized only a few phones to carry out its operational business. Each combat platoon was authorized only one telephone to report to company headquarters.

I was shocked to realize that not only had I inherited a platoon of fighting men but I also inherited a complete telephone network. My platoon was stretched out over a quarter mile of trench line with gaps of up to one hundred yards between some of the bunkers. Physical contact was nearly impossible; telephone contact was much easier. As I visited each bunker I realized what an efficient bunch of crooks I had—every bunker had a functional telephone. The phone in my bunker was the only legitimate one of the bunch. It was necessary to conduct periodic phone checks throughout the night. . . . The third platoon had its own check-in procedure. Instead of an actual physical contact, one of my sergeants or I conducted a telephone check. Bunkers were designated code names, and we decided to use colors for the code. The command bunker became Dog Red. During the first few weeks everything went well and Dog yellow, blue, white and orange covered the major bunkers. As more bunkers and attached units came on board, we began to experience some problems. Some bunkers got stuck with lavender, chartreuse and pink. Some macho Marines protested their effeminate color designations.

I did not look too closely at the unauthorized telephones or methods of acquisition. I did note a couple of U.S. Army designations and even a civilian phone or two. Ripping off the Army was perfectly acceptable, but some of the other phones may have been somewhat questionable. We had to hide some of the phones during inspections but found them a blessing during watches at night.[16]

PATROLS AND AMBUSHES

Patrols and ambushes were regular events on the outpost line. Both usually involved at least a reinforced squad and sometimes a larger group. "The main difference was that patrols moved and ambushes sat," a company senior NCO plainly stated. Clearly, that NCO should have been a general.

Instructions for Marine combat patrols, ambushes, raids, and reconnaissance (recon) patrols were spelled out in great detail in various manuals and orders. Unfortunately, the enemy failed to read them. In Korea, whatever the detail started out to be, it frequently became something else; the major practical difference being the number of men assigned to a task. And, of course, whether they "moved or sat." Subsequently, nearly all activity in front of the MLR became known by the generic term *patrol,* regardless of the specific mission for the night. Sergeant O'Hagan explained:

> Night time for darkness was thirteen hours. That is what we based our patrols on. During the summer months it was shorter, eight to nine hours. On an outpost we maintained constant listening posts and recon patrols. Sometimes the recon patrols would turn into ambush patrols if the situation was favorable. Conversely, sometimes the recon patrols were ambushed. A listening post consisted of two to four men just beyond the wire. Recon patrols could be six or eight men, up to a dozen.
>
> On the outpost there was no sleep for anyone during darkness. You're either on one of the patrols or on trench alert. When you finish with one you begin the other.[17]

To support the outpost defense, Division Headquarters insisted that all line battalions maintain an aggressive posture of patrol activity in front of the MLR. The tactic had two objectives: (1) to keep pressure on enemy positions, and (2) to return intelligence of enemy activity. Effectiveness of the latter objective was of questionable value, whereas the former objective was unknown altogether.

As the war progressed into late 1952, patrol routes became somewhat standardized. There were a finite number of trails and roads among the hills, paddies, and streams. The Chinese were able to avoid Marine patrol routes, which enabled them to close in, build up their forces, and attack an outpost when they were ready.

Patrols went out every night, and every Marine took his turn. For each, there was that "first night." 2d Lt. Howard Matthias of Dog Company, 2/5, recalled his first night patrol:

> My first night ambush was a personal disaster. During a meeting with the squad in the afternoon, I conducted all the preliminary actions as I should. The main objectives were outlined. The quick inspection at the point of departure went well. Then the dilemma: I could not see. No matter how hard I strained my eyes, I could not see even a few feet in front of me.

I had placed myself about fourth in the column of troops. I could not even see the Marine in front of me, and I could not see the trail. I stumbled and fell. I began to panic. "Lieutenant, hold onto me for a while," said the voice in front of me. For the next fifteen minutes I was led by the young private. Fortunately the squad leader knew the area, reached the ambush site, spread out the men and generally took charge.

I could not believe that it could be that dark anywhere. My eyes slowly became accustomed to the dark that evening, and I was able to finish the patrol as I was supposed to. What a horrible feeling, stumbling and groping in pitch darkness. "What must the men think of me, their leader, acting like a drunken, blind idiot?" It did not take long to realize that this was a typical reaction for most new Marines. As the weeks went by, my eyes became better and better at night. In just a few weeks, I could recognize people up to ten feet away in complete darkness. Darkness became a friend, as well as an enemy. For years afterward, I would judge the nighttime as a good night for patrolling or a good night for an ambush. A moonlit night was terrible for a patrol but great for an ambush.[18]

New lieutenants were mildly tolerated by the men and, until they earned respect, were usually along for the ride. It was the wise lieutenant who understood this fact and let his sergeants run the show until he learned the ropes and could ultimately lead his men with understanding and force of character, thereby gaining their obedience through loyalty. A mustang (commissioned officer who had risen from the ranks) recalled his first patrol in Korea:

At dusk I led a squad patrol forward of the MLR to "make contact." As we went out through the wire on the trenchline, I took the point. We were less than 100 yards out when a young, but combat seasoned lad approached and the conversation went something like this: "Lieutenant—you shouldn't be up front—when things start happening we are going to need your training and experience—we can't afford to lose you."

What he was really saying was; "Lieutenant—I don't have much confidence in you—move back and let a pro take the point."[19]

Quite naturally, the keys to a successful ambush were stealth and intelligence: Know where the enemy will be, and then stealthily get there before him. An ambush patrol tried to set up as early as possible on a known path or trail where the enemy was expected. The Marines approached the position as quietly as possible and then remained absolutely silent—watching and waiting.

More frequently than not, ambushes were unsuccessful. Sometimes they were not even as quiet as they should have been. 2nd Lt. Lee Cook recalls his embarrassing ambush:

> I took four or five men and out we went, down the reverse slope of the outpost and started to move around to the forward slope of "Yoke." Several times I stopped the men to have them hold down the noise. Silently we arrived at what appeared to be an ideal location for an ambush. We were all as quiet as a church mouse. As we moved into a semi circle facing a potential "gook" patrol route, I settled back and promptly fell head long into a pit, fully five feet deep. You could hear the noise all the way to the Yalu River. My helmet fell off and clattered against my carbine as we all parted company. As I landed there was more hubbub as grenades, ammo clips and canteens clanked and crashed into each other. So much for stealth. Two of my men picked up my carbine and helmet and helped me out of the hole.
>
> We resumed the ambush as if nothing had happened. Like the Chinese were deaf. As we sat on the ground, going through the motions with absolutely no chance of surprising anyone, one of the men handed me the magazine to the carbine. It had ejected when I fell. With it came the comment, "Here lieutenant, in case you need it."
>
> I had been sitting there with an empty weapon and hadn't even noticed.[20]

For two years, the war had eaten its way over and across the peninsula of Korea. Some in America preferred to call it a "police action." Others called it a "conflict." No matter the euphemism, it was war nonetheless. Soldiers from opposing armies were shooting at one another across, and within, a narrow strip of worthless, torn-up, burnt, and bloody land that neither side wanted to occupy anyway. Virtually nothing had been gained in two years of fighting. Though one must admit that little had been lost either, unless one counted the lives of several thousand soldiers, sailors, and Marines, not to mention two nations destroyed, tens of thousands of civilians killed, maimed, or orphaned, and buildings, factories, cities, and farms razed. It all seemed so futile. Across the table at Panmunjom, the negotiators could not come to terms and people at home seemed to have lost interest.

CHAPTER 3

JAMESTOWN LINE

I have seen war, and faced modern artillery
and I know what an outrage it is
against simple men.
—T. M. Kettle,
The Ways of War, 1915

On the 1st Marine Division's far left, the Korean Marine Corps sector was tank country—broad valleys with decent roads. Although the KMC regiment had a company of M-4 tanks, they were inferior to the M-46s of the U.S. Marine 1st Tank Battalion. The level of training was inferior as well. Men of the KMC had good spirit and were willing learners, but they simply lacked experience. Consequently, until they could get up to speed, one of the U.S. Marine tank companies supported their infantry and trained their tankers.

During April and May, frequent tank patrols, accompanied by KMC infantry, left the MLR and explored the area around the Sachon River valley. The patrols seldom met resistance from Chinese infantry but usually attracted incoming artillery.

Patrols were necessary because a countryside that could support Marine tanks was equally suitable for the Chinese variety. Intelligence reports continually warned of the presence of an enemy tank regiment located northeast of Kaesong, although it was seldom seen. The regiment was equipped with forty tanks or self-propelled guns, likely of Russian manufacture. The Marines also knew that the surrounding area had numerous covered revetments and assembly areas easily capable of concealing armored vehicles. The most probable avenue of armored approach was the Sachon River valley, hence the requirement for frequent patrols.

TANK COUNTRY

Monday, 19 May 1952 was hot and overcast. At noon, the sun was high and there was no wind. Humidity lay heavy on the skin. A Marine tank column of sixteen vehicles accompanied by two platoons of KMC infantry, reinforced with mortar squads, and a section of light machine guns was crossing no-man's-land and moving southwest. Returning to the MLR from a daylight fire mission against Chinese outposts, the column was led by five Patton M-46 tanks from the 2d Platoon, Able Company, 1st Tank Battalion. Five more Pattons from the 3d Platoon followed. A platoon of KMC M-4 tanks, with 76-mm guns, picked up the rear. M-4 tanks were World War II Sherman tanks, hand-me-downs to the Republic of Korea. The more modern M-46s belonged to the U.S. forces.

Tank A-41, commanded by Capt. Milt Raphael, was centered in the column between the 2d and 3d Platoons. Cpl. Lionel Durk was driving, and Sgt. Chris Sarno was the gunner. The crew had spent the morning in firing a full load of 90-mm HE (high-explosive rounds). The tanks were hot, the guns were hot, and sweat soaked through the men's uniforms. Tired and dirty, the men were looking forward to some chow, a sponge bath, and a little sack time. If they were lucky, they might even have some mail awaiting them at the CP.

Able Company was training a KMC tank company while supporting the Korean Marine Corps Regiment. One platoon of KMC tanks had completed training and was attached to Able Company for combat experience.

This was Patrol Number 190605 on 19 May. Albeit larger than most patrols, it was nonetheless typical. Intelligence sources had revealed that 25 miles northeast, in the Kaesong area, a regiment of forty Chinese tanks was assembled and primed for movement south. The mission of this patrol had been aggressive. The patrol had been ordered to attack targets of opportunity—gun emplacements, enemy bunkers, and tanks if they could find them.

Leaving the MLR on schedule at 0605, the column traveled southwest by a road that approximately paralleled the MLR. On their left, the Marines were covered from the high ground by five 90-mm guns of a platoon of Baker Company tanks. A section of flame tanks with 105-mm guns was also in position. The column traveled through valleys and abandoned rice paddies for two miles. Arriving at a fork in the road, the five tanks of the 2d Platoon split off and took a position on a low rise overlooking the river. The remaining tanks continued on the road for another mile before deploying in positions also facing north. At 0815, all tanks were in place.

Five minutes later, the 2d Platoon opened fire from the low hill and sent more than one hundred 90-mm rounds into enemy-occupied territory. From the road, tanks from the 3d Platoon and the KMC platoon contributed more rounds. The bombardment hit enemy shelters and observation posts and destroyed many yards of trench line. Regrettably, the rounds found no enemy tanks. Thirteen Chinese soldiers were counted killed or wounded. In return, Chinese gunners lobbed thirty-three 82-mm mortar rounds at the tanks, but they did no damage. The patrol encountered no enemy infantry or evidence of Chinese activity east of the river. By 1000, with no Chinese to engage, it became evident that there was little else to do but return from a relatively uneventful action.

Reforming, the column rumbled back down the dirt road toward the MLR. The Korean Marines were tired and not looking forward to the three-mile hike. The tankers stopped and offered a lift to the ground-pounders. The Korean Marines scrambled on board the tanks and the procession resumed, looking much like a line of giant green bugs carrying young on their backs.

The column soon arrived at a point where the road crossed a stretch of exposed terrain registered by Chinese artillery. Tanks regularly traveled this road on their way to firing positions. The Chinese sometimes fired at them, but often as not they did not bother. For the tankers, it was a crap shoot with a reasonable risk. A moving target is difficult to hit and the likelihood of damage to the tanks was slight. It would take a lucky strike to cause any real injury to the men inside. This time, however, the tanks had just spent two hours pounding enemy positions across the river, and the Chinese soldiers were not pleased. With Oriental patience, Chinese gunners bided their time. They knew that the tanks would likely return by the same route. A column of sixteen tanks loaded with exposed Korean Marines clinging to the outside offered an attractive target.

The first tanks entered the 200-yard stretch of open ground one at a time and reached a low hill in the middle where they were temporarily hidden from enemy view. After pausing momentarily, they continued 75 yards across a second portion of exposed road until they were safely out of sight of the enemy.

Leading the column, the 2d Platoon had alerted enemy forward observers. As the next group of tanks crossed the area, they attracted a deluge of incoming artillery fire. The next tank in line was Captain

Raphael's A-41. The crew watched as the tank ahead of them, with its load of Korean Marines, ran that gauntlet of dirt, smoke, explosions, and flying shrapnel. The tank crossed the open terrain and, incredibly, none of the exposed infantrymen was hit.

Now, it was A-41's turn. The crew buttoned up the hatches, Durk revved up the engine, and the tank began to move. Sarno, in the gunner's seat, was tightly shoehorned between the wall of the turret on his right, the breech of the gun on his left, and the tank commander's seat behind him. He could see precious little through his periscope, and his telescopic gunsight was of no value at this range. Sarno felt claustrophobic, uneasy. The experience of being inside a tank while receiving incoming artillery is never pleasant, but he had been through it many times before. This time, however, was different. Sarno had been in Korea for nearly a year and was due to be rotated home. A troopship with a bunk waiting for him was tied up in Inchon Harbor, and he did not want to miss it. And he sure as hell didn't want to return on a hospital ship.

Picking up speed, A-41 entered the impact area. Sarno heard explosions. He felt the armor absorb blasts of concussion and heard the ping, clang, and ricochet of shrapnel glancing off the turret. He had no idea what might be happening to the Korean Marines hanging on the outside.

Suddenly, the tank skewed to the right, lurched, and left the road. Durk began swearing. "Son of a bitch," he snarled, "I think we've picked up wire."

Discarded strands of communications and barbed wire, the debris of past patrols, emplacements, and defenses, littered all areas near the MLR. A moving tank, catching one of the wires, can entangle it in a sprocket and, as the tank continues to move, progressively reel it around a hub. The tightly wound wire, sometime miles in length, continues to grow in circumference until it finally grows larger than the sprocket. Like the proverbial straw added to a camel's back, something eventually has to give. Often, the steel track either stretches off its guides or breaks altogether, which leaves the tank immobile and vulnerable, a stationary target for artillery sharpshooters.

For obvious reasons, this was neither the time nor place for A-41 to become a stationary target. Over the intercom, Durk yelled to Captain Raphael that they had caught wire and were in danger of becoming stuck. Raphael replied that Durk should maneuver the tank and attempt to break the wire. He directed him to back up and try a neutral steer.

Neutral steer is a procedure whereby the driver applies power to both tracks simultaneously but each in an opposing direction. One track drives backward while the other is driven forward. The effect allows the tank to auger around in its radius—literally spin in a circle. This maneuver is risky because the side thrust of a tight spin has been known to throw a track. Also, the wire can become further entangled or, hopefully, simply break and free the tank. It was a gamble, but they had little choice.

Durk desperately began maneuvering the tank—backward, forward, spinning in a circle. Like an enormous crazed bug, the tank wriggled aimlessly around in the dirt. It soon became obvious to Chinese observers that, for whatever reason, this tank was in trouble. Consequently, enemy artillery began to impact in even greater concentrations. A round struck close and blew off a front fender. Inside, the crewmen heard more shrapnel strike the tank and felt concussion shocks against the armor. These were large artillery rounds, 105s and 122s, possibly even 155-mm. If any of them hit the tank, they would be in big trouble. By now, Sarno had decided that he was probably a dead Marine; the next round surely had his name on it. To make matters worse, he still could not see outside the tank. He imagined that he was already in his coffin.

Suddenly, Durk felt the tank break loose. He cried out, "I did it, we're free. Let's get the hell out of here." Returning to the road, the tank hightailed across the remaining open space leaving behind a cloud of dust and explosions.

Arriving behind the small hill, the crew took stock and prepared for the next leg of exposure. A quick 75-yard run down the road and they would be home. The tank crew found that the Korean Marines had wisely jumped off and made their way to safety on foot. They met the tank at the low hill. The young Americans felt pretty cocky by now; the longest run was over and not a man was injured nor a vehicle lost. Another quick run, and they'd be home free.

The tankers buttoned up and prepared for the last dash to safety. This time, two tanks would try it together. The Korean Marines, electing to remain on the tanks and take their chances with speed, climbed on board.

"Go for it." The drivers dropped their machines into gear, revved the engines, and raced into the second exposed area much as they had the first, hell bent down the dusty road. Midway through the area they began to receive incoming fire that was both heavy and accurate. The Chinese artillerymen were skilled at their craft and had plenty of guns to go around. The tanks ran the gauntlet at top speed. Unbelievably, they both made it safely to the MLR.

Next, it was the 3d Platoon's turn. The platoon leader, Lieutenant Johnston, in A-31, led five tanks. Picking up the rear was A-35, commanded by T/Sgt. John Alexander. Sergeant Alexander recalls that day:

We were buttoned up and as I squatted in the turret to adjust the radio to talk with the platoon leader I heard a heavy "thump" over the static in my head phones. We had been hit. Looking about I discovered that we had taken an enemy round on the engine compartment. The KMC infantry were blown off the tank into the dry paddies on our left. The armored engine doors were blown about in a hell of a mess. The housing of the transmission was cracked, and the final drive bent. The round had impacted about six or seven feet behind the turret. Had I not been crouched down I probably would have been killed.

The tank stopped dead in its tracks, a sitting duck. I ordered the crew to abandon the vehicle, and tend to the wounded KMC's. On the right side there was a bank six to seven feet high with a hill leading to the KMC wire and trenches. We moved the wounded to a protected position near the hill, gave them morphine and then hugged dirt. The incoming was heavy as Chinese tried to hit the tank but they remained off target. Finally, with the help of Korean Marines who came down from trenches we got the wounded and ourselves to the MLR.[1]

At the MLR, the tankers said a quick prayer of deliverance and looked back at the destruction in their wake. They saw bodies of Korean Marines who had been blown off the tanks or who had been hit while trying to cross to the MLR. From that distance it was impossible to determine the living from the dead, if indeed, any of the Koreans were still alive. As the commanders discussed the best way to rescue the Koreans, one of the battalion's jeep drivers, Pfc. Robert ("Shorty") Frohn, took matters into his own hands. Without orders or permission, he jumped into a nearby ambulance jeep and drove over the hill into the impact area. He was soon followed by Lieutenant Johnston and a corpsman in the company jeep. Together, they loaded all of the Korean wounded and brought them in.

Sergeant Alexander continued, "While all this was taking place, and the wounded were being evacuated, the incoming was horrific. Despite the danger, it did not prevent mechanics in the recovery tank from effecting a daylight recovery. Under fire, they drove out to the disabled A-35, hooked up, and successfully towed it back to the MLR."[2]

THE NEUTRAL CORRIDOR

The line that divided the KMC on the west from the 5th Marines on the east (the division's center sector) was the neutral corridor. Created by statesmen to facilitate peace negotiations, the neutral zone was an enormous impediment to pursuit of the war, while contributing little or nothing to its termination. In fact, it provided incentive to continue the war.

Established by mutual agreement in October 1951, the neutral corridor was a measured 400-meter corridor straddling either side of Highway One. The route was a north-south highway connecting Kaesong, North Korea, and Munsan-ni, South Korea. The corridor ran perpendicular to the lines of resistance of both sides. It cut through the UN Main Line of Resistance and the Outpost Line of Resistance, through no-man's-land, and through corresponding Communist defenses.

Neutrality rules in this corridor would not permit shooting into, over, or from it. No loaded weapons were permitted in the corridor except those carried by military police. Supplies to sustain the war could be transported on the road within the corridor. Outposts One and Two, sited deep in no-man's-land, were sustained because intercourse with the rear area was accomplished by way of a protected supply line inside the neutral corridor.

Between the two lines of defense lay Panmunjom, the site of the peace talks and the center of the neutral zone. Here, everything within a radius of 1,000 meters was neutral. At night, a large searchlight continuously shone straight into the sky to mark the zone for aircraft.

In typical military fashion, the commander of I Corps, Maj. Gen. John W. O'Daniel, had to go the diplomats one step farther. To be on the safe side, he "ordered that an additional area forward of the OPLR, be set aside. This megaphone shaped zone 'could not be fired into, out of, or over.'"[3] It was not long before the Chinese were aware of the addition of the "O'Daniel Line" to the restricted zone and used it to their advantage for assembly areas and gun emplacements.

The effect of the neutral corridor on the war was the introduction of complexities to the rules of engagement. Interpretation of those complexities would have perplexed a roomful of lawyers. To the men on and in front of the line, the neutral zone was an enormous pain in the neck.

RAID ON OP-3
On 3 May, the Marines on OP-2 watched as enemy activity increased on Hill 67 in front of them. The Chinese were digging the trenches deeper and appeared to be clearing or laying minefields on the slopes below. As dusk deepened, a red star cluster flare arced across the northern sky from the former OP-3, which the Marines had abandoned the previous month along with much of the OPL.

Early the following morning, 1st Lt. Ernest Lee led a reinforced platoon from Able Company, 1/5, on a reconnaissance of the old outpost.

Leaving at 0600, the column did not reach the base of OP-3 until 0845. The men had to walk carefully, not knowing if mines had been laid on the trail or if they were under enemy observation. Slowly, they picked their way around the east side of the hill until twenty mortar rounds fell in their vicinity. The patrol proceeded another hundred yards north, keeping the hill on their left, until the barrage increased in intensity and they could no longer move.

As mortars fell, Lieutenant Lee received a radio message that intelligence intercepts had picked up the following enemy message: "Fifty enemy were observed fifty meters from 102. Twenty rounds will be fired." Late though it was, this message accounted for those first twenty rounds. The time was 1120.

The mortars continued for forty-five minutes, and the Marines began taking fire from thirty enemy soldiers who had moved in under incoming fire. Simultaneously, the radio repeated another intercept indicating that the enemy was preparing an attack, but the message was too late. The Chinese were on them. The initial assault killed one Marine and wounded two others. A light machine gun was brought forward to cover the evacuation of casualties. As they moved back, the Marines counted fourteen enemy soldiers killed.

Under direction of an aerial observer, four F4U Corsair fighters arrived on station at the same time. The aircraft were able to silence four of the mortar positions supporting the attack. A subsequent radio intercept revealed that the Chinese had sustained ten casualties from the air strike.

The patrol, however, was still pinned down. A section of enemy machine guns had been moved to a position on their right flank, which prevented recovery of all the Marines. Unable to move from the base of the hill, they awaited a second air strike to cover their withdrawal.

At 1330, more Corsairs arrived to attack Hill 100 north of their position and neutralize two more mortar positions. Simultaneously, Marine machine guns were able to destroy the Chinese guns on the flank and kill ten more Chinese soldiers.

Under a barrage of friendly mortar and artillery, the patrol began to withdraw. Collecting their casualties, they worked their way south to a road between OP-3 and Three Fingers. Three more enemy machine guns were silenced during the move back and at least two Chinese killed. Another enemy group attempted to outflank the patrol on the west until it sustained a direct hit by Marine artillery. One enemy soldier was seen flying through the air when a round exploded.

Calling for smoke and more artillery to cover their movements, the Marines worked their way southeast along a road toward the MLR. They were not safe yet. Another Chinese machine gun was soon brought to bear on them but was quickly destroyed by artillery. Then, still under fire, some of the men carrying the wounded detonated a land mine. Two Marines were killed and three more wounded. The minefield had not been charted on their maps.

By now, reinforcements from Dog Company were able to work their way out to the Claw, where they laid a base of fire into pursuing Chinese troops. At 1545, the patrol broke contact and was able to load its wounded on jeep ambulances for transportation to the rear. Upon reaching the MLR, two of the wounded were evacuated by helicopter. At 1701, the operation was declared secure.

It was Sunday. Church services were held in the battalion CP.

Five days later, on 9 May, Able Company, 1/5, again led by Lieutenant Lee, attacked OP-3 in a company-sized raid supported by air, tanks, and artillery. The company sustained casualties of 7 killed and 66 wounded. Chinese casualties included 105 killed and 158 wounded. One enemy soldier was captured but died of wounds.[4]

CHINESE TRICKS

The Marines were learning that the Communist Chinese Forces in Korea were a formidable enemy. Their units absorbed massive punishment and continued to fight. Their tactics were clever and effective. The 1/5 Battalion Command Diary reported:

> . . . when friendlies marked targets with WP [white phosphorus], the enemy would immediately drop rounds of WP between the target and friendly troops in order to conceal the target and confuse friendly FO's [forward observers, Marine pilots on the ground who communicated directly with pilots in the air]; the enemy tried very hard to take prisoners, rather than shoot a friendly they would often attempt to knock him out with a concussion type grenade; counter attacks were made in waves of four to seven men deployed in a formation somewhat similar to the Marine Corps Wedge; snipers were deployed in holes that were mutually supporting; . . . In close in fighting the enemy used PPsh guns [burp guns] and grenades rather than bayonets; the enemy attacked behind well coordinated mortar fire; some enemy snipers were observed to have bushes tied to their backs; on several instances 76mm artillery was used to mark targets.[5]

Intelligence reports noted that a pattern of creeping tactics began to emerge at this time. Chinese troops crept forward during the night to occupy high ground that they could take without fighting. During

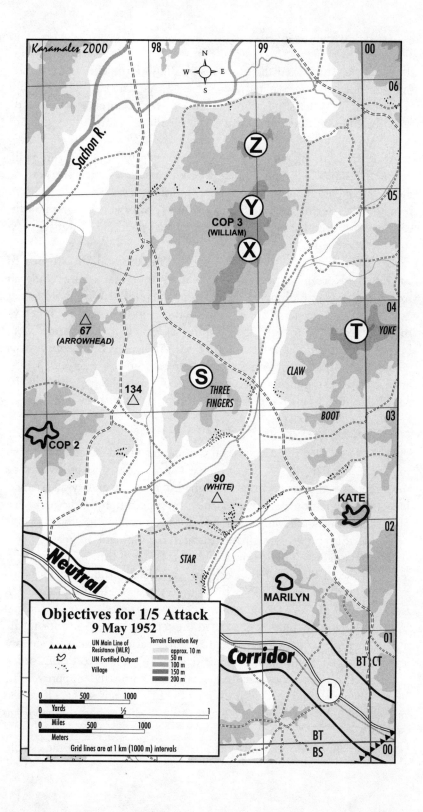

Karamales 2000

COP 3
(WILLIAM)

Sachon R.

Z

Y

X

67
(ARROWHEAD)

T   YOKE

CLAW

S   THREE
     FINGERS

134

BOOT

COP 2

90
(WHITE)

KATE

STAR

Neutral

MARILYN

Corridor

BT CT

1

BT

BS

Objectives for 1/5 Attack
9 May 1952

▲▲▲▲▲▲ UN Main Line of
        Resistance (MLR)

Terrain Elevation Key

approx. 10 m
50 m
100 m
150 m
200 m

♡ UN Fortified Outpost

∴ Village

0   500   1000
0   Yards   ½   1
0   Miles   500   1000
    Meters

Grid lines are at 1 km (1000 m) intervals

darkness, they improved the positions by digging trenches, tunnels, and fighting holes. Before dawn, they covered all evidence of their digging and withdrew. When a position was sufficiently prepared, it would suddenly be fully occupied and capable of defending against all attempts of dislodgment.

Another recurring trick was the Chinese monitoring of Marine radio channels. Chinese who spoke fluent English sometimes intervened on the radio net and attempted to disrupt communications. This tactic recurred repeatedly all during the war. (For some unexplainable reason, Americans continue to think that because they cannot speak a foreign language, neither can the enemy.)

On 13 May, A-21, a tank from the 1st Tank Battalion assigned to support the Korean Marines, was disabled by an antitank mine while on patrol. Subsequent probing by the tank crewmen located five more Soviet box mines. At one site, a mine set for detonation by a careless infantryman was placed on top of a second mine set for a tank. Both mines were buried in the path of a previous tank track. After covering the mines, the enemy traced track marks on the ground to camouflage their presence. At another site, a single mine had been placed under the tank path in the road by tunneling from the side so as not to disturb the track pattern.

HILL 67—A SUCCESS STORY

Hill 67 (later called the Arrowhead) was an arrowhead-shaped hill pointing at the jugular of Outpost Two near Panmunjom. The hill was to be the target of a surprise night raid designed to keep the enemy off balance. It would also demonstrate that Marines, too, could fight in the dark. The 5th Marine units, relieved earlier, had not been conducting night operations, and this raid was anticipated to catch the Chinese off guard.

The assault was a pet project of 2d Lt. James ("Jim") Vanairsdale's, leader of the 1st Platoon, Easy Company, 2/7. Vanairsdale had spent hours studying Hill 67 from OP-2, 1,000 meters away. He had watched it through field glasses and the twenty-power spotter telescope in the FO bunker. As he meticulously examined the terrain, he began to formulate a plan. A regimental directive had recently called for raids of various strengths on enemy positions. Vanairsdale's plan seemed to fit this order. After working out minor details, the battalion commander approved the lieutenant's plan and wanted it executed the following night. There was no time for a rehearsal, for mine recon, or for fresh air photos. It had to go on 17 May.

To his delight, Vanairsdale's platoon was selected to make the assault.

As he had conceived it, the raid was to be an unsupported, nonillumi-nated night operation. The Marines would bank on stealth and surprise to achieve success.

The previous day, intelligence from a friendly agent had confirmed that two platoons of Chinese defended the hill. The plan was to hit and run. Get there, surprise the enemy, hit hard, and get the hell out before the Chinese could recover and counterattack. To help with the surprise factor, artillery had been intermittently shelling the hill each night in an effort to convince enemy soldiers to remain inside their bunkers at night. The raiders did not want them out in the trench line where they might be warned of their approach.

In keeping with the tactics, the men traveled light. They wore flak vests, carried fixed bayonets, and left behind all nonessential accou-trements. Even their reliable but heavy Browning automatic rifles (BARs) were traded for carbines and submachine guns. Logistics involved sound-powered telephones with 2 miles of communications wire and more than six hundred 60-mm mortar rounds. The covering force of mortar and machine guns would operate from OP-2, where a forward aid station had been set up. The men were ready. The first platoon assembled in the neutral corridor and, at 2330, left for OP-2, their attack position.

Maj. Dennis Nicholson, Jr., 2d Battalion Operations Officer (S-3), later wrote an article, in the *Marine Corps Gazette,* that described many details of the raid. Of the action itself, he wrote:

> . . . The night was black. Lieutenant Vanairsdale's platoon had walked from the assembly area to the covering force position four times previously. Still it was difficult to follow the route. S/Sergeant Harvey Wright [Vanairsdale's platoon sergeant], a man with keen eyes, was leading the column, according to plan.
>
> The platoon was late passing through the covering force position. The pitch-black night had slowed its rate of march. An ominous bank of clouds covered the moonrise. Vanairsdale would have to attack without moonlight, but as black as it was, he realized that he and his men were slowly gaining night vision. He knew that his time sched-ule was off and comforted himself with the thought that stealth, not timing, was the key to his plan.
>
> At the line of departure and squad release point, Vanairsdale decided not to release his squads. He continued moving in column. It was the only way to maintain control in that murky blackness.
>
> When the column approached a road, which showed as a trail on the map, Wright signaled the column to a halt. The platoon quietly

settled down on its haunches while Wright examined the road. He found nuisance mines all over the road and the straw in his hand telegraphed back the delicate touch of a trip wire at the road's edge. Wright eased off to the left. Finally he found a spot where the road appeared to be clear.

The sergeant jerked the vest of the man behind him to signal him forward. The platoon crossed the road without being detected.

Once again Wright halted the column—he'd observed two enemy moving to his right. They were too far away to kill with silent weapons and shooting them would alert the enemy on Hill 67. The platoon members kept their heads down and held their breath intermittently, until they were signaled forward again. Then they resumed their stealthy approach to the objective.

Lieutenant Vanairsdale, who was moving in the center of the column with his second squad, could sense that his men were concentrating on one thing above all. They were making every effort to move silently. Wright was no exception. As he moved cautiously forward he encountered enemy wire. The first squad leader was immediately behind him. Together they cut through two double aprons and a single strand, careful to muffle the sound of their wire cutters. As the platoon passed through the breached wire, several men noted that it wasn't a good job of wire-laying.

At 0305, squads had been released and the platoon had eased itself down into an enemy trench, six feet deep and three feet wide. Entrances to enemy living bunkers were dug near the bottom. They were about three feet in diameter.

Men of the first platoon felt a slight relief. They had gained the enemy position without being detected. They knew, though, that a first-class fight was near.

Vanairsdale, in the center of the enemy position now, found time to be thankful that he hadn't yet had to use a pyrotechnic signal for the assault. That would have tipped his hand prematurely.

Wright could hear enemy talking in the bunkers along the trench sides. There was a pause in their conversation. The enemy had heard the first platoon. The chatter resumed. Wright, as he pulled the pin on his first grenade, imagined that the enemy was asking, "Who's there?"

As Wright's grenade went into the hole, an enemy head thrust itself outward and exclaimed, "Marines." That was the last word spoken by that Communist. He and his bunkmate were dead the next instant, as Wright's grenade completely filled the hole with deadly fragments.

Then Vanairsdale fired a white star cluster to signal the assault.

Hill 67 came alive with activity. Enemy came pouring out of bunkers rubbing their eyes, some of them even unarmed and stumbling around dazed and half-asleep. They were caught flatfooted. The cardinal sin had been committed; they were surprised! The first platoon had a field day. Grenades and demolition charges sailed into enemy bunkers. Bayonets found their marks. Carbines, M1's and tommy guns left enemy rolling in the dirt.

Artillery was falling in a prearranged pattern around Hill 67, seconds after Wright's grenade exploded. The little battlefield was nicely isolated.

Thirty-one minutes after the Marines entered trenches on Hill 67, the enemy began showing some signs of realizing that at last he'd been hit at night.

Enemy machine guns and mortars began firing on the objective from long ranges, but a spectacular friendly artillery mission knocked out the nearest enemy machine gun with what the covering force thought was the first salvo.

By 0345 it was getting lighter. The FO with the covering force spotted an estimated 30 enemy moving to reinforce Hill 67. They were clobbered. Not one of the group ever reached his destination.

By this time the enemy had finally succeeded in getting a few burp guns going on the north side of the hill. In knocking out the burp guns, the platoon sustained its first and only casualties. No one was killed, few were wounded, but the enemy losses were high. As he assured himself that the casualties were being attended to, Vanairsdale surveyed the area and noticed enemy dead everywhere. He was pleased to see that demolition charges had caused the deep bunkers to cave in.

Members of his platoon were moving through the position with no enemy left to shoot and no bunkers remaining to destroy. Twenty-five enemy had been encountered on Hill 67, 12 enemy dead and 13 wounded were counted. Few, if any, of the wounded would live. In addition, supporting arms had destroyed three active machine guns, five mortars and 50 personnel. With the mission accomplished, Vanairsdale decided to withdraw before the enemy recovered. His green star parachute burst overhead.

As the first platoon headed home, enemy mortar fire began getting thicker and hitting right along the route of withdrawal. The platoon moved forward down an old trench for protection from bursting mortar rounds, quickly mustering at the rallying point. A white star cluster fired from the M-1 of Vanairsdale's runner brought in the pleasant sound of friendly heavy machine guns covering the withdrawal.

Artillery and Lieutenant Samuel D. Arnspiger's 60mm's did their counter-battery fire according to plan, and the enemy mortars were silenced.[6]

Traditionally, American troops have never cared much for night fighting, but they learned new tricks of the trade in Korea. Driven by realities, tactics of the outpost war continued to evolve. Using its time in reserve wisely, the entire regiment trained in techniques of night combat. This had been one platoon's opportunity to use that training.

Sergeant Wright was subsequently awarded a Silver Star for this action. Lieutenant Vanairsdale received a Navy Commendation.

THE COMBAT RAID

Prohibited from advancing the MLR, yet having to endure harassing fire, probes, and creeping tactics of the enemy, the aggressive Marines found themselves in an intolerable situation. Consequently, they frequently used the combat raid as an offensive tactic in western Korea. Limited to small-unit actions, the squad-, platoon-, or company-sized raid became a frequently used technique to remind the enemy that the troops facing them were not becoming complacent. Further, as demonstrated earlier, the creeping tactics of the Chinese, if allowed to continue, would soon have them on the Marines' doorstep.

A raid, usually an assault against a fortified position, was a demonstration of firepower and of a willingness to fight. It was rarely used to gain ground but rather to deny it to the enemy or to make it dangerous for the enemy to occupy a particular piece of land.

Every raid, even a small one, was meticulously planned, thus leaving as little as possible to chance. Many disciplines and branches of the military were brought into play. Often, a raid was a textbook exercise played out in real life, and, like an examination, the after-action analysis, or "lessons learned," was as important to learning as was the original plan.

The Plan

On 10 May, the 1st Battalion, 1st Marines, prepared to raid a Chinese-held hill mass north of the Hook, above the valley of the Samichon River. Aerial reconnaissance had shown the target area to be a well-defended east-west trench line. To the rear of the trench was one known mortar emplacement, one machine-gun position, seven bunkers, and two personnel shelters. The photos revealed a trench arranged in such a way that reinforcements could be rapidly introduced from bunkers and shelters in the rear. Although the trench itself was held by only a squad, the readily available reinforcements from the rear shelters suggested that the exact number of enemy to be encountered would depend largely on the silence and speed of the Marines' approach.

The plan, titled "Battalion Operation Order 14-52" and issued on 8 May, designated the 3d Platoon, Able Company, as the assault element. Baker Company's 3d Platoon was to set up for cover fire on Hill 137, about 800 yards southeast of the objective. The 2d Platoon, Charlie Company, would occupy blocking positions south of the hill to furnish cover fire and to help with the evacuation of casualties, if necessary.

Fire concentration plans for supporting arms were prepared. The artillery fire plan consisted of neutralization fire and an isolation barrage designed to prevent enemy reinforcement of the objective area. Mortar concentrations of 4.2-inch and 81-mm tubes were targeted for all known and suspected enemy automatic weapon positions that could possibly bring fire to bear on the patrol. Two Canadian artillery batteries were aimed at targets to counter their mortar fire. Fire concentration plans included smoke and illumination on call to the assault platoon leader.

A platoon of five tanks from Charlie Company, 1st Tank Battalion, prepared to deliver direct fire missions from the MLR in support of the raid. Four aircraft would be on station by 0500 and available for direction by forward air controllers.

The communications plan called for radio, sound-powered telephones, and, if they failed, colored flares. Radio silence would be maintained until the assault group reached the objective or was detected. Sound-powered telephones were the primary means of communication in Korea and used extensively as a secure means of patrol communication. The instrument itself was little more than a standard telephone handset powered by the energy of voice waves spoken into the instrument. Attached to a speed reel was insulated, light copper wire, carried on the back of an infantryman, that unrolled onto the ground as he walked. Communication remained clear, quiet, and secure as long as the wire remained intact. Upon withdrawal, the wire was abandoned.

As best as could be managed without alerting the enemy, approach routes and assembly areas were checked for mines by clearing teams. Despite precautions, two men from Charlie Company detonated an antipersonnel mine while moving into their blocking position at 0245. Both men were evacuated.

The Execution

By 0300, all units occupied their assigned positions. Two minutes later, the 3d Platoon of Able Company moved out to begin the assault. Crossing the line of departure, the Marines picked their way north toward the entrenched enemy as quietly as a fully equipped patrol could move. The unknown locations of mines served to channel them into a column formation that followed a single trail.

In approximately thirty-five minutes, the assault force managed to attain the objective undetected. In the lead, the 1st Squad reached the top of the hill where they were finally discovered. Three Chinese soldiers opened up with burp guns and ran north toward the rear bunkers. The Marines returned fire and killed two of the soldiers. The 2d and 3d Squads arrived and began to sweep the west side of the hill, while the 1st Squad swept the east. When the 4th Squad arrived at the objective, enemy machine guns opened up on the Marines.

The assault force discovered that enemy strength had been underestimated. It found fifteen Chinese in spider holes in front of it and more in the trench behind the holes. (A spider hole is a form of foxhole dug into the earth to the depth of a standing man. It is often covered with a camouflaged, removable lid. The bottom of the hole can be enlarged to permit sitting or lying, thus enabling a soldier to live in that defensive position for days at a time.) As they attacked, the Marines came under fire by two machine guns on their right and three on the left. They called in artillery and mortar concentrations, which silenced the guns on the right. Concurrently, twenty-five more Chinese joined the fight from shelters in the north. Engaging the arriving enemy, the 2d and 3d Squads stopped their advance, while the 1st and 4th Squads destroyed the remaining machine guns with fragmentation and WP grenades.

The patrol leader observed about one hundred Chinese reinforcements rushing toward them from the northern trenches. Prudently deciding that it was time to retire, he called for another artillery concentration to turn the enemy reinforcements. Isolated by the curtain of artillery, the Marine patrol checked the battlefield for friendly casualties and organized for withdrawal.

With artillery maintaining pressure on the hill and preventing pursuit, the platoon returned to its lines along the planned route and, by 0450, had returned to the MLR. At 0530, an air strike hit the enemy's hill with bombs, rockets, and cannon.

Marine casualties were relatively light, seventeen wounded and none killed. Enemy casualties counted by the patrol before the air and artillery attacks were fifteen dead and wounded.

Lessons Learned
The thorough planning that preceded this action appeared to have been effective and likely accounted for success of the mission. Remarks in the

after-action report emphasized the teamwork involved in the planning phase. Other comments were both good and bad, for example: "It was found in this specific patrol that too many men were employed on the objective, causing crowded conditions and a problem in control."[7] This point was made partially in reference to the column formation approach to the objective. When the lead squad was hit, the trailing squads were too far back to engage the enemy.

A special report stated, "[M]embers of this patrol had confidence in their supporting fire, which in itself is important. When called down by the patrol leader, artillery and mortar fell at an average of seventy-five yards from friendly troops. To this end it is necessary that all concentrations and barrages be registered in by the crew firing the mission prior to D-Day. Corrections by map are not reliable as existing maps were found to be inaccurate."[8]

A complaint was made concerning radio communication when the SCR 536 and SCR 300 radios were found to have been compromised by enemy interference. It was further recommended that a simple word code be devised that would render transmissions meaningless to a monitoring enemy. Throughout the Korean War portable radio communications were rarely satisfactory, a fault primarily related to the state of the art. Sound-powered telephones worked reliably on this raid until the men became engaged in the firefight and the wire was destroyed.

RAID ON HILL 104

On the MLR east of 2/7, units of the 1st Battalion, 7th Marines, also took part in a raid. In that sector, Hill 104, west of Ungok and south of Tumae-ri Ridge, continued to be a thorn in the side. Daily patrols near the hill met enemy incoming, small-arms, and machine-gun fire. Hill 104 was a hot spot. Firefights occurred almost daily, and incoming fire and sniping at the MLR were constant. Marines were being killed and wounded with nothing to show for it.

A fourth Chinese strong point in the area was the Marines' former Outpost Five. Because of frequent contacts in both daylight and darkness, the Marines speculated that OP-5 had now been permanently occupied by the enemy.

On 28 May, the 7th Marines struck back in what would be the largest engagement thus far.

The Situation

Chinese forces opposing the Marine battalion at the time were believed to be the 559th Regiment, 187th Division, 63d Army. The Marines thought that Hill 104 was permanently occupied by elements of the 1st Battalion, but weapons and numbers of troops were unknown.

The estimated strength of the 559th Regiment was 3,157 men. Based on that estimate, intelligence assumed that all battalions were at full strength, with 647 men in each infantry battalion and 569 men in the Heavy Weapons Battalion, and that the enemy regiment was fully deployed with no internal reserve capacity. Possible reinforcements, if needed, were elements of the 189th Division, approximately 7 miles north. Possibly, two additional regiments from the 188th Division were also available in the vicinity.

The planning phase for raiding Hill 104 began on 24 May. The resultant Operations Order 16-52 detailed a twofold mission: (1) one platoon (reinforced) from Charlie Company was directed to bring the former Outpost Five under long-range attack by fire in order to divert attention from the main objective, and (2) the main objective, Hill 104 and Tumae-ri Ridge, was assigned to Able Company, with orders to penetrate the enemy MLR, destroy installations, and capture prisoners. After taking Hill 104, the assault force was to establish an effective firebase and then carry the battle across a terrain saddle to drive the enemy from Tumae-ri.

The operation would be well supported with artillery units of the 2d Battalion, 11th Marines, and two platoons of tanks from Dog Company, 1st Tank Battalion. Units of all regimental heavy weapons would be employed, including three platoons of 75-mm recoilless rifles, 4.2-inch mortars, .30-caliber heavy machine guns, and .50-caliber machine guns. Air support was arranged to be on call, and forward air controllers were assigned to the assault groups.

Able Company—The Assault

On Thursday, 28 May, at 0315, Able Company crossed the line of departure. The dark night was made worse by a moderate fog, and the going was slow. Each rifleman wore a flak jacket and helmet. He carried eighty rounds of M-1 ammunition in his cartridge belt and an additional bandolier of ammunition over his shoulder, as well as a package of C ration, two canteens, and an entrenching tool. The Marines had had little sleep before they shoved off. Between briefings and preparations, in addition to nerves, sleep had not come to many of them.

The 1st Platoon, led by 2d Lt. John Donate and followed by the command group, took a route to the left of Hill 104. The 3d Platoon followed a route leading to a small hill at the rear of the objective. At

0400, with the 1st Platoon in position, Marine artillery loosed a barrage on Hill 104. Five minutes later, the Marines charged the hillside with fixed bayonets. During the assault, they sustained casualties when they crossed a minefield and from a barrage of enemy mortar and artillery. All but one of the wire lines were severed by incoming fire, which left one telephone and two radios operational. By 0558, the 1st Platoon attained possession of the forward trenches but had yet to fight its way to the crest.

One fire team, led by Cpl. David Champagne, made it to the top of the hill through a curtain of fire. Bullets and shells of falling mortar and artillery fell around Champagne. Setting up a hasty defense, he distributed his men throughout an abandoned trench and prepared to repel a counterattack. Ignoring a wounded leg, the corporal remained with his men.

During the counterattack, a hand grenade landed in the trench. Champagne scooped up the missile and hurled it back at the Chinese. As the grenade left his hand, it exploded, blew off his hand, and threw him out of the trench. Before his men could reach him, a mortar shell landed close to where he lay and killed him instantly. Corporal Champagne was posthumously awarded the Medal of Honor.

After the 3d Platoon continued up the hill and mopped up the remaining enemy troops along the way, it was ordered to stand by to advance on Tumae-ri Ridge. Able Company attempted to consolidate in the abandoned enemy positions atop the hill, but incoming Chinese fire continued to cover them with a rain of exploding steel. At times, the tempo of falling shells was so great that casualties occurred at the rate of twelve men every five minutes. Adequate cover was minimal. Every bunker and shelter had been demolished by friendly artillery or heavily booby-trapped by enemy soldiers before they fled.

Air strikes, planned for first light, had to wait until the fog lifted. Without air support, the Marines were having difficulty locating the source of enemy artillery, hence there was no effective counterfire to silence the deadly guns. Artillery continued to pound Hill 104.

The Chinese mortar fire to the hill was amazingly accurate, which seemed to indicate that the Chinese had previously zeroed in on their own trench lines in anticipation of being overrun. Also, it appeared that booby traps had been set up well in advance and armed only when the Chinese withdrew. The Marines seemed to have walked into a trap.

The Marines received permission to scrub the assault on Tumae-ri; it was time to withdraw. A team of engineers cleared a road from the

MLR so that tanks could move forward to cover the infantry withdrawal. At 0745 on the MLR, the 2d Platoon of Charlie Company was ordered to reinforce Able Company. The platoon advanced to Hill 104 and aided with the withdrawal and the evacuation of wounded. By 0800, tanks were at the base of the hill and firing on Taedok-san. Once the road was opened, supplies could be brought forward and the wounded evacuated in DUKWs, amphibious trucks nicknamed "Ducks."

At 1100, an aerial observer arrived on station and was able to direct some of the Marine artillery at Chinese positions. An hour late, delayed first by weather and then by poor ground/air radio communication (too many radiomen had been wounded and their radios damaged), eight Air Force F-84 jets silenced the guns on Ungok. These strikes were followed by seven more sorties on Tumae-ri, Chirmung-dong, and nearby hills. At 1425, two Marine Corsairs appeared on station and laid a protective smoke screen to shield the route of withdrawal from enemy artillery observers.

With the arrival of friendly air, Able Company was able to withdraw from the hill. It is significant that, during the withdrawal, the company sustained no further casualties. This was attributed to the presence of the aircraft and their effectiveness in directing artillery counterfire and in attacking enemy positions.

Charlie Company—The Diversion

The diversionary force from Charlie Company, also heavily burdened with equipment, left the line of departure at 0300. The .50-caliber machine-gun section, in addition to two guns, carried twenty-two boxes of ammunition. The heavy machine-gun section carried two guns and thirty-five boxes of .30-caliber ammunition. Other men carried rocket launchers, flamethrowers, stretchers, medical supplies, rations, radios, and sound-powered equipment. Because of the heavy fog, visibility was almost nil.

The reinforced platoon, led by 2d Lt. Howard Siers, opened fire on Chirmung-dong and OP-5 at 0430, about the same time that Able Company on Hill 104 first began to receive incoming fire. As artillery began shelling OP-5, Lieutenant Siers received modified orders to attack the hill, rather than simply to keep it under long-range fire as originally planned. The platoon moved forward in a wedge formation with the 1st Squad on the point. The 2nd Squad was on the left, and the 3rd Squad took the right. The light machine-gun section held the rear. During the assault, the men discovered that ammunition for the rocket launchers had been left behind. Thus it was no value on this day.

Three fourths of the way up the hill, enemy soldiers began to resist with small arms and hand grenades. Lieutenant Siers ordered his men to continue the charge with bayonets. Reaching the trench line, the Marines overcame burp guns and hand grenades and, on the final assault, obtained possession of the trenches.

They were not out of the woods yet. Crawling through the trenches, the 1st and 3d Squads were stopped momentarily by ten Chinese soldiers with burp guns and hand grenades. Retaliating with grenades and finally a bayonet charge, the Marines broke through. Advancing a few more yards, they were stopped by twenty enemy soldiers and a machine gun.

With the Marines pinned down, the assault appeared to be stalled. Pfc. John Kelly, a radioman, requested and received permission to hand off his radio to another man and participate in an assault on the machine gun. Rather than simply participate, Private First Class Kelly became a one-man assault force. First, he single-handedly charged the machine gun and shot both operators. He then continued forward and assaulted another machine-gun bunker. Although wounded, he charged the bunker, destroyed it with a grenade, and shot the occupants. Taking on a third bunker, he reached the aperture and delivered point-blank fire into the interior until he was hit again and mortally wounded. Private First Class Kelly was posthumously awarded the Medal of Honor.

Private First Class Kelly's furious charge was all that it took to inspire his companions to continue the assault on the hill. Reaching the top, they quickly set up their machine guns and pursued the enemy with fire as they ran down the hill.

The Marines counted fifteen enemy dead on OP-5. They estimated that another fifteen dead Chinese lay on the hillside; other casualties would be anyone's guess. Considering the number of soldiers observed and counting the fighting positions, the Marines estimated that OP-5 had been defended by approximately one hundred Chinese soldiers. Examination of enemy dead revealed that the defenders were nearly out of ammunition. They all appeared to be very young, neat, and well turned out. The assumption might be made that this unit was new to the war, thus signifying that the Chinese replacement pipeline was still functioning—despite heavy and continuous air interdiction in the north.

As the enemy prepared to counterattack, the Marines inventoried their supplies. All automatic weapons were out of ammunition, rifle ammunition was low, and the grenades were nearly gone. They requested permission to withdraw.

Moving the wounded, the platoon left a fire team rear guard while enemy troops attacked the hill. When the Chinese attained the top, the last Marine had reached the base of OP-5. The platoon rejoined and made its way to the MLR. The Marines entered friendly trenches at 0930. Charlie Company casualties were one killed and fourteen wounded.

Afterward

The raid on Hill 104 resulted in a total of eight Marines and one Navy corpsman killed, with almost two hundred wounded, including seven Navy corpsmen. Able Company was particularly hard hit with seventy-nine casualties.

It was impossible to know exactly how many Chinese were killed or wounded, although forty-eight KIAs were counted. Marine ground troops estimated another eighty casualties, but no could speculate on the number of casualties caused by air strikes and artillery barrages.

The after-action report attributes the low ratio of Marine KIAs to the new armored vests worn by each of the 530 men on the operation. Of that number, the vests of 160 men were hit or damaged to some degree. Sixteen vests were destroyed. According to medical reports, shrapnel caused five of the nine deaths and 174 wounds. No wounds were discovered in body areas protected by the armored vests.

Noting that enemy shelling ceased when friendly air appeared on the scene, the findings recommended that future operations should be executed only under ideal weather conditions. They also noted that close air support was a critical asset in reducing the enemy's ability to provide artillery support of its troops. In this instance, it was speculated that had air support been on station at daylight, as planned, friendly casualties would have been reduced and both objectives likely would have been attained.

CHAPTER 4

RAID ON UNGOK

A soldier's time is passed in distress and danger
or in idleness and corruption.
—Samuel Johnson to James Boswell,
10 April 1778

In June 1952, the war began its third year without fanfare. At Inchon, the 21st Replacement Draft arrived by ship, and men were distributed to their respective units. A series of minor engagements, typical of the fighting at that time, took place. Sightings of enemy soldiers warranted the application of artillery or mortars, depending on interest, number, and ammunition allotments. Small units of Chinese attacked smaller units of Marines at various outposts. Nightly, patrols from both sides crisscrossed the barbed-wire–enclosed arena called no-man's-land and, like gladiators in earlier arenas, clashed when they met.

Intelligence reports repeatedly indicated sightings of Chinese forces in all sectors of the 1st Marine Division's front, with the largest concentrations noted in the Panmunjom-Kaesong neutral corridor. There were several reports of armor being concentrated in a large hill mass called Monghae-san, about 6 miles northwest of Ungok (Hill 31) in the area defended by the 2d Battalion, 1st Marines. Facing 2/1, a battalion of approximately 1,100 men, were 3,147 Chinese troops.

To bring out enemy troops in that area and induce them to expose some of their defenses, the 2d Battalion conducted a radio deception ruse over the battalion tactical net. Simulating preparations for a night attack on Ungok, the Marines engaged in heavy cross talk among units and acted as if they were moving on Ungok. They supported the illusion by firing mortars and artillery to simulate a preparatory bombardment of the objective and rifle grenades to simulate the detonation of land mines.

The ruse was partially effective. Reacting to the perceived attack, Chinese gunners fired mortars, small arms, and automatic weapons into the area. As rifle grenades exploded, enemy soldiers threw hand grenades in the direction of the detonations. When the ruse concluded, Marine patrols were dispatched to locate, capture, or kill Chinese troops investigating results of the "attack." The patrols met with negative results and returned empty handed. Nevertheless, it was a unique way to fight a war and probably left the Chinese shaking their heads and wondering, "What was that all about?"

The Marines needed to keep pressure on Ungok in any way they could. Situated 600 yards north of the MLR, the hill was a strong Chinese position. It served as a firebase for mortars and a jumping off point for enemy excursions into no-man's-land. From Ungok, enemy troops were a constant threat to Marine patrols and to nearby Outposts Bruce and Allen.

Typical of war tactics at this time, the Marines would never take Ungok because it had no strategic value. As an outpost, it was too far away from the MLR to be easily supported. Because UN troops were prohibited from moving the line forward, it would never be close enough for any other purpose. Thus, Ungok remained in enemy hands, a constant dagger pointing to the jugular of the Marine MLR. Were the enemy to be driven off Ungok, he would simply reestablish himself on an adjacent hill and the cycle would be repeated. Ungok became a killing ground—a place to bomb, shell, and shoot. The Marines did not want the real estate, but they did not want the Chinese there either.

On the night of 12 June, after completing rehearsals the previous day, Fox Company, 2/1, conducted a raid on Ungok. All three of its platoons were deployed in this action; the 3d Platoon would assault the hill while the 2d Platoon set up a firebase. The 1st Platoon would follow in reserve to be used where needed.

The raid did not get off to a smooth start. At 2300, shortly after the lead element passed the MLR, a land mine detonated and a Marine was injured. The advance was delayed briefly while the wounded man was evacuated to the MLR. Worse, the explosion alerted enemy troops on Ungok that Marines were in the area.

Resuming the advance on Ungok, the 3d Platoon soon began taking hand grenades. A few minutes after midnight, a Chinese platoon of forty-four men attacked the Marines with grenades, small arms, and a heavy machine gun. The 3d Platoon slowed as it became engaged in the firefight until the 2d Platoon had set and activated its firebase. As the 2d

Platoon engaged twenty-six more enemy reinforcements, the 3d platoon, under cover of friendly mortar concentrations, resumed its assault on Ungok.

Attaining its objective on top of the hill, the 3d Platoon succeeded in capturing a Chinese soldier. With the aid of friendly rockets and "box-me-in" mortar fire, the Marines returned to the MLR with their prisoner at 0130 on 13 June. There, they discovered that, in the confusion, eight men had been left behind.

An hour later, a tank-infantry rescue team set out for Ungok to find the missing men. The team consisted of two squads from Fox 2/1 accompanied by two tanks from the 3d Platoon of Charlie Company, 1st Tank Battalion. From the MLR, three more tanks fired support for the mission.

The tank-infantry team left the MLR under heavy enemy incoming fire. In return, the tanks devastated Chinese targets with more than one hundred 90-mm rounds. The recovery team reached Ungok and searched the hill but were unable to locate the missing Marines.

Recapping its casualties, Fox Company confirmed that three of the missing men had been confirmed dead, which left 5 listed as MIA. Additionally, the company counted 28 Marines wounded and another KIA. Chinese casualties were estimated at 103 KIAs, 2 WIAs, and 1 POW. The raid on Ungok would be the first of many more actions to occur on this annoying hill.

The Fox Company raid on Ungok was typical of the way that the ground war was conducted. It remained a war of attrition. Although casualties were one to four in favor of the Marines, it was not a good sign that the enemy was willing to absorb such losses, apparently without a blink. Conversely, the Chinese knew that American policymakers were gravely concerned. The enemy was mentally, emotionally, and numerically equipped to wait it out.

Earlier that week the 1st Battalion had been fighting east of 2/1's sector. On 7 June, near the Hook, a reinforced squad from Baker Company, 1/1, engaged a small group of Chinese near Hill 157 (Outpost Warsaw). Following a thirty-minute firefight accented with mortar and artillery, the enemy withdrew with nine dead. The Marines were unhurt.

Continuing on patrol under a bright moon, the Marines surmounted a small hill north of Warsaw that overlooked the Samichon River valley at 0255. Below, they saw a Chinese patrol of approximately seventy soldiers who were also observing them. The enemy patrol fired several white signal flares and began to ascend the hill in pursuit of the Marines, who called in friendly mortars and engaged the enemy with hand grenades and small arms. A Chinese machine gun on the right caught the Marines in a cross fire and began to rake their position. Enemy mortars and a 76-mm artillery piece entered the battle and began to shell the MLR in an effort to reduce Marine support from that source. The Chinese fired 240 rounds before friendly counterfire found their artillery position and silenced it. At 0410, two green flares arced across the eastern sky. The attack subsided, and the Chinese soldiers withdrew to the northwest. The Marines returned to the MLR by 0545 and reported thirty-three enemy KIA and fifteen wounded. There were no friendly casualties.

On 16 June, the 5th Marine Regiment left camp in the division reserve area and began replacing the 1st Marines on line. The move took three days to complete. By then, the right sector of the Jamestown Line was manned by men from the 1st and 2d Battalions of the 5th Marines. The 3d Battalion had moved to a forward reserve position off line and was poised to support either the 1st or 2d Battalion as necessary. On line to its left were two battalions of the 7th Marines. Leaving the line, the 1st Marines assumed the role of division reserve regiment.

A MATTER OF THE DEAD

Among Marines in battle, it was axiomatic: "We bring our dead and wounded back with us." Perhaps the finest and most conspicuous example being during the 1st Division's withdrawal from the Chosin Reservoir in December 1950, when it evacuated three thousand casualties. The rule was still being applied, only on a smaller scale. Lieutenants and sergeants followed examples set by their generals and colonels in a practice that continued throughout the war.

Vincent Walsh, a 2d lieutenant during the Korean War, expressed his view of this obviously painful aspect of command:

> To recover or not recover dead personnel—This is an agonizing question and taxes the action to be taken.
>
> Certainly the dead cannot do a thing to improve any military situation. Recovery forces engaged in retrieving the bodies most always present the potential for additional dead or wounded. However, offsetting that is the recognition that the Marines and other elite military units such as Army Rangers, "Take Care Of Their Own," as would any band of concerned, dedicated brothers. The Marines are and should continue to be such a society.
>
> Recovery action somewhat compensates a fallen comrade's dedicated disciplined performance in carrying out his assigned duty and

making the supreme sacrifice in that performance. It exacts an alliance to the fallen comrade's personal family that their loved one did not die in vain and that their comrades did care.[1]

This was the predominant view of the Marines in Korea. For better or worse, they expected to recover their KIAs. The belief that it is their duty to recover the bodies of their dead comrades is one of the major defining aspects of the U.S. Marines.

Although usually tempered with common sense, the practice was never more prevalent than during the outpost war. Time and again, rescues were mounted to return the bodies of dead Marines. Given the realities of war, it was occasionally necessary to abandon a body where it lay, but it was never acceptable to fail in trying to recover the body as soon as possible. If, after suitable attempts, a recovery appeared to be impossible or demonstrably too dangerous for the rescuers, the recovery operation might be abandoned.

Was the rule valid? Or was it a tactic that caused more bloodshed than could be reasonably justified? Lieutenant Matthias of Dog Company, 2/5, wrote:

> The enemy was aware of our pride in protecting our own. Case in point: A patrol from another platoon had been hit pretty hard. The patrol leader, a very highly respected Sergeant . . . was missing when the patrol finally made its way back to the lines. I was ordered to take a raid to the same area the next morning to find the body. My patrol took two more casualties and did not find the body. I was ordered back and wondered what the next move might be.
>
> Later that day I was told to go to the outpost and survey the area that I had been in earlier that day. On a hill behind the area that I had scouted, I noticed something. . . . Through binoculars I could see that the gooks had . . . stretched him over some barbed wire. They were daring us to come out and get him.[2]

2d Lt. Lee Cook of Easy Company, 2/5, led a patrol to recover the body on 22 June. In a letter to the author, he described details of the operation:

> From our position looking out across a road where a combat patrol had been engaged a week or more earlier, we saw a body. It was near the crest of a hill and appeared to be propped up, laying across the Chinese defensive wire. Field glasses confirmed that it was a Marine

uniform, and it was assumed that the body was that of a Marine missing from the earlier fire fight. The body was on display for virtually all of our company positions. . . .

Once the Marine was sighted it was clear that a plan would be developed to bring back the body, despite the obvious risk of additional casualties. There was a good chance that the Chinese had positioned the body near their strong defensive positions, feeling certain we'd come after our man.

I was called back to our company CP and given the general plan to retrieve the body. I was to select a squad to make the patrol, get familiar with the terrain approaching the slope and return for additional discussions with battalion operations [S-3] and a tank platoon commander. The mission was set for first light on June 22nd. I believe the mission was called "Operation Snatch."

After selecting Sgt. Kraft's squad for the mission, we reviewed the plan several times. We covered all of the potential pitfalls, everything that might go wrong. A mine detection unit checked the road we would cross on the night of the 21st. Our tanks moved up near the higher ground behind our platoon. Fifty caliber machine guns and all available 30's were quietly set up and trained on the summit directly above the body. We were assured that our company and battalion mortars were ready to support the mission.

With wire cutters, plenty of rope to pull the body free if booby trapped, and a body bag, we moved out quietly before first light to be set up at the base of the slope as daylight approached. We wanted our supporting fire, if needed, to see their targets. With a radioman and Sgt. Kraft's squad near me as a base of supporting fire, one fire team started to move slowly toward the objective 75–100 yards directly up the slope. The body became visible as they drew nearer, but there was still no way to determine if the Marine had been booby trapped, or if the Chinese had set a trap. The "snatch team" appeared to be well along recovering the body and were beginning to start their return to us when small arms fire broke the silence from the top of the ridge, followed immediately by incoming mortar rounds.

Our machine guns and mortars opened up, followed by the two tanks firing point blank from the MLR directly behind us. Two Marine Corsairs appeared, called in by forward observers. We were firing at the few enemy troops we could see, and I remember how grateful I was at that moment for those planes. The snatch team returned as planned with their mission accomplished as our supporting fire power including those beautiful gull winged airplanes pounded the crest of the hill and the reverse slope mortar positions.

As the snatch team joined us, we started to move back toward our lines. We counted heads and came up one short. We knew immediately that it had to have been one of the snatch team, though the other two had not seen him fall. I told the rest of the squad to start back to the MLR with the body bag and picked two men to go back up the slope with me to search for our missing man.

Our radioman passed the information concerning our return and requested that they hold their fire in that area. I knew where the man must have fallen and found him immediately. He was slightly built and I was able to pick him up and carry him down the slope and up the hill toward our MLR.

As we approached our trench lines, men from my platoon ran down to help carry the wounded man to safety. Scrambling into the protection of the trenches we found that the man was dead. He had sustained a single rifle bullet in the head, probably dying instantly.

Many might ask, was it worth losing a man to bring back a body? Every squad felt let down when they weren't called upon to make such a patrol, the feeling was that strong. Personally I was proud to have played a part. Was it worth it? We brought back a Marine, one of us, and that's what it's all about.[3]

Despite noble tenets, there were occasions when efforts to recover a body were not only impossible but foolhardy, especially when a body clearly had been left as bait for an ambush. In such situations, bodies had to be destroyed. There were no other choices. Though these cases were largely unreported, nearly every Marine on line knew what eventually happened to bodies left by the Chinese to tempt Marines into impossible recovery missions. The only alternative left to the Marine commander was to destroy a body by tank fire, artillery, or air strike. Imagine the inner turmoil. If the patrol had been unable to reach the body, how would the commander know for a fact that the Marine is dead? Yet, he had to act. The mental anguish was staggering.

A DAY ON OUTPOST YOKE

When the 5th Marines relieved the 1st Marines on line in mid-June, the units quite naturally assumed responsibility for the outposts, too. They included Outposts Royal, Nellie, Gertie, Digger, X Ray, and Yoke. Unfortunately for history, Outpost Yoke remains the only place name specifically identifiable by grid coordinates. The other outposts, although named in 5th Marine documents, had been unnamed by the 1st Marines, nor are the names located in any reports. Regrettably, this kind of omission is typical of battalion command diaries of the period. A reader must accept the errors and ambiguities of wartime reporting. This particular confusion is complicated by the fact that, months later, a strong Chinese position several miles west was also labeled "Yoke." The hill referred to in this section is the first Yoke, a position that later became Outpost Reno.

The names of the hills are not as important here as are the Marines' experiences on Outpost Yoke, which typify the slow process of the piece-meal war practiced during this period. With a change in outpost names, this process was repeated many times over during the outpost war.

When the OPLR was withdrawn and new outposts established closer to the line, Yoke was one of the hills selected. It was a medium-sized outpost 1,500 yards north of the MLR. Yoke held a garrison of thirty-four Marines.

Approximately 100 meters in elevation, Yoke overlooked the east side of a long north-south valley, a natural avenue of attack from the north. The terrain east of Yoke was dominated by a large hill, also an outpost, that was half again taller, 157 meters on the map. Later, this large hill would be called Clarence and finally Vegas.

Southwest of Yoke was another hill of the same approximate size and held by forty Marines, but it was somewhat closer to the MLR. Later, it acquired the name Allen, which was changed to Carson in September. Farther southeast, beyond Carson, was the Chinese stronghold of Ungok, approximately 1,000 yards away.

On 16 June, 2d Battalion, 5th Marines, completed relief of the 2d Battalion, 1st Marines, on line. The sector assumed by 2/5 was the left side of the division's right sector. Fox Company, 2/5, assumed responsibility for Outpost Yoke and a portion of the MLR.

By reading excerpts from the terse and generally understated Command Diary of 2/5 and selecting only those passages relating to Fox Company and Outpost Yoke on a single day, one can clearly see that the fight to retain the outpost was incessant. It is necessary to bear in mind that Yoke was not exceptional. In other sectors and on other outposts, the situation was all too similar. The following sample describes a typical day at Outpost Yoke:

> 24 Jun: . . . "F" Company reinforced squad set up a perimeter ambush. An estimated sixty enemy made contact and in the ensuing fight the enemy suffered two known KIA's, an estimated five KIA's and twenty estimated WIA's. Both sides withdrew at 2300. Fox Company suffered three WIA's two of which were evacuated by helicopter. . . . At 1520 "F" Company reported one WIA from hand grenade. . . . At 1530 "F" Company reported one WIA from fourteen rounds of 76mm artillery.[4]

Entries in battalion command diaries are brief and often confusing. They frequently fail to present a full picture of a given situation. Such is the case with Outpost Yoke on 24 June, when the defenders, attacked by a superior force, came within a whisker of losing the hill. Taking information from other sources, Meid and Yingling present a clearer version than that reported above. Their account follows:

Late in the afternoon of 24 June, the enemy began registering his mortars and artillery on MLR company positions of 2/5 and a portion of the rear area occupied by the battalion 81mm mortars. Chinese incoming, sometimes intense, sometimes sporadic, continued until shortly after 2130. By this time the CCF were moving down their trenches toward a key outpost, Yoke, . . . which was still occupied on daytime basis by the Marines and lay north of the Company F sector (Captain Harold C. Fuson). Moments later, the 34 men temporarily outposting Yoke saw the Chinese and opened up with small arms fire, but the Marine positions were quickly enveloped by the Chinese. The Americans occupying the forward slopes of Yoke suffered many casualties from the intense fire supporting the enemy rush.

While the initial attack was in progress, the Chinese were able to position and fire machine guns from behind the outpost and in trenches on the forward slopes. Communist mortars interdicted the Marine supply routes to make normal withdrawal and reinforcement measures difficult. The Marines moved into bunkers, called down preplanned fires, and continued the defense. Although the Chinese had overrun Yoke, they could not evict the Marines. At about 0300, the enemy withdrew. When the 2/5 troops followed to reoccupy the forward slopes of Yoke, the enemy renewed his attack and struck again. As before the Marines took to bunkers and called in defensive artillery fire. These boxing fires fell around the outpost perimeter until first light when the attacker withdrew for the second time.

. . . At Yoke alone, 9 were killed and 23 wounded [32 out of a force of 34 Marines]. Enemy dead were 12 known and 50 estimated. Chinese wounded were estimated at 100. At one point during the attack on Yoke, the outpost commander reported that the enemy were wearing gas masks and using tear gas grenades.[5]

STANDING AT EASE

The 1st Marine Regiment, having been relieved by the 5th Marines on 16 June, moved by truck and helicopter to the division reserve camp behind the Imjin River. The 1st and 2d Battalions encamped their respective areas and took up housekeeping chores, training, and continued building of the Kansas Line. Kansas was a fallback line in case the Jamestown Line fell. Each unit in reserve was responsible for creating fortifications and defenses for use in event of an enemy breakthrough. The work was arduous, largely trench and bunker building, all with picks and shovels.

When not digging, the men attended classes. A typical training schedule covered such subjects as squad formations, squad in the attack, attack on a fortified position, gun drill, map and compass reading, and other assorted infantry skills. Daily, patrols went out to search for infiltrators and other persons not authorized to be north of the military stay-back line.

Meanwhile, the 3d Battalion made preparations for a forthcoming amphibious exercise, called a MARLEX (Marine Landing Exercise), to be conducted on the Korean offshore island of Tokchok-to. The battalion would board a ship in Inchon Harbor and, two days later, storm the beach in a mock amphibious landing. After the men returned to camp, the 1st Battalion would conduct its MARLEX.

Reserve was not an easy place to be—it consisted of a lot of training and a lot of work—and there was always risk. On 28 June, a truck in a convoy hit the railing of a bridge and overturned. One officer, five Marines, and four Navy enlisted men were injured and evacuated to Able Med, the battalion aid station. (Each company in the Medical Battalion operated a small hospital—Able Med, Easy Med, etc. These were the Navy/Marine equivalent of the Army's MASH.)

Another problem in the reserve areas was North Korean agents, a minor but consistent threat. Reserve units were directed to put out frequent rear-area patrols and strictly enforce the stay-back line. In June, for the first time, selected areas south of the Imjin River began to experience occasional incoming artillery fire from the Chinese. The impacts were far enough behind the lines to have little tactical value relative to ongoing offensive operations, but they were accurate and well aimed. The shells fell on military installations, rather than randomly on rice paddies and towns, and appeared to be directed. Also, on occasion, unexplained blinking lights had preceded the barrages of incoming fire.

On 17 June, five Korean "civilians" were apprehended in the reserve area, where they were living in positions overlooking friendly installations. They were well stocked with food and supplies, more than the average Korean farmer was likely to own. The men, food, and equipment were turned over to counterintelligence for investigation. Two days later, intelligence officers reported that among the items found with the prisoners was a copy of the division code for 9, 10, 14, and 15 June. Near the location of the blinking lights, an unused bunker had been booby-trapped. Inside the bunker, the intelligence officers discovered a dead Oriental soldier with several stick grenades and an ammunition belt carrying nearly two hundred rounds. As a consequence, the division had to assume that the entire code for June had been compromised. Further, the regimental S-2 (intelligence) issued a warning that "there is no question that CCF and other unfriendly elements behind our MLR are armed."[6] Rear-area patrols of the reserve camps were increased and the warning widely disseminated.

While admittedly better than the South Koreans at infiltration techniques, the North Korean Communists had no corner on the market. Efforts to create South Korean partisan forces to infiltrate the north and work behind the lines had been ongoing since the war began. Many of the efforts were disasters, but some succeeded. In western Korea, there was a partisan command on offshore islands in the Han River estuary. Called Wolfpack, these groups were controlled by the U.S. Army's Guerrilla Division, Far East Command Liaison Detachment, Korea (FEC/LD[K]).

Even though the partisan forces were not a Marine operation, they took part in western Korea in the Marine sector. Wolfpack operations were supported by a platoon of Marine tanks located on one of the offshore islands. Because of the generally covert nature of partisan activity, little has been reported on this phase of the war by either the Army or the Marine Corps.

The comfortable side of reserve included hot and often tasty food, showers, clean clothing, and usually a lack of incoming fire. Beer was available to all enlisted men, and officers and staff NCOs had hard liquor as well. Life could be comparatively pleasant for the men when they were not working or training. Sports, card games, visits with friends in other units, frequent movies (in some camps, daily), and an occasional USO or Special Services show were common. Females were all that the men really lacked. A Marine tells of attending a USO show that starred a well-known Hollywood sex symbol:

> I was in the front row when out she comes, looking like a million dollars. She came to the edge of the stage leans over to talk to me. Christ, her two boobs are practically hanging out! I figured she must really like me, because she knows I'm looking right at those watermelons she's throwing around and she has this big smile on her face with the most beautiful set of teeth you've ever seen lighting up the place.

Jeez, then she goes to the next guy and does the same thing. Before she was through, she worked over the whole row. ·

...The guy next to me was killed a month or two later at an outpost called Vegas. I think it was damn nice of that beauty to show him her knockers. Might have been the last pair he ever saw.[7]

With the shortage of suitable females, the world's oldest profession thrived. Though off limits and despite active efforts to drive them away, Korean whores found ways to prosper. In June alone, Marine MPs arrested eighty-nine pimps and prostitutes.

Korea was not Paris, however, and the local ladies sometimes proved to be more depressing than satisfying. A lieutenant tells the story of catching one of his own men leaving an off-limits cave known to be a crib for prostitution. Pleading to be let off, the young man stated that he had just experienced the ugliest, most depressing, and most humiliating moment of his life. He went on to say that, while on line, his buddies had made the discovery that he was a virgin. Arriving in reserve, they decided that it was their duty to correct that flaw in his education. Passing the hat, they all chipped in to pay for a "short time" with one of the local beauties. As financial arrangements were consummated with a pimp, the friends never laid eyes on the lucky lady. When everything was set up, his friends took the young man to the designated cave and pushed him inside.

As his eyes adjusted to the dark, the young man noted that the girl was barely into her teens, flat-chested, and nearly hairless. She smelled heavily of garlic, fish, and sour cabbage. Her clothing and blankets were filthy—sticky and soiled with dirt and other unidentifiable stains. As the lad gamely attempted to fulfill his part of the hellish bargain, the girl lay back on her thin mattress, unwrapped a candy bar, and noisily began eating. She was completely unconcerned. This was the last straw. Our hero gave up and fled from the cave into the waiting arms of his lieutenant. Rationalizing that the young man had suffered sufficiently from the trauma of his experience, the officer released him to make peace with his buddies. Our swain had no doubt escaped his "fate worse than death" and would be safer on an outpost dodging shrapnel.

CHAPTER 5

BLIND MEN
AND ELEPHANTS

Men rise from one ambition to another;
first they seek to secure themselves from attack,
and then they attack others.
—Niccolo Machiavelli

On 2 July 1952, George Company, 3/7, conducted a raid on an unnamed hill northeast of Three Fingers in the vicinity of Outpost Two. Three Fingers itself sporadically functioned as a Chinese position. Although the unnamed hill was not garrisoned constantly, it was occasionally used to launch night attacks on OP-2 or other nearby Marine positions. Truly a no-man's-land, it changed hands frequently, but, tactically, the location had no useful purpose.

George Company's raid was comparatively routine. Recently, numerous sightings had been observed on the objective hill. It was felt that the Chinese might be trying to improve defenses and occupy the hill on a more permanent basis, a manifestation of the creeping tactic. The Marines planned to use Three Fingers as a springboard and drive the Chinese from the hill.

Accounts of historical events written from the various participants' points of view often leave one with a question, "Am I reading about the same event?" Nowhere is this more true than in military history because so many people, under varying degress of stress, have participated in a given action. Each person, it seems, has a positive, unshakable belief that he knows what happened because he was there. Largely, he is correct but not to the exclusion of other observations. The phenomenon reminds one of the fable of ten blind men describing an elephant. Each man was correct because he described only that portion of the animal that he experienced, but each one argued that the other nine men were wrong. The raid from Three Fingers is a similar example. Several versions exist. They offer greater detail in proportion to the physical proximity of the writers. All versions are accurate but some more so than others.

The 7th Marines Regimental Command Diary for 2 July reported the following:

> Four ambushes, three listening posts, two combat patrols, one of two squads (reinforced) and one of company strength (minus one platoon) were sent forward of the MLR. *The latter patrol made contact with the enemy;* all other units returned to the MLR with negative contact.[1] [emphasis added]

In its command diary of the same day, the 3d Battalion, 7th Marines, parent battalion of George Company, elaborated somewhat on this patrol contact:

> During this period a night raid and dawn attack were conducted against the enemy Fwd of the MLR in the "G" Company sector with the mission of capturing prisoners. The raiding party was composed of two platoons from "G" Company. One platoon of the raiding party proceeded to Vic BT 987034 [Three Fingers] with Neg enemy contact and then withdrew to BT 9878036 and set up a base of fire. At 0624I the other platoon passed through the base of fire and made contact with the enemy at BT 987036 [the objective hill]. The enemy employed small arms, automatic weapons, hand grenades, mortars and artillery; Friendlies employed small arms, automatic weapons, hand grenades, mortars, artillery, 4.5 rockets, 3.5 rockets and flame throwers. Contact was made with the enemy at 0700I and broken by the friendlies at 1030I. Enemy casualties were estimated to be 50 KIA and 150 WIA; Friendly casualties were 4 KIA and 40 WIA. There were negative prisoners taken. Intercepted enemy radio transmissions substantiated 60 enemy casualties during the first hour of the action.[2]

Based on this report, it might be fair to summarize this action by saying that a platoon left the MLR very late at night and was in position on the slope of Three Fingers by nearly 0630. Another platoon passed through the first and, thirty minutes later, engaged the enemy on the next hill. The firefight lasted three and one-half hours until the Marines withdrew. Marine casualties were moderate and Chinese casualties much greater.

Another view of the elephant is obtained when one reads the words of 2d Lt. William A. Watson. Assigned to George Company, 3/7, Watson was present on the raid, his first time in combat. He related:

> On 3 July, the quiet war ended. Someone . . . decided that G Company of the 7th Marines should assault a fortified Chinese position immediately next to Three Fingers, a piece of terrain which appeared on the map as a "hand" with three fingers pointing south toward the Panmunjom road. Across a deep depression from the round part of the "hand" of Three Fingers was another hill of about the same elevation upon which was located a clearly visible Chinese trench with some bunkers. . . .
>
> . . . I was still an extra officer in the company. My job was to take out a squad on the previous evening, near dark, and occupy a hill just off the neutral corridor from which both Three Fingers and the objective hill could be seen. Our artillery FO would be with me and would adjust fire from there during the fighting. After the assault began, I would go down and assure that the base of fire people were re-supplied with ammo, candy and fruit juice, and see to the evacuation of wounded. We would have Korean civilian bearers helping with the labor. . . . During the night, our engineers would check the route for mines, using metal detectors and probing with bayonets. If they found something, they marked it with little white strips of cloth in an X pattern. It seemed a good plan for the purpose.
>
> . . . We moved out near dark with just enough light to see clearly, and occupied the hill where the FO would set up his operation. There were about twenty men, including me. The hill had no tactical importance except for this mission and was not occupied, so we just walked in, carefully though. We sent a code message to the Company Commander, Capt. Anton Froelich, announcing we were in place, and then it got dark, black dark. Now there was nothing to do but wait for first light. Down below, on the trail leading to Three Fingers, the engineers would be at work clearing the path and marking any mines they found. . . . [W]e saw the product of their work next morning, several little white cloth X's at intervals going out toward the objective hill.
>
> Up on our position it was quiet except for one black Marine, some distance from me, who was heard to mutter audibly, from time to time, "Mother Fucker" this and "Mother Fucker" that. I acknowledge the urge to kill him, but he fell silent, and across that broad valley there was really not a sound, not even frogs. . . .
>
> That night, as always, we did not sleep, not even a little. I sat in the trench, cold, my legs drawn up with my carbine between them. I lis-

tened for sounds which would tell us our presence was betrayed. But none came. Much later, about 0300 hours, we could hear the frogs again and we knew that all must be well with the engineers, and with the troops who would be moving into position for the assault.

The sky lightened and we began stretching in the trench, a sterno capsule was produced here and there and canteen cups of water were heated for coffee. There was a lot of moisture in the air, fog, very dense fog. By 0600, it was almost light and the fog seemed to settle down into the valley. Looking up, the sky was clear. It would be another hot day. Then, in a few minutes, we could see across the valley. Three Fingers and the objective were under a deep fog. By now the first platoon and the machine gun sections must be in position as a base of fire. The third platoon was waiting to move through for the assault. The fog was a thick white mantle. A man would have trouble seeing a few yards ahead of him. No one said anything before that about fog, not to me anyway. I wondered if our planning included such a contingency. Did we have meteorological input? Would the assault platoon jump off without artillery preparation fire, or the air strike? Time passed. It became apparent they would not. They were waiting until the fog cleared. I discussed it with the FO, mentioned it to the Company Commander on the land line. My opinion was noted, no response. I suggested respectfully they should go now, a silent bayonet attack. I thought the troops would achieve great surprise by going up the hill under cover of the fog. It was really thick, but who can say? Artillery and mortar fire break up mines and barbed wire. I suppose this was deemed necessary. But the waiting dragged on and I retain some doubt to this day about the delay. It seemed a long time until the mist began to dissipate. Slowly the terrain materialized through the fog, like Brigadoon come alive after a hundred years. But, no gentle people awaited our coming here.

Then, after the fog cleared, we heard our shells come in. The trench on the objective became obscured by exploding shells and dust, ground and air bursts. It was difficult to believe Chinese soldiers there could have survived our barrage and fight but, as we learned, they did, and fought well. After a few minutes, the barrage lifted and the air strike began, two hundred fifty pound bombs delivered by AD 4's. They made several runs. The bombs sent shock waves through the clear air, across the valley. The entire Chinese position was obscured by dust. Then machine gun fire, ours or theirs. The assault had begun. I started down the hill from where I had spent the night, to join the Korean bearers. A corpsman had established a position to the side of the hill where I had been. In just a few minutes, the first casualty came back, a young Marine on a stretcher, face down, a throat wound. He was choking on his own blood. A grenade wound. He had been part of the assault platoon. As I watched, he gagged and blood came out of his throat and mouth. I thought I would be sick. I felt nausea and turned away. It was the only time in Korea when I felt that way. The first and the last time. After that I shut it up inside me. The corpsman did what he could for him and sent him on. We heard later that surgeons at the aid station did an emergency tracheotomy on him, got him aboard a helicopter to Easy Med., and that he survived. Our surgeons were the finest men in the war, Navy doctors. I wondered if they ever got a medal. They deserved it. Wherever Marines were getting torn apart, they were there, doing desperate things, and saving most of them.

I could not simply stand there and watch the casualties go by. I loaded a stretcher with candy, canned fruit juice, and extra bandoliers of M-1 rifle ammo, and some boxes of belted .30 caliber ammo for the machine guns. The Koreans carried it and we set out across the paddy. The morning was clear and bright now. Soon it would be warm, and then hot. The rattle of machine gun fire was constant, mortars crumping, and rifle fire. Who was winning?

. . . Along the trail we stepped around the little white X's left by engineers. We were across the open ground in a few minutes, then started up the middle finger through the scrub growth. The sound of our machine gun fire was very close to us, but I couldn't hear much M-1 rifle fire. When we got to the crest of the hill where the base of fire was situated, I saw why. Our machine guns were on the forward slope, set up on graves and they were firing actively. . . . The 1st Platoon, most of whom were in defilade on the reverse slope, strung out in a line a few feet apart, doing nothing. . . .

I distributed the M-1 bandoliers to men whose guns were cold. Then, exasperated with their apparent lack of purpose, or concern for the damage a single mortar round could inflict, I ordered them to spread out. Their platoon commander was on the ridge, but he wasn't commanding many of his troops. Whether the intense, concentrated rifle and BAR fire of three full squads would have turned the tide in the assault, I don't know, but I have to believe it would have done so. You can't look over the side of a trench and fire effectively at people coming up at you if you are receiving a steady volume of accurate fire, especially at 250 yards or less. That is what they taught us at Parris Island. The Chinese were well within the range of our weapons and our machine guns had to be supplemented by rifles from the 1st platoon, the entire platoon, else the barrels would burn out. Maybe some did. They seemed to be firing constantly during the entire morning.

I lay on the crest of the ridge for a couple of minutes after we spread the ammo and snacks around. There was a sergeant lying there beside me and we spoke. Chinese bullets were zipping past me, just above our heads. Then I got up and went back to get some more stretcher people and ammo. Before I made the second trip back to the base of fire, that particular sergeant came by on a stretcher, a bullet went clean through his upper right arm. There was a bandage on it, stained with blood, and he had his left hand behind his head for support. He laughed when he saw me. "You lucky son-of-a-bitch," I said. He put his head back and laughed again, and went home, all the way home. I got some bearers and went back out to see about the casualties.

It was hot now. I was thirsty and hungry. Going across the paddy I heard some slugs striking a few feet from me. I hit the ground, using the dike upon which the trail was located for cover. The slugs could have come from anywhere. Picking a spot in some trees a hundred yards away I ripped off a burst from my carbine, probably hit nothing, but I felt better anyway. I got up and trotted on out to the troops.

...The troops pulled back in an orderly way, strung out but with no undue haste, and we got another air strike to cover us. Marine pilots in close air support just make you feel good about what you're doing. They came in low, strafing with the .50 caliber guns. I was near the base of Three Fingers with a stretcher. My Koreans were off somewhere. The sky was blue and the air was getting hot indeed. The stress of the firing and the constant physical exertion was now palpable. But we were young. . . . A short distance away a sergeant from the 1st platoon had a casualty by the arm, a young Marine with a fragmentation wound in his leg. The sergeant was calling for help and talking to the Marine. I told him to take it easy and we would get the man out all right. I opened the stretcher and we got him on it. Four men started back with him. We were some of the last to pull back. I got some people organized to cover the flanks of Three Fingers by fire if necessary, while the main body traversed the open ground of the paddy. It seemed there was no staged or phased withdrawal and things got a little ragged, but the Chinese weren't following, not in broad daylight and we had our air cover. . . .

The last elements fell back across the paddy and soon were back in the neutral zone. I remember a field ambulance parked there with the right hand door of the cab open. We were all beginning to feel a release of tension by now and I said something to the black Marine who was sitting in the passenger seat. When he just stared straight ahead, I looked again. There was a neat bullet hole right between his eyes. He was quite dead.[3]

Another perspective of the elephant emerges on examination of the account of tank support by Dog Company, 1st Tank Battalion. Here, the tanks failed to achieve their mission because of a lack of prior route reconnaissance. To support this raid, five M-46 Patton tanks of the 1st Platoon left the MLR under cover of darkness at 0440. They traveled a good road, flanked by marshy rice paddies, and passed between hills that were later named OP's Kate and Marilyn. The road crossed a ditch that was impassable because of overflow from rice paddies and a swollen stream. The heavy, flat-bottomed tanks lost traction in the muck and bellied up. They could go no farther. The remainder of the night was spent in extracting the tanks from the mud. Not a shot had been fired.

Ironically, the impassable ditch probably saved the men and machines from serious casualties and damage. Discovered across the ditch about fifty yards up the road was a Soviet box mine buried 4 inches underground. The mine was active and indications were that more were secreted nearby. Had the tanks crossed the ditch, they would have run into a minefield.

Later in the year, a special tank reconnaissance team would be established to avoid the circumstances encountered at the ditch. After the spring thaw, all of the paddies, stream crossings, and many roads turned into impassable mush. It nearly always took a man on foot to check out a contemplated tank route in front of the MLR.

ATTACK ON OUTPOST GARY

Early July found the 1st and 2d Battalions of the 5th Marines remaining on line in the right division sector. In sequence, east of the 7th Marines was 2/5. Next came 1/5, abutting the Samichon River, and the British Commonwealth Division. Opposing the two Marine battalions of approximately 1,000 men each were 3,100 soldiers of the Chinese 354th Regiment, supported by five artillery battalions.

Guarding the Marine MLR were fourteen outposts manned in varying degrees of strength. Common to all of them was a shared view of no-man's-land as the troops stared down the throats of the enemy. Taking umbrage at these positions, the Chinese reacted strongly during the first week of July by simultaneously striking five outposts.

During the day of 5 July, Outposts Bruce and Gary and Fox Company's sector of the MLR began receiving incoming mortar and artillery fire. It continued throughout the day and, by 1830, had spread to George Company's MLR sector and Outpost Clarence. Falling continuously, the barrage had the appearance of preparatory fire intended to soften up the locations for an assault.

At 2200 hours, incoming fire reached maximum intensity on the MLR, with concentrations also falling on Outposts Gary, Bruce, Allen,

Clarence, and Felix. One officer estimated that the Chinese directed more than one thousand rounds at the Marine defenders within a period of ninety minutes. The greatest number fell on Outpost Gary.

Gary, which was later to become Outpost Frisco, was manned by Marines from Dog Company, 2/5. At 2050, between lulls of incoming fire, a preplanned ambush patrol left the outpost to seek enemy activity in the vicinity of Hill 98. A reinforced squad was left to defend Gary.

When the barrage was heaviest, an enemy company attacked the hill. Chinese soldiers, moving through their own artillery, breached the protective wire. In the trenches, Marines fought off the Chinese with small arms, bayonets, hand grenades, and shovels. Chinese troops almost exclusively used concussion grenades. The soldiers wore special vests fitted with pockets to carry twenty-five or thirty hand grenades. (A common Chinese tactic was to arm many of their assault troops with nothing but grenades. They were expected to use captured enemy small arms to finish the fight.) Then, at 2245, the enemy broke contact and withdrew.

The ambush patrol was able to return to Gary at 2315, and the men reinforced the defense. Incoming fire had ceased, and the men breathed a little easier, though they stayed alert.

At 0030, the Marines heard unusual noises in front of their position and sent a fire team to investigate. The team found four wounded Chinese soldiers, left behind during the retreat, who were hiding in the bushes. The Marines took the prisoners to the outpost and later captured another Chinese soldier.

Twenty-three enemy dead were counted on the ground around Gary, and one hundred more were estimated killed and wounded.

View From the MLR

Lieutenant Matthias was among the Marines fighting on Outpost Gary that night. This was his first night on line. On June 11, Matthias had arrived in Korea on a special flight of seventy-seven brand-new second lieutenants, fresh from The Basic School (TBS), who had been assigned to the 1st Division. The division needed replacements because junior officers were getting killed a little too regularly.

Matthias had reported to the Company Commander of Dog Company, 2/5, 1st Lt. Charlie Lee, who said that Matthias would be assigned to a platoon in a few days. In the meantime, he was to stow his gear in a corner of the command bunker known as the guest room. Feeling a lot like a new kid on the block, Matthias relaxed on his cot and waited. Evening fell, and activity in the bunker increased. Communication men

became very busy as they talked with Marines assigned to platoons, outposts, mortar and machine-gun sections, and battalion headquarters. From
the bunker, Matthias could hear explosions of incoming artillery.

Activity in the command bunker became feverish. It was evident that
something unusual was happening. The communications men furiously
manipulated their equipment, swore, dialed, and passed messages all at the
same time. Then the radio went dead. No one knew what was happening on the outposts or on line. Fear of the unknown was rising.

Standing near the main entrance, trying to stay out of the way yet
interested in the activity, Matthias was startled by the arrival of a sergeant
whom he had met earlier in the day. "He was the nearest facsimile of a
black ghost that I could imagine. The first thing I noted were his huge,
frightened eyes. His helmet was on and buckled. He had attached his bayonet on his carbine. He was ready. He looked at me but addressed Lt. Lee
and stammered, 'Lieutenant, all hell is breaking loose out there, we better get some help.' The sergeant was due to be replaced, and he was my
first example of a true short timer."[4]

As reports came in, it became apparent that heavy fighting was going
on at Outpost Gary. There was concern for a patrol in the vicinity of the
battle, and the CP was receiving no communication from the outpost.
Military terminology includes a phrase that quite accurately describes
events such as this: "The shit has hit the fan." Unfortunately, Marines on
many outposts found it necessary to repeat the phrase—frequently.

Events during the remainder of that night are related in the words of
Lieutenant Matthias, as he became involved:

> . . . It was now nearly morning and Charlie [Lieutenant Lee] came
> over to me and said, "I do not want to do this but I have no choice.
> As soon as you can find your way, take a relief force and as many
> 'chiggie bearers' (Korean laborers) as we can muster and get out to
> the outpost."
>
> My first "command" was a motley crew consisting basically of
> cooks, clerks and other service personnel. An old mustang of a techni-
> cal sergeant I remembered from California brought up twelve very re-
> luctant Korean laborers. They were heavily laden with ammunition,
> stretchers and medical supplies. One of the messengers from the pre-
> vious night was assigned to guide me to the outpost.
>
> Before we even left the MLR (Main Line of Resistance) we began
> to meet some of the gory aftermath of the previous night. Several
> wounded Marines had been helped to the "gate" and were waiting for
> assistance. We also met a couple of Marines roughly herding three

prisoners of war. Everyone was dirty, disheveled and gaunt. I noticed for the first time how thin and tired everyone appeared to be. The Marines were angry and the prisoners were pale with fright.

The outpost was across a rice paddy and up a fairly steep hill. The path across the rice paddy was well traveled and clearly evident. It was unprotected and open to enemy observation. The total distance was probably less than a third of a mile but it took about twenty minutes to negotiate. We were very cautious. We had been warned about stragglers and possibly lost soldiers. In addition, we always had to be concerned about an ambush. The biggest problem was the Korean laborers. They had to be constantly prodded to keep moving.

We were moving along quite well when I experienced the most frightening sound in the world—the scream of an incoming shell. It was my first experience. Everybody hit the dirt, with me leading the way. The shell passed overhead and hit the hill behind us. We were in the open and had to keep moving. More shells followed as we crossed the open rice paddy. Fortunately, we had no casualties.

A new problem developed: the Korean laborers would not move. In fact, a couple started to move back toward the main line. One of the Marines to the rear quickly moved toward the retreating laborers, yelled, "Idi wah, you son of a bitch," and fired his M-1 so that several shells hit right between the Korean's legs. The retreating men stopped, came back and continued the climb. I noticed we were moving faster than before.

It was a steep climb up to the outpost. As we neared the top I noticed the first smell of death. It is a very definite, distinctive odor, a combination of blood, rotting flesh and perspiration. A putrid, stagnant air hung over the outpost. Mingled with the sickening smell was the faint odor of garlic. At the time I could not understand this sweet odor intermingling with the ugly smell.

As we reached the summit, we were challenged. I returned the countersign and moved through the barbed wire. . . . Several Chinese prisoners were sitting on their haunches under the watchful eyes and guns of the Marines. Most of them were wounded.

. . . The first priority involved two seriously wounded Marines. Two stretchers, a corpsman and eight Koreans were hurried down the hill to medical help back at the main line. I asked the corporal in charge if there were any more casualties and he said, "No more except the guys around the corner." This was the second reference to "around the corner." This time, I noted tears in the eyes of the corporal. He said, "Follow me and stay low. You can be seen by the gooks."

At the corner of the trench line was a makeshift bunker with a machine gun emplaced. A dead Marine was still slouched over the gun. His buddy had already been removed. I said, "Let's get him out of here." As I started to reach for the dead gunner, the corporal said, "First, look out there." I saw bodies piled on top of each other lying on top of the barbed wire. Other Chinese had broken through the wire and were killed charging toward the gun. A couple of bodies were less than eight feet in front of the emplacement. The body count, we learned later, numbered over thirty in this one section alone. These two Marines had single-handedly stopped the attack and saved the lives of the remaining dozen Marines on the hill. They must have been killed by the last of the attacking wave of Chinese. God, what a sight. What courage it must have taken to stay at their post when faced with such odds.

. . . The corporal and I dragged the dead Marine back to the rear of the outpost. It was my first touching of a dead person. It would not be my last.

The rest of the day involved bringing in replacements, removing bodies and making preparations for the night. I was greatly relieved when I was finally ordered back to the command bunker. My first night and day in combat. I had been fired upon, fired my own weapon for the first time, came in contact with real heroes, handled my first prisoners and made some of my first decisions while under fire.[5]

THE MATTER OF PRISONERS

Records do not disclose what became of the five prisoners captured on Outpost Gary that day. Treatment of prisoners by the men who had been fighting them moments before was not always predictable. In Matthias's narrative, he mentions that one Marine slapped one of the prisoners around and threatened him. To the lieutenant's credit, he immediately ordered the man to stop. The conduct, however, was not that unusual on either side. Marines are taught and ordered to treat prisoners of war (POWs) humanely. In practice, however, there are human failings. One does not hit a foe in the face with a shovel to prevent him from killing you and then pick up his injured body, offer him a cigarette, and show each other photos of the family. That's the fiction of which movies are made.

In front of the MLR, prisoners were a nuisance. They had to be watched or carried if wounded. They were in the way and took up scarce resources. Also, they were a threat. Prisoners could call out to their comrades, make noise, steal weapons, or simply jump someone in an un-guarded moment. Outposts did not have jails and patrols did not carry handcuffs.

It is one thing to capture a man who has been actively trying to kill you and quite another to accept the surrender of a passive, unarmed enemy. Most prisoners were taken when they voluntarily surrendered to an outpost or a post on the MLR. Typically, the soldier walked into the open with his hands raised and waved a surrender leaflet. Covered by several weapons, he would be ordered to strip naked and only then allowed to enter the wire. Once inside, he would be searched and briefly questioned if a translator could be found.

After capture, prisoners were removed to the rear as soon as possible. They were interrogated by American and South Korean counterintelligence agents and then placed in the division POW stockade, a temporary holding facility guarded by Marine MPs. As soon as practical, POWs were transferred to an Eighth Army prisoner of war stockade far to the rear.

Intelligence personnel generally found Communist POWs to be cooperative, and they learned much from their interrogations. Often, prisoners were so talkative and knowledgeable about enemy plans and strategies that American interrogators questioned the validity of their information. With experience, however, American interrogators learned that Communist officers, as a matter of doctrine, customarily shared a great deal of high-level strategic and tactical information with their men. The purpose apparently was to bolster morale and convince the men as to how well prepared and equipped they were, compared to "those imperialistic warmongers from America."

In any case, enemy prisoners were a valuable intelligence resource and in great demand by Headquarters. Later in the war, a bounty of one week's R&R (rest and recreation) leave in Japan was offered to any Marine who captured a prisoner.

The matter of prisoners was a difficult one. It was paradoxical. Everyone agreed that they were beneficial to the pursuit of the war. Headquarters (Division, Corps, and Army) were continually requesting that greater efforts be extended to capture enemy troops. The men did not want the bother on line, R&R or not. It was far easier to shoot the enemy than to capture him; it was also less dangerous. 1st Lt. Stan Rauh, with A/1/7, wrote:

> One early morning as I was sipping my C ration coffee, I noticed a small patrol of Korean Marines moving along the Panmunjom Corridor with three Chinese prisoners in tow. The prisoners had their hands tied behind them, were blind folded and tied together by ropes around their necks. Within minutes I started for the Korean command bunker to determine if I could gain any useful information. Shortly

before I arrived at the bunker I heard three shots. The KMC captain informed me that the Chinese wouldn't cooperate so he shot them. So much for intelligence gathering.[6]

That first week in July was a busy time. The attack on Outpost Gary was only part of the picture. Simultaneously with the assault on Gary, the enemy launched a two-battalion sustained attack against all defending outposts in the 5th Marine sector and on the MLR itself. As most fighting occurred on outposts, a heavy assault on the MLR was an infrequent event of high strategic concern. Because it was so thinly held, any attack on the MLR always carried a threat of breakthrough, the potential for disaster. At battalion headquarters, a provisional platoon was organized to counterattack a possible breakthrough, but by 2400 on 5 July, all contact with the MLR was lost and the enemy artillery bombardment ceased. As suddenly as they began, the Chinese withdrew. For that day, the fighting was over.

During the battle, 2,300 rounds of mixed mortar and artillery incoming rounds had saturated Charlie and Baker Companies' sector on the MLR, but the line held.

Throughout July, fighting continued from hilltop to hilltop with monotonous repetition, like a well-rehearsed stage play—one performance after the other. Only the cast of players changed as the nights and the hills blended into sameness. Unlike a performance, however, the players dropped from bullets and shards of steel. The months ahead would only worsen the situation.

CHAPTER 6
BUNKER HILL

Don't fire until you see the whites of their eyes.
—William Prescott, at the battle of
Bunker Hill, 17 June 1775

Late summer is the monsoon season in Korea—hot and humid, and always wet. In 1952, the rains of July continued through August. Widgeon and Honker Bridges, crossing the Imjin Ruver, were washed away as the water rose. Dirt roads turned into brown mush as trucks and jeeps traveled back and forth to the line. The resupply of ammunition, food, people, toilet paper, and other necessities became difficult but never stopped. Ingenuity and manpower prevailed as the requirements of war continued despite the weather. Also continuing, in defiance of the weather, was the fighting. The Korean War version of king of the hill played through on the outposts.

Since the end of July, two battalions of the 1st Marines had held the center sector of the MLR. The 3d Battalion was on the left abutting the KMC regiment and the neutral corridor, and the 2d Battalion was on the right next to the 5th Marines. The 1st Battalion was in regimental reserve.

Opposing the Marine battalions were two regiments of Chinese, the 352d and the 580th. These units were described as well supplied, with excellent combat efficiency. According to the 1st Marines command diary, "The enemy maintained an active defense characterized by limited objective attacks, small probes and a slow but continuous forward extension of his defense system in conjunction with an aggressive and tenacious resistance to friendly attacks or patrols."[1] In other words, the Chinese tactical defense was much like that of the Marines, active and combative.

On 17 June 1775, the first major battle of the American Revolution was fought in Massachusetts Colony. The battle actually was on Breed's Hill, next to Bunker Hill, but history has chosen to disregard that fact. Breed's Hill was an outpost, fortified to oppose the attacking British. After three British assaults, which included hand-to-hand fighting in the trenches, the colonists retired to the adjacent Bunker Hill. The minutemen sustained fewer than half the casualties endured by the attacking redcoats: 441 Americans versus 1,124 British.[2] The men who fought that outpost battle were regarded as heroic patriots.

Nearly two centuries later, on the Jamestown Line in Korea, another generation of patriots fought on an outpost called Bunker Hill. This battle was also bloody, close, and costly in terms of casualties, but the Americans prevailed and Bunker Hill remained a viable outpost facing enemy forces. Coincidentally, this battle for the second Bunker Hill was the first major battle fought by the Marines in western Korea. The casualty figures for Bunker Hill reflect several days of fighting and the effect of modern military equipment—Marines, 732; Chinese, 3,200. Like the battle for its namesake in Massachusetts, the fighting for Bunker Hill in Korea also began on an adjacent hill—Outpost Siberia.

Late on Friday, 8 August, Easy Company, 2/1, reported incoming fire on its portion of the MLR, as well as on Outpost Siberia. The incessant barrages of incoming mortar and artillery fire were soon recognized as the preparation for an attack. Well over one thousand rounds fell on the 2d Battalion's area of defense. Then, at 0100 on 9 August, the reinforced squad on Siberia, about fifteen men, was attacked on three sides by a company of Chinese. The squad held on for twenty-five minutes until it was forced to abandon the position or be annihilated. The Marines returned to the MLR with eight casualties, more than half of their manpower. Buying time for his squad, Pfc. Ramon Nunez-Juarez remained behind to cover the evacuation. An article in *Leatherneck* magazine recorded the following:

> Pfc Nunez-Juarez, had been in a forward position [Outpost Siberia] and once the attack started he remained there squeezing off round after round of well aimed .30 caliber M1 rifle rounds. He kept the attacking Chinese at bay until an empty clip ejected from his rifle. His ammunition pouches and bandoliers were empty.
>
> Sensing it was time to leave, Nunez-Juarez crawled down a slope, hoping to find someone among the wounded with a few extra rounds. He eventually did, but was by now unable to return to his old firing position.

He quickly set up his new position near the crest of the hill and continued to deliver devastating fire upon the enemy. Aware that his squad was unable to evacuate its casualties without covering fire, Nunez-Juarez waved them out of the area and poured accurate fire on the oncoming Communists, thus enabling his squad to withdraw.[3]

Private First Class Nunez-Juarez died that night. He was posthumously awarded the Navy Cross.

After withdrawal of the Marines, the Chinese held Siberia. They were a serious threat to Marine defenses. The outpost had to be retaken. Therefore, at 0400, after five minutes of artillery fire, a reinforced Easy Company platoon attempted to take back the hill. An hour and a half later, the attack was stopped fifty yards from the crest by defending small arms, grenades, and artillery. After two more unsuccessful attempts, the platoon withdrew.

At daybreak, another effort to retake Siberia began. Four air strikes saturated the hill and surrounding positions with napalm and explosives until 1025. They were followed by a ten-minute artillery barrage. Then, a second Easy Company platoon charged the hill. In ten minutes, the Marines were heavily engaged and, five minutes later, at 1050, pushed the enemy over the top of the hill. Fighting continued, however, as enemy soldiers fighting from the forward slope tried to regain a foothold on the crest.

It was a tenuous victory. To hold Siberia, Able Company, 1/1, moved forward from reserve to replace Easy Company atop the hill. Twenty minutes later, the Chinese counterattacked under a barrage of artillery and mortar fire. The reinforced Marines on the outpost sustained 75 percent casualties and were driven 50 yards off the hill. An artillery duel developed with battery and counterbattery fire, each side trying to silence the other and deny the hill to opposing troops. Trying again, unsuccessfully, to attain the crest of Siberia, the Marines broke contact at 1210 and retired to the MLR.

Determined to retake Siberia, the Marines planned another effort. Charlie Company, 1/1, was brought forward from regimental reserve to make the assault.[4] At 2300 on 9 August, Charlie Company, minus one platoon, began the assault. The route differed slightly from previous attacks; the men crossed the northern slope of Outpost Samoa, which had been abandoned while Siberia was being contested. Reaching the foot of Siberia, the Marines fought through the artillery, grenades, and machine guns and carried the day by attaining the crest of the hill with a wild bayonet charge. One platoon followed Chinese soldiers over the top and fought them down the forward slope. On the outpost, other platoons closed with the enemy in tough hand-to-hand fighting. Finally, at 0130, the Chinese retreated, and Charlie Company held the hill. An hour later, Charlie Company's 3d Platoon joined the others to reinforce the hill against a counterattack.

An indication of the ferocity of the fighting thus far may be inferred from the heavy fusillade of enemy artillery and mortar fire absorbed by Easy and Charlie Companies. "During the period, the Battalion was subjected to seven thousand, one hundred seventy-nine rounds of mixed mortar and artillery fire. Most of this falling in the Company 'E' sector."[5] This was only the second day of battle for the outpost. More days like it would follow.

Tanks, too, were vulnerable to severe artillery barrage. In one of his letters home, Lieutenant Colonel Williamson, commander of the Tank Battalion, wrote:

> The Chinese snipped off one of our outposts and repeated efforts to regain it have been to no avail. Tanks have been giving a little support but haven't helped much. One of my lieutenants was hit in the head by a shell fragment yesterday and isn't expected to live. He was a fine boy named Hannigan. He was mess officer here for a while, and I thought him completely undistinguished, but he turned out to be a good platoon leader, and his men loved him. Several other of my men were wounded, but none seriously. I hauled a couple of them back to an aid station in my jeep when I was coming back. One had a tooth broken off when a shell blew his turret hatch shut. The other had a small fragment in his back that came in through the pistol port.[6]

At 0220 on 10 August, enemy mortar and artillery fire began to fall on Siberia. The artillery lifted when a company of Chinese infantry assaulted the hill. Fighting became furious as both sides exchanged fire and hand grenades. Several times, the Chinese charged the Marines but were beaten back.

The sparring began to take its toll. Each side suffered heavy casualties. Because of terrain considerations, however, the enemy was able to reinforce its troops after each assault. Charlie Company, on the other hand, began to run out of ammunition and able-bodied men. At 0530, after four hours and thirty minutes of fighting, Charlie Company withdrew to the MLR. Again, the Chinese occupied Siberia.

Captain Peterson, the forward air controller on COP-2, often alternated his duties between the Bunker Hill area and COP-2. On the afternoon of Sunday, 10 August, while the Chinese held Siberia, Peterson wrote his wife about the fighting on the outpost and the sadness that he felt upon seeing so many young men with bodies and lives abused by war:

> The 2nd Bn/1st Reg, flanking us to the north (right), has been receiving many casualties from over 3000 rounds of mortar and artillery logged in the past 24 hours. They made a platoon sized push on a Commie OP in front of their position and were driven off. A second platoon attempted it and were also driven off by the enemy. Then this morning after (17) 4-plane air strikes on that hill, our forces made a company (300 men) push on it and received many more casualties. I get weak and sick whenever I look upon those pitiful youths—17, 18, 19 years old—lying there on those stretchers biting their lips to hold back their great pain. I have seen the hill they are fighting for and am at a loss to find in my heart the need and worth of their great suffering. From a fighter pilot's viewpoint, I know how I could have covered it with napalm and made it impossible for a human being to survive there. However, with our own troops so close, it would have been very difficult to put an air strike so near them.
>
> I went to church this morning and sat there and prayed with all the rest to bring a cease-fire to end this bloody mess. As we sat in the makeshift church under canvas, the bomb blasts from the unending air attacks would puff out our tent interrupting the chaplain's every other word. I couldn't help but feel very deeply moved and I felt very close to God as I searched for a justification of this horrible killing. Pray, dearest, for peace, for we need it. God, how we need it.[7]

At this juncture, it became clear to Marine planners that Siberia was not going to be retaken without a long, hard fight. The situation called for a significant change in tactical thinking and a hiatus for Marine infantrymen.

By 11 August, the men of the 1st Marines were tired and needed a rest. With the CCF fully entrenched on Siberia and dominating the Marine lines, however, a real rest was impossible. The regimental commander, Col. Walter F. Layer, attempted to interdict the Chinese positions in order to gain a brief respite for his command. The colonel turned to the aviation half of the Marine air/ground team for this support:

> Jet fighters flew 12 air strikes throughout the day. Pilots claimed a few dozen enemy casualties, many bunkers destroyed, and much damage to the enemy system of trenchlines. The aerial attacks forced the CCF to take cover during the day while Marines on the MLR spent their time improving their trenches and sniping at enemy emplacements with .50 caliber machine guns and 75mm recoilless rifles. The enemy retaliated in kind, but casualties were negligible.[8]

At a regimental staff conference that day, it was noted that the successive Marine withdrawals from Siberia were due chiefly to the intense enemy shelling. Following this line of thinking, it was further determined that the key to the artillery's effectiveness was the observation afforded the enemy from their outpost on Hill 122, called Bunker Hill by the Marines.

Study of the situation convinced regimental tacticians that shifting the battle from Siberia to Bunker Hill presented major advantages to the Marines. As an outpost, Bunker Hill offered excellent observation of the enemy's rear forces. Occupation of the hill would provide dominating terrain that was more defensible than Siberia. Moreover, Bunker Hill offered an excellent opportunity for an attack employing the element of surprise. Temporarily, at least, the Chinese could keep Siberia and the Marines would go after Bunker Hill.

To maintain surprise, the Marines would direct an elaborate feint toward Siberia in an effort the keep the Chinese believing that Siberia remained the principal objective. A plan was developed for a night attack on Siberia by a reinforced rifle platoon supported by flame and gun tanks. When the enemy was well committed, a reinforced company from 2/1, heavily supported by artillery and tanks, would conduct the main attack on Bunker Hill. Because of this operation's high priority, tanks and artillery from the 5th Marines sector, east of Bunker Hill, would create another diversion in the Ungok hills in an attempt to draw more Chinese from the main attack. Elements of two battalions would thus contribute to the battle.

The operation began at 2030 on 11 August. The night was clear and dark; moonrise would occur at 2230. Four M-4 flame tanks and four M-46 gun tanks from Charlie Company, 1st Tank Battalion, moved from their assembly area behind the MLR. Two of the gun tanks were equipped with the new "fighting lights," 18-inch searchlights equipped with shutters to instantly turn illumination on and off. Reaching Changdan Road, the armored vehicles turned north and crossed the MLR into no-man's-land.

Reaching a point on the road about 700 yards northeast of the MLR, the gun tanks suddenly turned left and stopped. Pointing their 90-mm guns at Outpost Siberia and Chinese observation positions on Hill 120, the tankers opened fire.

Nine more tanks were positioned on the MLR to provide support for Marine infantry assaulting Siberia and Bunker Hill. Six armored personnel carriers (APCs) stood by for casualty evacuation and ammunition resupply.

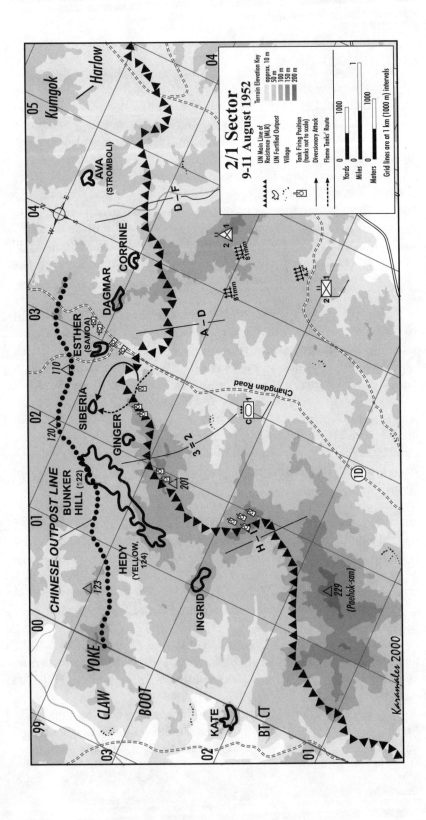

Meanwhile, two flame tanks, led by 1st Lt. Buckley, turned left off Changdan Road and made their way along a streambed by using short bursts of flame to illuminate the way.[9] The tankers traveled with hatches open in order to see where they were going. Arriving at the base of Siberia, the tanks ascended the slope to extend the reach of their flames so that the fire would fall into trenches on the hill. On reaching their objective, the tankers burned over the crest and reverse slope in a series of crisscrossing bursts of napalm. Simultaneously, machine guns raked the area to inflict maximum casualties on enemy soldiers flushed from their position by the flames. "Listening to the tankers' conversation on the radio, the commander of 3/1 remembers hearing the tank commander ordering his men to hold fire until the last minute. Then as the Reds filed into the open, 'they were mowed down.'"[10] The supporting gun tanks on Changdan Road moved their fire to Hill 110 to allow the flame tanks to burn Siberia without interference from enemy artillery.

Reserving enough napalm to light the way back, the first section of zippos looped back toward Changdan Road in time to see off the second pair of flame tanks. With a fresh supply of napalm and ammunition, they retraced the route of the first section and poured flaming gasoline on enemy positions. When the napalm was exhausted, the tanks returned to the road. Completing their part of the scenario, the four tanks returned to the assembly area to rearm and stand by for any subsequent mission. The time was 2330.

At that time, the 3d Platoon of Dog Company, 2/1, advanced on Siberia from the MLR. Led by 2d Lt. James Dion, the men swept over the top of Hill 56A (Samoa) and charged the slopes of Siberia as tanks illuminated the hill with their fighting lights. The infantry assault encountered light opposition and, after a ten-minute firefight, Dion reported that the outpost was again in Marine hands. The time was 2345. Fifteen minutes later, the 3d Platoon was ordered to return to the MLR. The main attack on Bunker Hill had begun.

For the main assault, Baker Company, 1/1, had come from regimental reserve by motor march to an assembly point behind the MLR, where the Marines waited to be deployed.

At 2305, with the attack on Siberia at its peak, Baker Company had received orders to move forward on foot. It was quite dark, and the Marines had set a fast pace in order to retain an element of surprise. By 2318, two squads were moving up Bunker Hill. Ten minutes later, a platoon was on the ridge and started its advance to the crest. Another platoon was at the base. Both units advanced forward and swept the slope, base, and top. Near the end of their sweep, they came under small amounts of rifle fire from Chinese defenders. Soon, the fire increased, accompanied by supporting mortars and artillery. Enemy soldiers on top of Bunker Hill began throwing hand grenades down at the advancing Marines. Failing to stop the attack, the Chinese fought back briefly at point-blank range before giving ground and climbing toward the summit. They were pursued to the top and over the eastern side as they escaped to rejoin their units. With the exception of a bypassed pocket of resistance, Bunker Hill belonged to the Marines. That pocket was soon dealt with by two fire teams, and the real fighting was finished. In all, Baker Company's casualties were light, one killed and twenty-two wounded.

While the Marines dug a tenuous foothold atop Bunker Hill, working parties from the MLR began hauling fortification material, sandbags, picks, shovels, and timbers to the site. Off and on, enemy mortars landed on Bunker, but the Chinese effort seemed to be one of harassment, rather than a serious attempt to dislodge the Marines. For the remainder of the morning, the men dug fortifications into the hill and waited for a Chinese counterattack. Administratively, Baker Company was passed to operational control of the 3d Battalion. Although this action had no effect on defense of the hill, it did help to tidy up the command and logistical situation.

The terrain referred to as Bunker Hill was, in fact, a ridgeline. A saddle between two promontories jutted from the MLR at a lower elevation. Physically, it was possible to walk or drive to Bunker from the MLR by following the exposed top of the ridge. Tactically, it was impossible—anyone trying such a maneuver undoubtedly would be shot.

The northernmost promontory was Hill 122 (Bunker Hill), and the southernmost Hill 124 (later to be named Hedy). The ridgeline was often referred to as the 122–124 line, which roughly paralleled the MLR at an angle jutting northeast. Years later, Pfc. Frank Walden described the hill as he remembered it:

> It was impossible to dig in on Bunker as it was solid rock covered with a couple of feet of top soil. Once past the top soil you couldn't get anywhere. To make matters worse most of the top soil had been blown away or turned to dust by the repeated shelling. Even that dirt disappeared as time, erosion and more shelling scattered it to the winds.[11]

While Baker Company dug in, Item Company, 3/1, sent a reinforced squad to set up on Hill 124 and cover Baker Company's rear. Marine Col.

Russell E. Honsowetz wrote that "taking these places was easy but hold-ing them under heavy Chinese artillery and mortar fire was extremely costly."[12] Yet, hold it they must.

HOLDING THE HILL

At 1405 on 12 August, Bunker Hill began receiving incoming fire. The fierce shelling of men in their incomplete fortifications was gruesome. Casualties mounted, and Capt. Sereno S. Scranton Jr., Baker Company's commander, soon received permission to withdraw from the forward slope of the hill and begin a reverse slope defense from the other side. No sooner had the men begun their move than incoming fire lifted and an enemy platoon attacked the left flank (the northern slope, out of view from the MLR). The attack reached monumental proportions as four hundred enemy soldiers attacked the company of Marines. Shortly after 1700, the Chinese broke off the attack and dug in on the northern slope of Bunker Hill. With the Marines dug in on the southern slope and the Chinese on the north, the crest became a no-man's-land.

Meanwhile, Item Company, 3/1, on the MLR, was ordered to relieve Baker Company on Bunker Hill. Item Company, 3/7, was brought for-ward to replace Item Company, 3/1, on line. At the same time, the entire 3d Battalion of 7th Marines was brought forward to support the 1st Marines. The Marines were determined to keep Bunker Hill.

At 1600, Item Company, 3/1, left the MLR and began to relieve Baker Company. By 1820, Item Company was digging in as rapidly as possible. Fortification materials were in short supply, but all available personnel were employed to resupply the outpost. Even the battalion's Headquarters and Service (H&S) personnel were sent forward to assist with the situa-tion. All KSCs who could be mustered were trucked to the supply area and formed into supply trains. In the midst of the fighting on the north side of the hill, the KSCs, supervised by Marines, carried supplies to the south side. On their return, they brought out the dead and wounded.

From his FO bunker on the MLR, Captain Peterson watched as fresh troops from Item Company arrived, formed up, and began their trek to Bunker Hill. In a letter to his wife, he wrote:

> I watched the faces of those kids as they passed through our trench line on the way to Bunker. Oh honey, this is a horrible war—worse than anything I have ever imagined possible. Everyone is shook. Major Bill and I controlled the 4.2-inch and 60 and some 82mm mortar as well as all the air today because nobody was up there to take over the control when the battalion control switched from the 2nd to the third.

Bill controlled the whole show for a while, then I took over. We really saved the day for a bunch of those kids but couldn't help a lot of those poor devils. Haven't eaten but one meal today, at 1300.[13]

Like a calm before the storm, the situation lulled for the remainder of the day, though sporadic incoming fire continued into the night. At 0130 on 13 August, the storm broke with a full regiment of Chinese attacking Item Company on its center and right flanks. Enemy soldiers attacked the hill in a tight skirmish line. It was the first wave of a sustained methodical assault by more than one thousand Chinese. Ducking behind rocks and a few remaining scraggly bushes, enemy infantry charged across the open ground. They ran single file up a 6-foot trench that debauched in front of a row of Marine fighting holes. A handful of Chinese popped out of the trench, caught four Marines in their holes, and killed them with hand grenades.

The attack against Item Company was largely within range and sight of the MLR. Supporting tanks and artillery were used to advantage to place accurate fire into enemy forces. Box-me-in fires by artillery were fired on demand, and nine rocket ripples[14] were brought to bear on the advancing enemy. From the MLR, thirty tanks fired more than eight hundred rounds of 90- and 105-mm and thirty-two thousand rounds of .30-caliber machine-gun ammunition. Seemingly oblivious to the danger and their companions dropping around them, Chinese infantrymen ran through the screen of flying earth and metal thrown up by the impact of artillery shells and broke through Item Company's defenses.

Pfc. Gus Mendez of Item Company recalled the battle:

I shot five of the enemy there. One caught fire when his ammo blew up. He was about 10 yards from my fighting hole. I didn't even have to get out of my hole, the enemy coming towards my position at about 10 and 11 o'clock in front of me. The first Chinese I shot was sneaking behind a water can and I blasted him with my BAR. Two or three more followed and I got them too. Everyone got a chance to fire their weapons that night.

Sometime during the fighting, I heard a voice saying "Eti wa," (Korean for "come here"). I looked to my left and I saw a figure standing there, I said, "Is that you Waldron?" I pointed my BAR at him. When he repeated himself I knew it wasn't Waldron. I pulled the trigger, but the bolt only moved slowly forward. The BAR wouldn't fire so I shot him with my second weapon, an M-1 rifle. He fell right in the hole with me, and I had to get out to pull the body out.

. . . Dawn came and it was difficult to see or breathe because of all the firing. It was like a very heavy fog. I spotted "Willie" (Wilson from St. Louis) in his hole to my right. He was bleeding from a laceration on his right cheek and trying to smoke a blood soaked cigarette. He said, "Wanta smoke Bad Ass?" He pulled a wet package of three cigarettes from his flack vest pocket. I did not smoke but I lit an "OLD GOLD" cigarette for each of us. . . .

It was about eight in the morning when Capt. Connally ordered us to place a helmet on each of the wounded and dead men and place them in a fighting hole. Then he told us that battalion wanted us to assault the top of Bunker Hill. We had less than 20 men who were not seriously wounded.

I had small punctures on my buttocks near my groin and another on my right waist from two pieces of shrapnel that hit me in the back the night before. My flak vest saved me from serious injury. My vest was destroyed. A corpsman pulled the shrapnel with forceps and bandaged me up but my pants and underwear were all torn and bloody.

I estimate that the top main trench on Bunker Hill was no more than forty yards from the base where we were. When we got the word, we ran up in a wedge formation towards the top of the hill. Except for pieces of barb wire entanglements here and there, the hill was clear, bare of vegetation. The dirt was loose, nearly ankle deep due to the repeated bombings, tank cannon, artillery and mortar fire. . . .

We were twenty yards from the top trench which ran parallel to our formation when fifteen or twenty Chinese soldiers suddenly stood up and one hell of a firefight started. When this happened, "French" from Bay City, Michigan, and I were the last two men on the left flank. We shot two of the enemy as we jumped into their trench. Our main party, which had hit the deck when the Chinese stood up, were shooting it out. French and I were shooting at Chinese in a trench about fifteen yards away. Our party started to take casualties and began dragging the wounded downhill, firing as they went. French and I were still firing at the Chinese in the main trench, but it was difficult to determine how many we were hitting because some heads popped up and some did not.

Suddenly, a Marine Corsair made a swing towards the top of the hill and released a 500 lb. bomb dropping it toward the top of the hill. As the plane came over the hill very low, Chinese started shooting at it. French and I just looked at each other knowing that it was the time to go.

We jumped out of the trench and ran downhill, zig zagging. We could feel the bullets around us. I saw Capt. Connally covering us with his M-1 as we ran. He was in a kneeling position just like on the rifle range, pumping rounds out of that rifle. Suddenly, the bomb exploded sending me through a patch of barbed wire. I became momentarily entangled but soon broke loose. When we reached the bottom of the hill I had to laugh. What did the Chinese think when they saw me running down the hill with a torn and bloody rear end. My skivvies, originally white in color, were all torn and red from bleeding.

That afternoon we were relieved by another company and what was left of us withdrew to the rear, walking two miles to the trucks. We were tired and hungry, but alive.[15]

During the battle, George Company, 3/7, was moved forward from reserve to reinforce Item Company. From the MLR, Marine tanks opened a path of fire through the swarming enemy. With two companies on the hill and massive support from the MLR, Bunker Hill held.

Lieutenant Watson and his platoon spent twenty-four hours on Bunker Hill. George Company had been off line in division reserve for twelve days. Suddenly on 12 August, the men were uprooted and trucked to a place behind the MLR where they unloaded and began walking toward the sounds of war. Watson described the battle:

. . . Our route was up and down one ridge, across a valley, and up the reverse slope of the MLR, a very steep mountain. With the weight of the extra ammo, it was a demanding hike. . . . The First Platoon went first, which I thought appropriate. We left our packs where we had dropped them and I remembered, I left an orange in mine.

. . . We did not know the status of the activity on Bunker Hill, although as it happened, a Chinese infantry attack was then in progress. All we knew then was that we were to go down the forward slope of the mountain, move on to Bunker Hill, and relieve the people there. A guide from the unit would lead us down the slope, which was just as steep as the one we'd just climbed, and the trail was rocky and difficult to negotiate in the intermittent darkness. My platoon would go first. I passed the word, and we fixed bayonets.

A young Marine came over to us, our guide. I couldn't see his face. He was carrying an M-1 rifle with a bayonet fixed and a flak vest over his fatigue jacket. The vests were standard equipment, we all had them. He started toward a notch in the hill which led to our trench on the forward slope, up some wooden steps and down the outside of the trench, and down the forward slope of the mountain. We could see the flares up in the sky now, strung out in an uneven line, somehow holding your attention as if you wanted just to watch them, and they seemed to sway from side to side in a jerky fashion as they descended, like tiny lanterns being carried on invisible sticks.

I followed the guide. My runner was behind me, PFC. Reuben ["Ruby"] Robledo from San Antonio, a fine young man, and a good Marine. The trail was steep and rocky, more like a natural drainage area that had been pressed into service as a trail. It was full of loose stones that you would step on and they made you fall down. In places the trail would drop down sharply and men would slip and sit down hard, or some would trip and fall forward on their faces, rifle and ammo cans clattering. It was difficult and slow, and around us was the thick scrub growth of the mountain in which might easily have lurked Chinese soldiers in ambush. Shells burst occasionally on either side of us and the bits of shrapnel whined through the brush. We would have been excellent prey for an ambush, but fortunately the enemy were spending themselves on Bunker Hill. As the flares burned out, others popped open to replace them. I looked back from time to time and could see the faces of the men, apprehensive in the pale bobbing light. Everyone was conscious of the potential for ambush, looking left and right, falling down and getting up, always descending. . . . We were going very slowly, however, and I sensed a hesitancy in our guide. I think he was simply quite afraid of going back to where he had to take us. Then his relief arrived on the scene, as if he had come to find us by some instinct.

He was a stocky Marine, no fatigue jacket, wearing his flak vest over bare skin, carrying his rifle with fixed bayonet in his right hand, casually, helmet strap unbuckled. "Where you headed, Lieutenant?" he said, and I told him we were relieving Item Company, First Marines. He said, "Come on. I know the way," and he took us forward with authority. Also, he spoke in the familiar vernacular of eastern Kentucky. I knew the sound the minute he spoke. Unfortunately, the urgency of the moment prevented a discourse about his place of origin, a coal camp or a mountain farm I suppose. But he was calm and had courage, which was right well needed at the time. It was only minutes after that encounter that we reached the bottom of the mountain, came into a more open area, and he cautioned us to be alert for Chinese. A couple of wounded Marines limped past us, and mortar shells were now exploding a short distance away to the right and left. In the flare light, we could just make out a low ridge to our front, the place of our desperate encounter. Of course we had no idea where we were or what our position would be, but our new guide did. We started angling to our left and we walked a fairly gentle grade as we cleared the reverse slope of the hill. The place was simply littered with dead men, some Marines, but mostly Chinese soldiers in their pale khaki uniforms, their bodies arrayed in the limp and awkward positions which men can assume when they have died in a shattering burst of gunfire. Lying there, arms flung out, twisted. Ragdoll men. I presumed they were all dead and learned later that this was true. . . . I marked the time at 0300 hours.

We moved along the reverse slope toward the crest, now stringing out, looking for holes to occupy. We couldn't be sure if they would attack again. I got to the crest and looked down the forward slope whence had come the attack. Just a few yards down the slope we found individual Marines in foxholes at intervals of ten yards or so. They were glad to see us and left without ceremony, one of my men replacing each of them. You may imagine the tension, walking a strange ridge line in that eerie light, trying to find Marines, uncertain if the enemy were lying in the scrub growth just below us waiting for a clean shot by the light of our flares. One thing I noticed was that our single line of forward slope foxholes was just yards from the thicket of trees and brush on down the slope. There was no field of fire. They would come out of the ravines and the brush in the darkness and you try to shoot them before they covered that last few yards to get you. Defense against vastly superior numbers under these circumstances was almost an impossible task. Thus each company kept leaving its machine guns until we could pour such a volume of fire into the night that their numbers could be somewhat neutralized. But nothing, of course, neutralized their mortar and artillery fire as we learned, even through the next day. We learned too, that our foxholes were not deep and we had to set about that job at first light, trying to dig them deeper under intense shelling. For the time being, however, we tried to find our holes and get the men in them quickly, anticipating another infantry attack. In the course of this activity, my platoon took its first casualties within three or four minutes of arriving on the hill. I should note, I had gone out to Bunker Hill with an understrength platoon. A normal complement was forty-four men and me. I had thirty-two men when we left the MLR.

We were going along, searching for our positions when we heard a mortar coming down and knew it was going to be close. Ruby and I hit the deck side by side, a few yards between us. He was on my left. A squad leader and my radio man were nearby. The explosion was close enough to lift us off the ground and raise dust in our faces. I heard Ruby cry out, "Oh, shit!" He had taken a piece of shrapnel in the upper right arm. I don't understand how it got between us to hit him and yet miss me. I tied his bandage on and told him to go back, but not alone. The squad leader and the radio man were hit also. The First Platoon was already down to twenty-nine men.

I kept crawling through the scrub, placing men. Other rounds hit close, not an intense barrage, but a lot of them. It was a surreal scene, the faint light, the dead, the limping wounded. Once I stepped into a small pool of blood, slipped and fell down awkwardly. I had not known it was slick. While my face was close to the ground, I learned the smell of it also. A young Marine lay dead beside me, and I kept smelling the burnt powder where shells had exploded. It seemed my face was near the ground almost all the time I was on that place, and the smell of powder and blood was all over it, everywhere.

Finally the twenty-nine men of the First Platoon were in place. I found a hole just on the reverse slope, about in the center of our sector, on the left flank of the company. The hill seemed to drop off into a gully of some kind on our left and I didn't know what was down there at the time. Sgt. Thompson and I decided to share this hole, which seemed intended for two, rather then start a separate one at the time. Principally, we wanted to be ready for another infantry attack if it came. Our foxhole was about deep enough to kneel in and rest your elbows on the side of it to fire our weapons, but not much protection from shrapnel.

Shells kept falling around us, and we would duck into the hole to avoid the metal splinters. The flares continued to illuminate the scene. We kneeled with our weapons directed at the likely point of attack, the forward slope. My people were staying in their holes, just waiting apprehensively. We were having a respite now from any really heavy fire. That did not last much longer than first light, when we would start to organize the position in a serious way, under fire. . . .

After a time, our guns stopped putting up the flare shells. Presumably someone in command decided they would not hit us again that night, and this proved to be true, but we were keyed up for it and no one relaxed. God, we were wound up tight, and a fight right then might have been good for us, a catharsis, but we were not to be so fortunate.

Finally the sky began to lighten in the east. The Chinese would not be likely to attack in the daytime. Marine air and artillery would prevent the massing of their forces, although a great many of them were undoubtedly just down the forward slope of the hill, in the little ravines and the dense scrub, probably just yards away from us. Maybe they were down there munching on dough balls and rice, their standard field rations. We found plenty of little sacks with draw strings by the bodies, and inside little cooked balls of dough with some kind of meat in the center, and cooked rice. Very efficient, easy to carry. In passing, we had no rations, and only the water in our canteens. They brought some water cans out about the time the sun came up and some direct hits by Chink mortars took them out. We had been marching, carrying extra ammo, up and down some pretty steep terrain, and then crawling around in the dark, a lot of stress and sweat and it wasn't even hot yet.

. . . Throughout the day on 13 August, remnants of Item Company, First Marines, were still trying to sweep the Chinese off the high ground at the other end of the hill, and never did. That was one of the places from which they directed fire on the rest of the ridge. . . .

On our left, the depression I detected in the light of the flares during the night was in fact a trail passing between us and the next ridge, which was ten or fifteen feet higher than the crest of Hill 122. It was readily apparent that a few Chinese soldiers up there could put enfilading fire on us for the entire length of the ridge. I don't know why they hadn't thought of it. This fight was in its fourth day. I called a squad leader and told him to get up there and dig a perimeter to protect the flank, support the troops below, and keep the Chinese from occupying that high ground, deny them the opportunity of bringing us under fire from there. I don't remember how many men that squad had left, but out of our twenty-nine man platoon, it wasn't more than eight or nine, I would think. So there was maybe twenty or twenty-one of us left on our ridge, but it was the right thing to do. Curiously enough, the men up there didn't draw a round of incoming after that.

We spread our remaining people out, and now we really were thin. The sun was clear of the horizon and even though it was no later than 0700 hours, you could start to feel the heat of it already. The temperature went above 100 that day. The mortar fire had never stopped, up and down the length of the ridge, constantly. I thought I detected an increase in the intensity of the fire. We were also getting sniper fire from somewhere. Out where Item Company people were still fighting, or they were behind us. One round kicked dirt in my face as I was standing in my foxhole giving instructions to the squad leader about the high ground above our flank. I didn't point anymore.

Tommy and I also did some digging, but the first job all of us undertook was to clean up the area, the bodies. They were everywhere. Our Korean bearers took the Marines out, but we had no time to spend on the Chinese except to get them out of the way. The incoming dismembered some of them. The men started dragging them down the reverse slope. All of them had a huge hole through the center of their forehead, courtesy of some Marine who went among them with his M-1 rifle and administered a coup de grace after they had been cut down during the sweep over our positions the night before. We didn't get rid of all the bodies. There were simply too many, but enough to make the area passable and hold down the stench.

There was one body near my foxhole, to the left, and every time I looked that way, he was there, laid back, mouth, arms and legs open to the sky, his head turned, eyes wide open, staring at me, and that huge hole through his head. I got used to him.

One Marine yelled at me and I looked up. He was holding the severed head of a Chinese soldier by the hair, then lobbed it down the reverse slope underhanded, as you would a sack of garbage. It bounced. "Jesus Christ," Tommy said. We dug some more, trying to deepen our hole and fill sand bags to put around the edge of it. I had laid my cartridge belt on the side of our hole. As mortar rounds came in, we sat down quickly in the hole, then got up and dug some more. Once I noticed my ammo belt was full of shrapnel. The fuckin' stuff just never let up. Larger rounds were coming across the ridge now too, not just mortars.

I was standing in the hole using an entrenching tool to fill a sand bag which Tommy was holding as he sat in the other end of the hole when a shell came over the crest, a .76 mm round, the kind you know if you heard it then it missed you. I mean screaming toward impact at the end of its trajectory, and the goddamn thing didn't miss my head two feet, the entire projectile. It detonated down the reverse slope among the Chinese bodies. Both of us knew what had happened. I had seen the shell, literally, out of the corner of my eye, and Tommy saw it. I just sighed and sat down in the hole. "Jesus Christ." We just looked at each other. Talk about one with your name on it. But that one didn't have my name on it. It had Ling Ling's name on it, down in the ravine, but he was already dead. I don't think I stood up in that foxhole again.

Then a welcome sight appeared. Marine Air. I saw an F4U (Corsair) coming out of the sun, down the long axis of the hill, and I could see the napalm under his belly. He was going to burn the forward slope, dropping down to no more than a hundred feet above the crest of the ridge and he let it go so it splashed the ground right in front of the First Platoon. Beautiful, also very hot. I could feel the heat of the flames as they boiled and roiled across the gullies and ravines just below our forward foxholes. Right on target, and what a psychological lift. We were not alone. Someone cared! We sent up a yell from the First Platoon. The pilot didn't hear it, but it made us feel good. Bless his heart, I hope he killed a thousand of the bastards. He did an encore and we yelled some more.

Perhaps buoyed by the air strike, I decided I would go find the Captain and see if he knew anything. He was somewhere toward the center of the ridge. It was an interesting trip, get up, run a few feet, hear the rounds coming down, hit the deck, face in the dirt. Crump! Wham! Whir!, missed me! What a fucking game. At that rate it took me more than ten minutes to go a hundred yards, with time out to catch my breath. It was also now getting hot and I was not quite as full of energy as I was last night. Also, I visited briefly with some of the foxholes along the way.

I found the Captain in a sort of hole on the reverse slope among a cluster of people, all appropriately supine. I'm really not even sure they all had foxholes. He had no news at the time, keep digging and they'd send word when they knew something. And no, there's no water to give out.

On the return trip, I took the scenic route, up to the crest and over to crawl along my line of forward slope foxholes. Along the way, I was on the ground just after a round hit close, facing up the reverse slope, and found myself looking into the disemboweled guts of a Chinese soldier. His intestines had spilled out where his genitals used to be. Oddly, this one didn't have a hole in his head. His eyes were wide open, staring at the blue sky, just a boy. I bet he wasn't seventeen. Some Marine had ripped him open with gunfire, and I wondered if the Chinese sent telegrams to the family. What an odd thought.

There was an automatic rifle beside him, and a potato masher type grenade. The first one I'd seen up close. I picked it up, put my finger through the loop on the end of the string that hung out of the handle, pulled it, and let the thing fly through the air down the forward slope. It really sailed a long way, and it made a nice big explosion. About a five second delay, just like ours. Another new experience. What a fun place.

I crawled over the crest, down to the forward foxholes. A knee and elbow crawl, face down, looking down the slope into the thick brush. How close were they? The napalm must have hurt, but those people were tough and persistent. We didn't have a monopoly on courage. All of us were living at the edge of life just then, beyond accepting death, past worrying about it. . . .

The men were sitting in their holes, unable to dig much because of the shelling, squatting there with their rifles with bayonets fixed, held between their legs. "Hey, Lieutenant," they said. I touched them, said something encouraging, and crawled some more. I was dust-covered from crawling. The oldest one of them was nineteen, and most were younger. I went to the last hole, then slithered back to mine. The sun was just a little higher, and hot. The incoming never stopped. I had run a gauntlet.

Tommy was digging some when I got back. We filled another sand bag or two, made a complete row of them around the edge of our hole, and then sat facing each other to rest. "What in the fuck are we doing here?" I asked, and he made an open handed shrug of the shoulders. Our MLR loomed behind us, secure, virtually impregnable. We were down here, suffering the rashness of someone's judgment, or lack thereof. It was beginning to anger me. Black humor does not mitigate the wasting of young Marines.

Then I heard the sound of one of my men's voices. He was crawling toward me from the left and when I turned to him, the Chinese soldier with the hole in his head was still there. More rounds hit close and we ducked down. "I'm hit," he said. I could see the wound, shrapnel in the left thigh. "Can you get back?" I asked. He said he could. "Go ahead," I said, and he got up and ran off. I didn't know whether to laugh or shoot him. Another one of those grand wounds. Now we were down to twenty-eight men.

One man who was out in the open, all that morning, was our corpsman. I don't remember his name. I heard the calls for his assistance and he honored every one. It is a wonder he wasn't hit. I told him later I wanted to write him up for a Silver Star, but he refused the idea adamantly. He had not done it for glory. So I did not write the citation, though often later I wished I had. But heroes have their own reward, and what they do will shine inside of them, as long as they live.

After a time of just sitting in the hole and taking fire, it occurred to me I hadn't been up to check on the squad I sent to the high ground on our left flank. So I crawled off in that direction. Tommy covered me as I disappeared down into the ravine where the trail went through between the two ridges, and up the other side. The vegetation over there was undisturbed. As I climbed up, I looked back on Bunker Hill. The trees and bushes along the crest and on the reverse slope were gone, denuded by the exploding shells. Only a few splintered stumps remained along the entire length of the hill. I could see the camouflaged helmets of Marines in the holes, and the bodies of dead Chinese scattered on the ground. A shell was bursting somewhere all the time. But up where I was now, I found another world.

The squad leader had done a good job organizing his position, a perimeter to secure them, fire support for the ridge below. It was cooler in the brush and trees up there. The Chinese either didn't know they were there, or were not concerned with them. I took a breather. "You guys are on R&R," I said, and they laughed. They kept digging and I looked to the east again, along Bunker Hill. The Chinese would come back that night in large numbers, and Marines would meet them with rifle and machine gun fire, and courage. To what end I don't know. . . .

I told the squad leader to keep digging and I left that haven as I had arrived, on my stomach, and went back down to the real world. My initial appraisal of the situation had been correct. A single Chinese sniper up there, firing from the underbrush, just a round now and then, would have done immense damage to the men on the ridge below. I made it to my hole, dragging dust and gravel. Crump! Whir! I hoped the men were in their holes. Then here came Sgt. Twitchell from the forward slope, wide-eyed, speechless, and simply pointing at the barrel of his M-1 rifle, arriving at my hole on his knees in a cloud of dust. The mortars seemed to let up some, so he could talk to us. But he couldn't talk. He just pointed. A piece of shrapnel had passed right through the barrel and the gas cylinder of his rifle as he sat in his fox-hole with the rifle held in front of his face, just inches from his eyes. He was frightened to the point of near hysteria. Coming back to us was a way of coping with the surge of fear he was experiencing. We talked to him, told him to get another rifle. There were a lot of weapons lying around on the ground. After a minute or so, he seemed to sigh, threw the weapon aside and picked another one up as he disappeared over the crest on his knees and elbows, going back to his hole. Another brave young man coping with high stress.

I wondered how many more casualties we had taken. Later I would learn that we had one dead, three more were wounded by shrapnel, just sitting in their holes. The one who died had part of his skull taken off by a piece of hot metal. A few days later, I had to explain this to a chaplain who was writing his family a condolence letter, telling them that he died without suffering, quickly. Of course he did. When your brains are shattered, you are quickly dead. There really is no better way to die. It is not tidy, and your friends are anguished by the sight of you, but the victim feels nothing.

So the First Platoon was down to twenty-four men, one dead, seven wounded, and we had not fired a shot in anger. We were angry, but we could not assuage it in the killing of Chinese. We merely prepared for the killing which was to come, that night, when the Chinese massed to attack, and surged out of the forward slope brush under cover of their own mortars, to be splintered by their own fire, and ours, and Marines would gun them down, and die, by the light of the dancing flares. It was no longer a matter of purpose, but pride.

...At 1200 hours, the word came down, we were relieved. H Company of our Battalion was moving in. By the grace of God, or some other natural law which I do not understand, the incoming seemed to abate somewhat as fire teams and squads from the relief company came quickly into our area and my men left as rapidly as they could. No one bothered to take the souvenirs with them, the Chinese automatic weapons and the potato masher grenades which littered the ground. We were, to a man, physically and emotionally exhausted. We were dehydrated with little left to sweat. There were some cases of heat prostration on the way back and our corpsman tended them, as we climbed the steep trail to the MLR. The Chinese mortars marked it for us. I walked just in front of four men carrying a stretcher with our dead comrade on it, and each time I looked back, I watched his brains dripping out as the head jerked limply from side to side. I tried not to see it, but I couldn't avoid it. I remember the color of his brain matter was gray. I kept seeing it. I still do.

It was a struggle now to walk, to move up the rocky trail. Men stumbled and fell going up as they did coming down, even in daylight. Fatigue, no food or water, it sapped our strength and our will. I thought about the orange I left in my pack.

With shells bursting on either side of the trail, we climbed back to the MLR, sometime just lying there to get our breath and cool down. It was very hot, and it was a hard climb now. Going down we had energy, quickness, a spring in our walk. Climbing back we forced our legs to move and the breath came hard. It was a long time getting to the main trench. Just before I got there, a 76 mm shell came into the brush beside me and I flung myself down hard, face in the dirt. Another Marine coveted the same spot, and he landed half onto me. After the shrapnel went away, I rolled over on my side and saw a smiling black Marine. "Hey, Lieutenant," he said, "got any water?" I had some left in my canteen and we shared it.

I climbed on up to the top, crossed the main trench, and walked through the notch in the hill. The men were gathering in the lee of the hill until we started back, standing there with their bayonets still fixed, sweaty, dust caked on them, and I remember one young Marine was so stressed he was crying uncontrollably, sobbing. An older Marine, a year or two older, had his arm around him giving comfort. The company formed a column of two's. We still had about five miles to go to where we dropped our packs. The sky was clear and the sun was hot. I hoped there would be trucks, but there weren't. We slung arms and started back. Feet dragged and raised the dust. The men talked about their fear, anger, and frustrations. That's O.K. That's the way you do it. Of course this time we were going down the big mountain.

. . . Finally some empty trucks did come by, going to the rear, and we caught a ride. The First Platoon, now reduced to twenty-four men and me, were able to get on one truck, sitting on fenders, and I stood on the running board. I had just enough strength to hang on as we jolted along in the dust, over the next ridge and down, and we came in sight of our packs, still neatly lined up where we left them the night before. We got off the truck and fell out. Other trucks would come for us. It had not been twenty-four hours since we arrived at that spot the day before.

To a man, we all slumped down by our packs and then just laid out on the ground. The fatigue we felt was utter, bone deep exhaustion. These men had been in the base of fire at Three Fingers, when many of them did not fire their weapons, and they had taken incoming before, lost sleep, been hungry, and experienced some degree of fear. This time they had been wrung out physically in a relatively short period of time, been subjected to intense and unrelenting shelling, seen a lot of death and gore, and now they knew what it was to be afraid. All of which would make each of us a better Marine. But we had been shaken by the experience. It was hot and we were still exposed to the open sun, but we just laid there and breathed, and sighed, and tried to sort things out in our minds. Then I remembered the orange in my pack. I sat up and got it out, pinched one end off, and sucked the juice from it hungrily. In just seconds, I was transformed. It was as if some part of me had left and now it came back. The natural sugars in the orange rejuvenated me. I was not so exhausted. I breathed more slowly. Some of the fear and anger left me. I tore it open and ate the pulp, more deliberately now, but aggressively. I dropped the peels on the ground between my legs and just sat and looked at them, arms across my knees.[16]

The relief of George Company progressed in increments. Throughout the day and afternoon, the weather turned hot and humid. Private First Class McClure, the communications wireman attached to How Company, remembered when he relieved George Company:

It was about mid-day on 13 August when we arrived on Bunker Hill. The day was stifling hot. Many of the troops, including an older gunny sergeant, suffered from heat prostration.

I talked with a young Marine that acted like he was in shock; he told me he was a machine gunner with George Company. He was bleeding from his forehead and though it wasn't a serious wound, had bled down his face and over the front of his dungaree jacket and flak vest. He told me that he had been on Bunker for only a few hours and that his company had been hit pretty bad. He went on his way in pain and shock, carrying no weapon.

Our first task after selecting a shallow foxhole was to establish wire communications to our three platoons. My partner was Pfc. Gene Fuhrman, Milwaukee, Wis. After repairing the line back to the MLR we began receiving sporadic incoming to the hill. Our skipper, Capt. John Demas, passed the word to dig in, which we did as much as we could between wire laying activities. In that heat the only drinking water available was in one gallon Lister bags. It was hot and tasted like water from a garden hose that had lain out in the sun all day.[17]

With How Company ensconced on the outpost, the situation temporarily lulled. The relieved units were returned to their respective reserve areas for a shower, hot chow, and rest, but they remained on standby. Regimental reports indicated that, to date, the fighting for Bunker Hill had resulted in 24 Marines killed and 214 wounded. Chinese known dead numbered 210 plus an estimated 470 killed and 625 wounded. Artillery observers estimated that between five and ten thousand rounds of incoming fire had fallen on Marine positions.[18]

At 2100 on 13 August, How Company reported hearing sounds of Chinese troops approaching Bunker Hill from the east. Attacking the center and right flank, a Chinese company probed the hill. Although defensive fire held off most of the Chinese, a few broke through to Marine fighting positions. Marine artillery and mortars began countering the attack. Box-me-in fires surrounded Bunker Hill with shrapnel, and Chinese artillery retaliated by shelling the Marines with equal vigor.

From the start, Captain Demas, How Company commander, had continually exposed himself to danger while seeing that his men were well positioned on the hill and equipped with sufficient supplies to fight off an attack. When the Chinese began their assault that night, he was again characteristically exposed. A round exploded near him. Those who saw the impact figured they would be lucky to find his dog tags. As the dust cleared, Demas popped up and shouted orders. His utility uniform, nearly blown off, hung on him like an ancient shroud. Although almost naked and dripping blood, Demas was all right. He continued to direct and reassure the Marines around him and even found time to help with the wounded. That day, he earned his Navy Cross.

At 2215, the enemy withdrew and left behind twenty bodies on the slopes of Bunker Hill. How Company sustained seven killed and twenty-one wounded. Division intelligence later reported that this attack had been made with an enemy battalion using a reinforced company for the assault.

Among How Company's dead was HMC3 John ("Doc") Kilmer, a Navy corpsman, who was posthumously awarded a Medal of Honor for his bravery. Doc Kilmer's actions, recounted by author Edward Murphy, give a little more insight into the fighting that night:

> Leaving his place of safety, Jackie Kilmer dashed across the hilltop. Ignoring the carnage around him, he went from one casualty to another. All through the first CCF infantry assault, Kilmer dauntlessly administered life-saving aid to the wounded. While rifle fire cut the air around him, he repeatedly exposed himself to reach wounded marines. He carried several men to safety, giving that extra effort that saved several lives.

The Chinese fell back, their ground assault beaten back by the tenacious marines. But they weren't giving up. They again loosed a barrage of artillery and mortar fire on the hill.

Within seconds a cry for help reached Kilmer; a marine had been caught in the open. Badly wounded, unable to move, his pain-filled calls for help continued.

Kilmer started for him. A sergeant grabbed him.

"You can't go out there," he shouted. "You'll die."

"So will he unless I do something," Kilmer stoically replied.

Hugging the fire-swept ground, Kilmer snaked his way toward the casualty, about twenty-five yards away. Halfway there a mortar shell erupted just feet from him. Metal fragments tore into his side, blood poured from a dozen holes. The pain was intense but Kilmer had a casualty to treat. He continued forward.

As shells hit all around him, Kilmer reached the man. He pulled battle dressings from his pouch and began first aid. He had almost completed his task when enemy shells shattered the immediate area. Intent only on saving the marine, Kilmer unhesitatingly threw himself over the man, shielding him from danger with his own body.

While covering the man, Kilmer was mortally wounded by flying shrapnel. The marine lived.[19]

Again that night, a peace of sorts descended on Bunker Hill. As one historian noted, "By midnight one man out of every two man foxhole was dozing with his weapon at hand. His partner was peering intently into the enveloping blackness, straining all senses for some sign of the enemy. For more than two hours the night was silent."[20]

At 0225, 14 August, a small band of Chinese, under cover of long-range machine-gun fire from Siberia, successfully achieved the crest of Bunker Hill and began to throw hand grenades on the defenders. As a feat of bravado intended to harass the Marines, it succeeded but the Marines drove off the Chinese in less than four minutes.

In retaliation, tanks from the MLR illuminated Siberia and immediately destroyed the offending machine gun. Enemy artillery took the tanks under fire, and a deadly artillery-tank duel commenced. The tankers fired more than 200 rounds from their 90-mm tubes and 12,000 rounds of .30-caliber bullets from their machine guns. Not to be outdone, Chinese artillery countered with more than 150 rounds of mixed 82-mm and 122-mm mortars and 76-mm artillery. One tank crewman was wounded and a fighting light damaged.

In one of the letters to his wife, Lieutenant Colonel Williamson mentioned how, in spite of the danger, Marine morale remained high:

. . . You have no idea how eager some of these lads are to fight. The reserve regiment [7th Marines] had to have a bed check every night to be sure none of their men sneaked off to the front. Some of my men drew lots to see who would get to go up, really splendid Marines.[21]

Privates First Class McClure and Fuhrman returned to Bunker Hill early that morning. McClure's account continued:

. . . About mid-afternoon it began raining artillery and mortar rounds. It was not the whistling sound depicted in the movies but the unbelievable sound of freight trains screaming and rumbling overhead. It covered us with dirt and debris upon impact. The concussion took your breath away.

The incoming continued for ten or fifteen minutes then a pause for a time, and then it would start again. During one of the pauses Capt. Demas came out of the CP bunker to call, "Wireman up!" One of the platoons was out, and it was my turn to trouble shoot.

As I climbed out of my hole, a sniper hidden on a nearby ridge began to dig dirt all around me. I couldn't move out. Capt. Demas immediately saw what was happening and yelled for our 81 mortars to "eliminate that God damn sniper." Within minutes our mortars zeroed in and solved the problem. I was on my way, and shortly thereafter had wire communication restored to the platoon.

Enroute from the platoon I heard a young Marine calling for help. He was lying on his stomach near a pile of sandbags about ten yards from our hole. I crawled out to him and saw that he had been hit in the butt, lower back and legs. There was so much dirt over him that the wounds weren't obvious. He was scared and probably getting close to going into shock. I spoke with him and he told me that a corpsman had treated him and told him not to let anyone move him while he, the corpsman, went for help. I lit him a cigarette and he told me he would be OK, so I returned to my hole.

Within minutes the bombardment resumed. I looked out at the Marine and realized that he was in the open. I couldn't stand to see him being pelted with rocks and dirt, or shrapnel, so when I had the opportunity I crawled back out to him. As best I could, I covered him with an extra flak vest. He had retained his own vest and wore his helmet so I felt he was reasonably well protected. He again told me that he would be OK. I hope so. I feel confident that he was evacuated and survived. I never found out.[22]

Bunker Hill remained free from assault for the remainder of August 14, but the incoming fire indicated that something might be in the wind.

A platoon from Able Company, 1/1, was sent out to reinforce How Company. Whoever was responsible for that decision was omniscient, or close to it. A few hours later, the Chinese struck again.

About 0100 on 15 August, a firefight developed along the ridgeline between Bunker Hill and Hedy. Two companies of enemy soldiers attacked from the west but were held back by accurate box-me-in fire around the outpost. After ten minutes, the Chinese withdrew, but the attack had been a diversion. From the east side of the hill, hidden in the draws and canyons and well camouflaged by the scrub growth, a mass of Chinese awaited the signal to charge the hill. The attack might have succeeded had not a fighting light from a tank on the MLR focused on the soldiers below. Within seconds, fire missions were called and a fusillade of artillery, mortar, tank fire, and machine-gun rounds fell on the soldiers and drove the survivors away from the hill.

Countering with a devastating barrage of mortars an hour later, the Chinese pummeled the men on Bunker Hill with one hundred shells per minute. Again, it appeared to be a preparatory shelling intended to keep the Marines down while the hill was assaulted. Indeed, the soldiers who had been scattered earlier regrouped and were again preparing to advance on the hill.

The assault began under shell fire that lifted as the Chinese moved forward. Without the mortars to contend with, Marines manned the fighting holes and another deadly firefight began. Communist infantry, using rifles and machine guns, moved up the hill. Returning the fire in kind and adding more box-me-in fire, the defenders fought off the Chinese. Finally, by 0315, the intensity of the fight began to wane as the enemy withdrew. Forty-five minutes later, the night was quiet.

Enemy losses were placed at 350, with 40 counted dead. How Company had 7 killed and 35 wounded. Lt. Col. Norman W. Hicks wrote:

> This whole struggle was an excellent example of coordination between infantry, artillery, and air. Pre-arranged artillery concentrations were first fired almost on top of the defending Marines. As the enemy withdrew, the fires were lifted forward to follow and harass him. Because of the pyrotechnics below, pilots of the attack planes on station above were able to orient themselves on the enemy muzzle flashes or any other lights available and then drop their explosives and napalm. The enemy [prisoners] expressed surprise that American planes were able to seek out and attack his infantry during the night.[23]

Just before dawn, How Company was relieved on the outpost by Baker Company, 1/1, returning to Bunker Hill for its second tour. During the relief, Chinese mortars claimed four Marines from How Company and six from Baker Company. If anything, the Chinese were a persistent lot. The fight was never really over.

For its next attack, the enemy changed tactics. Attacking in the midst of a thunderstorm at 1640 that afternoon without artillery preparation, the Chinese stormed the hill again and tried to wrest Bunker Hill away from Baker Company. The firefight lasted for an hour as the Marines and Chinese exchanged hand grenades and small-arms fire. Then, as suddenly as they came, the Chinese retreated, with thirty-five of their dead left behind. Of notable interest is that after the firefight, four Marines were evacuated from the outpost with battle fatigue, an indication of the extreme physical and mental exhaustion that the men were suffering. The strain of Bunker Hill was becoming acute. Fortunately, the remainder of the evening was quiet, which allowed the Marines a little physical rest. It would not last, however, and the men knew it.

Attacking again, the enemy gave up on stealth and reverted to its former tactics. At 0206 on 16 August, another bombardment began to fall on Bunker Hill. Advancing behind the artillery was a battalion of infantry, firing as it advanced up the hill. Despite the box-me-in fires, a company of Chinese attained the crest of the hill and began using hand grenades and small arms against the Marines entrenched on the slope below.

As the fighting continued, a platoon from Item Company, 3/7, was dispatched to reinforce the defenders. Arriving at 0255, it had ample opportunity to join the fray, and, in fact, its arrival might have turned the tide. Thirty minutes later, incoming fire began to diminish. By 0430, the Chinese had disengaged.

The following day, Charlie Company relieved Baker Company on the outpost. For the next two weeks, Chinese troops made no further serious effort to capture the hill.

Bunker Hill and the MLR were subjected to intermittent disruptions by mortar and machine-gun fire that wounded several Marines, but this activity was a standard form of harassing fire practiced by both sides. On 19 August, Dog, 2/1, relieved Charlie, 1/1, and, on 24 August, Fox Company, 2/1, relieved Dog Company. At sundown, Fox Company fought off a two-company assault, during which the Chinese managed to breach the defenses in one place. In hand-to-hand fighting, the Marines turned them, and the enemy withdrew.

BUNKER HILL RECAP

Like that of its namesake, Bunker Hill's tactical significance was not great. Yet, also like the original Bunker Hill battle, it was the first time that each side in the war took a real measure of one another. The bottom line was that the Marines wrested Bunker Hill from the Chinese and held it. Despite everything, the enemy could not get it back.

Bunker Hill was not the worst or the largest battle fought during the outpost war, but it was one of only a few prominent battles of that war. Also, on this occasion, the 1st Marine Division ran out of men. Division casualties for the month were 144 killed, 15 missing, and 1,237 wounded.[24] To replace losses from Bunker Hill, 58 men from the Amphibian Tractor Battalion were immediately transferred to the 1st Marines. Then, on 21 August, in an emergency draft, 500 men from the 3d Marine Division at Camp Pendleton, California, were transferred to the 1st Division and hastily airlifted to Korea.

Was Bunker Hill worth it? Who knows. Much depends on which part of the elephant one has examined. To men who lost limbs, eyesight, or their minds, the battle was likely the worst experience of their lives. To others, it might have been thrilling—pilots flying air strikes, tankers on line who were protected from incoming fire, and others who participated from positions of safety. Artillerymen might remember those days as a time of unbelievably exhausting work. The survivors of the battle for Bunker Hill, however, have earned the right to question its value. They and the dead are the men who paid the price.

On the plus side, the trade of Outpost Siberia for Bunker Hill turned out to be a good deal. First, it was larger and more defensible than Siberia. Second, it was easier to supply. Third, it offered better observation into Chinese lines and provided an improved defense to the MLR.

Also, during this battle, Marine commanders had an opportunity to assess their opponent's tactics and methods. From observations, after-action reports, and intelligence gained from prisoner interrogations, they learned the following:

• The elements of the 118th Chinese Division that were opposing the Marines had an extra artillery regiment attached. This fact seemed to account for the extremely heavy incoming fire during the period. It also confirmed the greater than usual number of enemy artillery positions reported by air observers.

• The Chinese attacks were heavily supported by mortar fire. It was learned that they relied heavily on 60-mm and 82-mm tubes that could be frequently moved from one site to another before Marine observers could pinpoint their location and retaliate. Many mortars were fired from deep holes in the ground that were covered and camouflaged. A small aperture in the ceiling of a hole permitted the round to pass through but concealed observation of the smoke and flash. To the Marines, these mortars were virtually invisible. On a few occasions, CCF mortarmen brought their weapons out into the open, fired a few rounds, and then quickly retired to cover before the Marines could fire their mortars to retaliate.

• Unlike UN forces, the Chinese obviously did not suffer from ammunition rationing. Their rates of fire with mortar and artillery were generous. A Marine artillery officer reported that, because of ammunition shortages, counterbattery fire from the 11th Marines (artillery) was often ineffective because the Marines were limited to one to eight rounds per tube per day, depending on the kind of weapon.[25]

Counteracting some of the miserly ammunition allocations, however, was the close support of Marine air. To achieve close air support, the flying leathernecks were controlled by forward air controllers (FACs), who were Marine pilots on the ground. FACs worked in the trenches alongside infantrymen and called air strikes sometimes as close as 150 feet away from Marine troops. Captain Peterson recalled:

> August was to become the record month for the 1st MAW [Marine Air Wing] attack and fighter pilots during 1952, with a total of 5,869 sorties flown. . . . At any rate, Major Mill Biehl and I would like to lay claim for having controlled more aircraft in a single month than anyone else in the war, or perhaps any war. Lord we were busy![26]

To deceive the enemy, the Marines were also able to pull a few rabbits out of the hat. One of the most obvious, of course, was the highly successful deception of 13 August on Siberia. That operation enabled the capture of Bunker Hill itself.

Another successful ruse was employed on 13 August, just before the Chinese main attack. Heretofore, it had been a general UN practice to precede all assaults with an air strike, followed by smoke. An artillery barrage would complete the pattern, and then attacking infantry would make the assault.

This time, the procedure was followed except that no troops charged the hill. The Chinese, thinking that an assault was under way, reacted as usual by sending their troops into the battle zone to meet the assault. As the Chinese were the only troops in the field, the only damage done was to Chinese soldiers. Adding insult to injury, Marine artillery opened up on the troops and caused still greater damage.

Much of the great disparity in casualties was attributed to the armored vests and steel helmets worn by the Marines and to the swift evacuation by helicopter. Medical facilities behind the American lines were also much improved. In many cases, forward aid stations were set up on the reverse slope of the MLR, which enabled quick treatment of the wounded.

Finally, the reverse slope defense used on Bunker Hill after 12 August was credited with saving many more lives than the original forward slope defense would have done. The quantity of incoming ordnance that fell during the battle virtually obliterated positions on the forward slope of the hill. Had the positions been manned, the casualties would likely have exceeded the availability of replacements.

Second Lieutenant Howard Matthias, Dog Company, 2/5, on the MLR after a night patrol in July 1952. HOWARD MATTHIAS

First Lieutenant Stan Rauh, Able Company, 1/7, aboard the hospital ship USS *Repose,* after being wounded retaking the Hook in October 1952.

STAN RAUH

Staff Sergeant Dave Evans, George Company, 3/1, returning from a rescue patrol carrying weapons of wounded Marines, about June 1952.

DAVE EVANS

Captain Bernard Peterson *(right)* and Major Bill Biehl *(left)* controlling an air strike from the MLR.
BERNARD PETERSON

Sergeant John J. ("J.J.") O'Hagan, Able Company, 1/7, surveying damage to Outpost Dagmar after a June 1952 shelling.
JOHN O'HAGAN

Private First Class Don McClure, a wireman with How Company, 3/7, taking a break as his company resumes its MLR position on Hill 229, June 1952. DON MCCLURE

Second Lieutenant Lee Cook, platoon leader in the Reconnaissance Company, September 1952. LEE COOK

Staff Sergeant John R. Alexander, platoon sergeant in Able Company, First Tank Battalion, standing on a ridge-line overlooking enemy territory during the winter of 1951. JOHN ALEXANDER

Tank A-41 disembarking LST 1068 at Inchon on 16 April 1952 after making the trip from the east coast. Private First Class Durk *(driver)*, Sergeant Chris Sarno *(standing on right)*, and Second Lieutenant Wilson *(standing on left side of turret)*. U.S. MARINE CORPS PHOTO

Second Lieutenant Jim Vanairsdale, platoon leader, Easy Company, 2/7, the day after his platoon's successful raid on Hill 67 in May 1952. JIM VANAIRSDALE

First Platoon, Easy Company, 2/7, after the raid on Hill 67. The men are leaving OP-2, returning to their company Command Post. JIM VANAIRSDALE

Three Kentuckians meet in Korea, August 1952, while in reserve: Second Lieutenant William Watson, George Company, 3/7 *(center)*, Corporal Mickey Williamson, 3/7 *(left)*, and Bill Conners, Eleventh Marines *(right)*.
WILLIAM WATSON

Private First Class Gus Mendez, Item Company, 3/1, while in reserve, July 1952. Mendez is holding the Browning Automatic Rifle (BAR) that he used on Bunker Hill the following month. GUS MENDEZ

Second Lt. Hunt S. Kerrigan, Platoon Leader, Able Company, 1/5. Photo taken in 1953 after he was awarded the Silver Star. Note the Purple Heart ribbon with four stars. HUNT W. KERRIGAN

Private First Class Tom Lavin *(left),* and Private First Class Miller *(right)* of Fox Company, 2/5. Miller was killed in action on Yoke on 24 June 1952. TOM LAVIN

First Squad, First Platoon, Fox Company, 2/5, on the Panmunjom Road (Highway 1), preparing for a daylight patrol. Private First Class Tom Lavin *(second from right)* with a BAR.

TOM LAVIN

Sergeant Glen Dye, Dog Company, 2/1, receiving a Gold Star in lieu of his second Purple Heart at the U.S. Naval Hospital, Yokosuka, Japan, October 1952. He was awarded the medal for wounds received in the fighting for Outpost Bunker Hill. UNITED STATES NAVY PHOTO

(Left to right) Corporal Peter Beauchamp and Private First Class William Freyer, George Company, 3/1, packing to move off the line for a reserve area, spring 1952.
PETER BEAUCHAMP

Private First Class Chuck Burrill, Reconnaissance Company, with his M-2 carbine, October 1952.

CHUCK BURRILL

Sergeant Robert J. Thornton *(right)* and Private First Class "Red" Garden *(left),* How Company, 2/7, June 1952, on the line at Hill 229.

ROBERT J. THORNTON

Second Lieutenant Henry Conway, George Company, 3/7, was captured 6 October 1952 on Outpost Detroit. HENRY CONWAY

Private First Class Howard Davenport, Reconnaissance Company, in the company area near Munsa-ni in August 1952. Davenport was evacuated with wounds four months later.
HOWARD DAVENPORT

Private First Class Andy Frey *(right)*, George Company, 3/1, September 1952, in the reserve area. The Marine on the left is unknown. ANDY FREY

Captain Fred McLaughlin, Able Company, 1/7, at his CP bunker after retaking the Hook in October 1952. FRED MCLAUGHLIN

Sergeant Arthur Lipper III, First Platoon Guide, Reconnaissance Company, 1952. Lipper is holding an M-3 .45-caliber submachine gun, often called a "grease gun" due to its appearance.

ARTHUR LIPPER

Private First Class Gene Thomas, George Company, 3/1, outside his bunker on the MLR, December 1952.

GENE THOMAS

CHAPTER 7
ELMER AND IRENE

Few men are born brave; many become so
through training and force of discipline.
—Vegetius, *De Re Militari*, iii, 378

Six miles northeast of Bunker Hill was a small outpost bearing the
rather prosaic name of Elmer. During August, this tiny hill was occupied
each day by a squad of men from Dog Company, 2d Battalion, 5th
Marines. Elmer was situated in such a way that it protected the larger
Outpost Felix (later known as Outpost Detroit). Felix was located about
1,000 yards north of the MLR, and Elmer was about 700 yards northwest of Felix.

Elmer was one of the positions that would be lost to Chinese forces
that month. Whenever a lull in the fighting at Bunker Hill occurred, the
enemy, like a petulant child, seemed to take out its anger elsewhere.
More likely, the Chinese were simply probing for weak spots in hopes of
drawing Marine reinforcements from the Bunker Hill area.

Dog Company, 2/5, on the battalion's left flank, had Outposts Felix
and Elmer and its assigned sector of MLR to defend. Felix was a large hill
with a commanding view of two large valleys for 270 degrees north, east,
and south. Elmer was useful for observing the rear of a Chinese position
on Hill 123, but, more importantly, it offered an excellent view of Felix's
forward and western slope. Although not a critical position, Elmer was
nice to have.

Elmer was not constantly maintained. It was a daytime outpost. Generally, a squad of Marines left the MLR before daybreak, hiked to Felix,
and then proceeded to Elmer. Once there, the men checked the hill for
enemy soldiers, mines, and booby traps and, when finding it clear, took
up residence for the day. At dusk, they returned to the MLR. This prac-

tice of manning an outpost for a day and then abandoning it at night has been shown to be flawed. Elmer was a vivid demonstration of the impracticality of that arrangement. Like "hot beds" in a flophouse, no sooner did one group leave the hill than another took over. Chinese soldiers occupied Elmer each night, and Marines took it over during the day. It was bizarre; if this had been the American Civil War, the men would have left notes and presents for one another or become pen pals.

On one occasion, a squad was en route to Elmer and noticed prints of tennis shoes entering an abandoned bunker adjacent to the trail. As no prints were shown leaving, the men suspected that the owner might still be inside. A grenade thrown into the bunker was rapidly thrown back. The squad rushed the bunker, seriously wounded the lone Chinese soldier inside, and took him prisoner.

Five days later, at 0515 on Thursday, 7 August, the 2d Squad of the 2d Platoon, Dog Company, left the MLR en route to Elmer. Leading the squad was S/Sgt. R. H. McCray. As usual the squad checked in at Felix and then proceeded northwest toward Elmer. Sergeant McCray was cautious because he knew that only the night before, sounds of digging had been reported as coming from the outpost. Obviously, the enemy had been there then. Had the Chinese been secreting mines? Digging fortifications? Or maybe they had set up an ambush and were now waiting for his squad.

Following a small trail toward the hill, McCray placed one fire team with a light machine gun in position on a small ridge overlooking the route winding its way toward Elmer. This team would establish a base of fire covering movement of the other two fire teams as they moved up and secured Elmer. With two fire teams remaining in the squad, one moved along the high ground of Hill 123 on the left, while the other followed the footpath to Elmer.

Suddenly, a whistle sounded. The enemy opened fire from Hill 123 on the left, from Hill 125 to the left rear, and from Elmer at their front. They had been ambushed! Both advancing fire teams took casualties, and McCray immediately ordered his men to return to the base of fire. Six men were wounded and one was missing.

At 0615, McCray called for High Explosive (HE) and White Phosphorus (WP) on Hills 123 and 125 and Outpost Elmer. Artillery, 4.2-inch mortars, and 60-mm and 81-mm mortars all responded to the sergeant's call for help. In seconds the targets were saturated with bursting explosives. Concurrently, 1st Lt. Charlie Lee, Dog Company commander, dispatched a squad under the command of Lieutenant Matthias to reinforce the engaged squad and, if possible, to overrun enemy positions and secure Elmer.

Matthias's unit reached McCray's squad in fifteen minutes. Using the base of fire already set up, Matthias moved up Hill 123 with two fire teams on the enemy's flank. The remaining fire team engaged the enemy with a frontal assault. As the men approached the crest of the hill, the assault stalled approximately thirty yards short because of the heavy volume of fire. Holding back the team, Matthias placed two BARs in position to cover the advance of the flank teams and enable them to move to positions of greater support. Because of increasing enemy fire, one of the flank teams was unable to move forward and had to drop back to a more favorable position for supporting the assault.

Eventually, the assaulting fire team succeeded in reaching the crest of Hill 123. Two Marines of the team were wounded and a third pinned down by enemy small arms. Two of the men reached the trench line and immediately became engaged in hand-to-hand combat. The Chinese withdrew. The assault squad returned to its base of fire and withdrew its casualties. Both squads then retired to Felix.

A few hours later, at 1215, the 1st Platoon of Dog Company left the MLR to locate and recover the missing man from McCray's squad. The platoon, reinforced with two light machine guns, was led by 2d Lieutenant Crabaugh. While searching for the missing Marine, the platoon began to receive small-arms and automatic weapons fire from Hills 123 and 125. The Chinese troops had returned. On request, artillery and regimental 4.2 mortars placed smoke on Elmer and Hill 125 in preparation for another assault on Hill 123. For a brief period prior to the assault, the 1st Platoon lost all communication when incoming fire damaged its radio and cut land lines.

Despite the lack of communication, the platoon prepared to attack Hill 123. Lieutenant Crabaugh used one squad with the machine-gun section as a base of fire and assaulted Hill 123 with two squads. As the assault force neared the crest of the hill, it came under a fusillade of hand grenades thrown by the defenders. Nonetheless, it reached the crest of the hill and engaged the Chinese hand to hand. For the second time that day, the Marines held Hill 123. Fifteen enemy dead were counted as a result of this engagement, with an additional twenty wounded. The right assault squad, however, had sustained casualties. The platoon withdrew to the base of fire.

After creating a perimeter defense to protect the wounded and re-establishing radio contact, the platoon notified Outpost Felix that litter bearers were required for the wounded. A nose count revealed that the platoon had fifteen known wounded and three missing. As the original missing Marine had not been located, there were now four MIAs. Under enemy fire, the remaining effectives from the 1st Platoon returned to Hill 123 to search for their missing companions.

In the meantime, all available personnel on Felix were occupied with evacuating the engaged platoon. Ten men from the MLR, led by Lieutenant Matthias, were sent out to reinforce the 1st Platoon and assist with the wounded. After the Chinese were driven off at 1730, all Marines withdrew to Felix and thence to the MLR forty-five minutes later.

This was a minor engagement, compared with that of Bunker Hill, but Dog Company suffered five killed, twenty-nine wounded, and four missing. The enemy lost three times that number, but a war of attrition always favors China. The Marines lost Outpost Elmer and never garrisoned it again—night or day.

Many years later, Lieutenant Matthias recounted his recollection of the loss of Elmer. He felt that he and his men had been let down by a failure to reinforce their efforts, "a most unfortunate incident." In his view, Elmer should not have been lost. He wrote:

> The account of the battle was essentially correct [Special Action Report of 2/5, 7 August 52] but I doubt if the enemy casualties were ever that high. I was one of the two identified in hand to hand combat with the enemy. That was a side account that I have not told many people.
>
> I was leading a fire team up the hill. Suddenly we had several grenades rolling down at us, and one of them exploded between my legs. Fortunately it was a concussion grenade and lifted me up but caused no major harm. Before the second wave could be thrown I signaled to my men, "Charge up the hill." I cleared the trench only to see a gook running away. He left about a dozen grenades. I started throwing the grenades along the trench, all the time yelling for my men to come on up. Only one made it, and he not for long. As I was throwing, a gook came around the corner of the trench with a captured M-1. I had laid my carbine down so I jumped him, took away his M-1 and shot him as he ran away.
>
> Still no reinforcements from our troops. I was now armed with an M-1 and after scouting out some trenchline and hearing a lot of firing, I jumped back down, rejoined the men at the base of fire and picked up the casualties that we had. We returned to Felix and got help from Korean litter bearers.[1]

The following day Charlie Company, 1/5, relieved Dog Company on Felix and the MLR. Dog Company, having been on line since June, was removed to a quieter sector.

In mid-August the sector defended by the 5th Marines had a small respite from fighting while the Chinese again focused on the 1st Marines. Bunker Hill was not the only headache in that sector. The enemy also demonstrated against other nearby outposts as it tried to draw reinforcements from Bunker.

At dusk on 13 August, Chinese mortars began to fall on George Company, 3/1, when it was occupying Combat Outpost Two. Simultaneously, the MLR began receiving incoming artillery in preassault proportions. The shelling lasted for ninety minutes.

As firing lifted on COP-2, Chinese infantry targeted it with machine-gun and small-arms fire and commenced what appeared to be an assault. Before the Marines were seriously involved, however, the firing broke off. The attack had been a feint.

OUTPOST STROMBOLI

About 2½ miles east of Bunker Hill at the extreme edge of the 1st Marine regimental sector, there was a small outpost on Hill 48A called Stromboli. Hill 48A was a rise of ground between the MLR and the high ground of the enemy on Hill 104. At night, it was garrisoned with a squad, which was reduced to a fire team during the day. Stromboli was 250 yards forward of the MLR. A half mile beyond it loomed Hill 104. Stromboli served as a useful warning and observation post for enemy activity.

Minutes after midnight on 13 August, a Chinese company attacked a Fox, 2/5, squad on Stromboli. The assault came without prior artillery preparation and progressed immediately to a hand-grenade and small-arms firefight, followed ten minutes later by a mortar barrage. The fighting lasted for thirty minutes before the attackers withdrew. During the attack, the MLR behind Stromboli was also subjected to a furious barrage of mortar fire.

A squad from Fox Company was sent to reinforce Stromboli, but it arrived at the base of the hill while another firefight was in progress. An unknown number of enemy troops had initiated a second probe of the outpost. By 0130, the reinforcing squad was engaged in its own battle. Unable to reach Stromboli, it was forced to return to the MLR.

On the MLR, Fox Company was suffering casualties from mortars.

Among the wounded were all three of the company's platoon leaders. A provisional platoon from H&S Company went forward to reinforce the MLR, and, by 0220, there was fighting on the MLR. Chinese troops had stormed the line, and the fight spread laterally as the mortar barrage increased in vigor.

Finally, about 0305 the fighting began to subside, and Fox Company formed a rescue effort for the men on Stromboli. Radio communication from the outpost indicated that the enemy had surrounded the position and made repeated efforts to take it. At one time, it appeared that Stromboli might have been overrun, but that observation later proved to be false. At 0325, a platoon-sized rescue party, led by Capt. Clarence G. Moody Jr., Fox Company Commander, left the MLR and, at 0336, was itself heavily engaged in a firefight at the base of the outpost. Ultimately, Moody's platoon prevailed. By 0500, it had penetrated the enemy encirclement and relieved the besieged men on Stromboli. Captain Moody organized and reinforced defenses on the hill and then returned to the MLR with all casualties. A reinforced squad from the rescue platoon remained on the outpost.

Captain Moody was awarded a Navy Cross for his defense of the MLR, his leadership of the platoon reinforcing Stromboli, and his subsequent rescue of the wounded men. Outpost Stromboli remained in Marine hands and was later named reOutpost Ava.

GOODNIGHT, IRENE

Well east of Stromboli lay Irene, another part-time outpost formerly known as Rome. Irene was a little closer to the MLR but still in the sector controlled by Fox Company, 2/5.

Irene was not a well-developed outpost; the trench lines were narrow and relatively shallow. There was only one bunker on the entire hill. On the near slope, trenches were deeper than those on the southwest and east sides. Direct observation from the forward slope required extreme care because the Chinese zeroed in on that slope.

Like Elmer, Irene was manned only in daylight by a squad of Marines reinforced with a light machine gun. Each day, around first light, a detail of men left the MLR to garrison the hill. Times of departure were varied in hopes of avoiding an ambush, but there was little that could be done to vary the route. A single trail traveled down the forward slope of the MLR, crossed a tank road, passed over some abandoned rice paddies, and began to climb the hill that was Irene. The rice paddies and other features of the terrain pretty well dictated the location of the trail.

On 17 August, the outpost detail from Fox Company left the MLR as it had done countless times before. This day would be different. Some of the Marines would be killed and more wounded; three would remain on the hill forever.

Pfc. Tom ("Tot") Lavin was in Fox Company's 1st Platoon.[2] He was a fire team leader but often doubled as radioman. That morning, he was standing radio watch on the MLR as the Irene detail prepared to leave.

Shortly after 0400, Sgt. ("Mac") McComber was to lead the Irene detail up to the platoon CP. Before leaving, Mac talked for a few minutes to Tot about the previous night's ambush and whether or not the detail could do without pyrotechnics on the hill. Mac was tall and thin, a squared-away Marine. Even on the MLR, his dungarees were freshly washed and looked pressed. If he was at all worried about leading his patrol to Irene, it did not show. He had been there a dozen times before.

Mac checked out his men, reported their departure by telephone to the company CP, and said, "So long," to Lavin. Tot reminded him that there were lice in the bunker on Irene and to stay out of it if he could. Mac replied, "You got it, Ace!" and left the CP. The time was 0435. Lavin would never again see Mac alive.

Some fifteen or twenty minutes later, as Lavin was getting ready to heat up some chow, the radio came up. Mac said that he had heard a tank and requested a rocket-launcher team. He reported that his radio was unable to raise the company CP and asked that the message be relayed. Lavin verified Mac's request for the rocket launcher, woke up his lieutenant, and notified the company CP. Then, Mac came back on the air and said that his detail was getting ready to move through the little draw that fronted the base of Irene. He would contact them again when they arrived on Irene. As the message was being relayed, the sound of burp guns and grenades broke across the rice paddy. The Irene detail had been ambushed.

During the night while the outpost was abandoned, a Chinese platoon had worked its way to the trenches from the far side and set up on the hill. At 0505, as the squad of Marines reached the top, the enemy struck. Surrounded, the Marines were confined to a small defense perimeter in the inadequate trenches of Irene. Mac's radioman came on the air and requested immediate help from the MLR.

In the CP, Lavin could hear the firefight across the valley. The distinctive rapid staccato of burp guns followed by the slower but more authoritative burst of a BAR echoed through the hills. Flashes and sounds of exploding grenades punctuated the night. Frantically, Lavin tried to raise

Mac or his radioman on the air. 2d Lt. Ernie Northcutt, the platoon leader, rose from his bunk in the CP and settled down Lavin as a voice on the radio again requested help. Lavin recalls that the voice was "plaintive, pleading and etched with fear." Immediately, the lieutenant motioned for Lavin to get ready and then left to gather up some men. They were leaving for Irene.

In just a few minutes, Northcutt had assembled a reinforced squad of sixteen volunteers, including himself, Lavin, a light machine-gun crew, and two corpsmen. Lavin looked over the small group of men. After ten months of combat, he had learned to pay a lot of attention to the people around him. He felt good about whom he saw. He had worked with most of them before and knew they were dependable. Lavin was ready. The lieutenant told him to pick up the radio and they moved out.

The lieutenant, radioman, and corpsmen dropped in line behind the second fire team and began the little climb that would take them to the crest of the hill and the forward slope of the MLR. Lavin had not moved more than ten feet when a voice to his rear said, "Tot, stay away from me. You radio guys draw too damn much fire." As he shuffled toward the gate that would take them to Irene, Lavin tried to think of a biting reply. Instead, he just grunted over his shoulder the response that Mac had given him earlier, "You got it, Ace."

The column moved down the crest of the hill, through the trench line to the gate. Through the break in the wire, the path opened onto a steep little slope that carried them a short distance to the valley floor and a rice paddy. As the rear of the patrol started down, the point was already in the rice paddy and headed for the tank road. The lieutenant had called for a 10-yard interval between men. They were giving him that and more. He also told them to move out as quickly as possible across the open paddy, almost 200 yards, until they were under cover of a finger ridge extending out from the flank of the Hook. Each man ran, trotted, or jogged toward that ridge as fast as he could move.

Lavin remembers a man they called "Sir Archibald the Degenerate" or, more commonly, "Dog Fucker." The nickname had apparently been bestowed on him because he loved dogs. He talked about them constantly and carried pictures of favorite dogs in his wallet. Sir Archibald was a meticulous and thoroughly competent point man, who, if the occasion called for it, would get on his hands and knees and smell his way along a patrol route. None of the men quite knew what he was smelling or, rather, trying to smell. When asked, Sir Archibald would only grin, coo, and touch his head in a slightly daffy manner. That night, he ran across the rice paddy in grotesque leaps and bounds as he raced for the finger ridge. The men smiled. The fact that they were heading straight into a firefight was momentarily forgotten. Dog Fucker looked absolutely ridiculous.

The squad had crossed the tank road and moved well into the next paddy when it began receiving mortar fire. The men took some casualties but kept moving. Despite the fact that the trail was zeroed in, they could not get off it for fear of tripping mines. They did the best they could to present a moving target for the mortars—run a little, take some incoming, move a little further, and take more incoming. Lavin remembers there was no place to hide. "All that one could do was hit the deck, attempt to pull your whole body under a helmet, and pray. Sometimes it worked; sometimes it didn't." By the time the men reached the relative safety of the finger ridge, they had taken more casualties, including one KIA.

The squad wasted little time preparing for the assault on Irene. Lieutenant Northcutt told his men that they would be going up the part of Irene that had been used as a garbage dump. He ordered one corpsman to stay in the draw with the wounded and had the remainder stand by while he contacted the company CP. The Marines spread out across the reverse side of the little finger ridge that they were to cross. They checked their intervals and weapons and waited for the word to advance.

Lieutenant Northcutt gave the order and they pushed off. There were four or five men in front of Northcutt and Lavin and four or five behind. Lavin recalled, "I stepped over the crest of the ridge and started a diagonal movement right and down the hill that fronted Irene. I thought to myself that there was no way I was going to survive this one, but I kept walking, actually more of slow trot, as did the other Marines with me."

The men moved down that little slope. Everywhere, they heard the horrible and continuous sound of small arms, mortar, and artillery. The air was filled with smoke, dirt, and the smell and flash of burning powder. Some men could see little puffs of dirt rise and fall as bullets and shrapnel swept through the ranks. Lavin continued, "We were moving at a good pace when two, maybe three Marines down the hill from me and to my right began to move up the base of Irene. The heat was terrible and I was conscious of being miserably dry and thirsty." In his haste to leave the MLR, Lavin had neglected to fill his canteen.

Lavin stopped for a moment to respond to a radio transmission when he saw the lieutenant wave him to the deck and move farther down the hill. A man who had been behind Lavin moved up and touched him on the shoulder. "As I started to speak to him, I saw a sudden white flash and the world went away." A mortar round had landed close by and knocked Lavin unconscious.

He awoke flat on his back. He had not been out more than a few seconds. The man next to him had been hit and was struggling to get up. Lavin had a massive headache, and his ears were stopped up. As he rolled over, he saw that the stock of his M-1 rifle had been smashed by a piece of shrapnel. He began helping the wounded man back to the reverse slope of the finger ridge. "The journey wasn't simple as the wounded Marine kept screaming that I was hurting him. I couldn't help it; there was no way I was going to leave him on that forward slope exposed to more incoming." Soon, two other Marines came and took the wounded man over the crest. Relieved of his burden, Lavin turned and made his way back down hill.

He had gone only a few yards past his previous position when he saw that several Marines from the relief squad were withdrawing and moving back up the hill. Tom Nash, one of the corpsmen was helping Lieutenant Northcutt, who had been wounded. Lavin joined a second knot of men also headed uphill with another wounded man. As he assisted them, he saw two Marines, maybe 15 to 20 yards away, who were obviously dead. "They were 'frozen,' almost 'wooden puppet like'—not moving," he said. "They had the 'look' that I recognized."

Mortar and small-arms fire continued to pursue the men as they made their way up the hill with their wounded, twelve in all. Cresting the hill where they were protected from direct fire, they carried the wounded down the draw to relative safety. Northcutt had been badly hit. Blood flowing from under his flak jacket was staining his dungaree jacket and trousers. Seeing him sitting there among the other wounded men, Lavin "felt such a despair. He was truly a fine officer." In the draw, the wounded were spread out in places that would be the most protected.

Trapped in the draw, the rescue detail knew that they, too, now needed rescue. They did not have the manpower to withdraw with their wounded, and they would not leave them. Even without communication, however, the men knew that a relief squad would be there to help. That was how the Marines fought the war.

The walking wounded and remaining able-bodied men, a total of four, took up defensive positions on the crest of the ridge facing Irene. If the enemy were to counterattack, they would be met with bullets. To reduce the odds, the Marines spent their time firing at occasional enemy soldiers on Irene to make their presence known. It was important to let the Chinese know that there was still fight left in the small group. Some of the men began praying that the relief column would arrive soon.

Perhaps an hour passed.

Incoming fire was heavy in the draw, but the narrow area afforded some measure of protection. Small-arms fire from Irene began to diminish but was soon replaced with long-range machine-gun fire from Hilda, two ridges away. After a while, Lavin crawled off the ridge seeking a drink of water. Reaching the place where the wounded were resting, he began searching for a canteen when he heard a familiar voice say, "Tot, you look like hell." It was Sgt. John ("Woody") Wood, Jr., Lavin's platoon sergeant. The relief column had arrived. Lavin recalled that he had never been so happy to see anyone in his life and all but embraced him.

Sergeant Wood, older than his men, was a natural leader. The men looked up to him. Gazing about, Woody knew immediately what had to be done. He began to organize an orderly withdrawal. He assembled stretcher bearers, set up a rear guard, and put out a point. Forming the men into a column, they began to walk out. Lavin remembered that, as they began to step out, he felt a hand on his shoulder. Turning, he saw that it was Woody. Slowly, and with great care, Woody took the heavy radio from Tot and slipped it over his own shoulder. Without saying a word, he gave Lavin a smile and they stepped out together—heading back.

As the column of men headed out of the draw toward the MLR, Lavin carried the front of a stretcher containing one of the wounded Marines. Woody walked beside him. Suddenly, they heard the ominous "whoosh" of a falling mortar. He looked up and saw the round falling. It was wobbling slightly.[3] The round hit approximately one yard in front of them. It was a dud. No explosion. Nothing. Woody and Lavin simply looked at one another and continued on.

The column reached the MLR and safety. Lavin reported to the aid bunker. A corpsman removed a small piece of shrapnel from his calf and closed the wound with a butterfly clip. Next, Lavin found a priest who heard his confession. After that, he threw up.

The fighting for Irene was over. It had lasted ten hours. Fox Company, 2/5, had sustained casualties of five dead and thirty-three wounded. Chinese casualties were approximately the same. Outpost Irene, however, was yielded, its value apparently less than the cost of holding it.

In support of the morning fight for Irene, Baker Company tanks, firing from position forward of the MLR, had neutralized enemy support fires emanating from the former outpost on Hilda. Their guns had killed more than twenty-two enemy soldiers. One wounded Marine infantry-man was so grateful for the help of the tanks that he shouted, "You great big pig-iron bastard, if I could, I'd kiss your ass."[4]

There was more to do. During the fighting on Irene, four Marine bodies had been left on the battlefield. Among the dead were two men with the 1st Platoon, Pfc. Milton West and Pfc. Lawrence Lee. Lieutenant Northcutt reported that West and Lee were killed when a mortar round landed between them as they charged Irene. A machine gunner had both legs blown off from the same round. Because of their own wounds and the intense enemy fire, the survivors were forced to leave the dead men at the base of Irene while they withdrew.

During the days following the battle for Irene, two efforts were made to locate and retrieve the bodies of Marines lost during that action. One body had been retrieved with the wounded on 17 August, but three remained unaccounted for. As the dead men had been in Fox Company's 1st Platoon, it was by preference that men of that platoon chose to bring them back. Lavin was among the group that went out the following night shortly after dark. He wrote:

> Woody, who was acting platoon leader, was in charge. Hack Weis, myself, Charlie Kivette and Woody were the snatch team. Other first platoon members came along as stretcher bearers and their replacements. Hack and I rotated point, Woody came next, then Charlie, who was to be the snatch man, came last.
>
> Our movement across the paddy was slow, methodical and extremely cautious. Woody relayed our progress at pre-established check points. As I once again climbed the hill above the draw that was the sight of yesterday's fighting, I found myself strangely calm. We held up at the ridgeline as Woody placed a fire team in position to give us supporting fire on Irene in case we got into trouble. We moved down the right flank of the finger ridge that we were on yesterday. Woody, armed with a BAR, took a position on the nose where he could deliver covering fire. Hack and I moved down to a little slope that overlooked the bodies.
>
> Charlie was to make contact, visually check the area and, if possible, tie a rope around one of the limbs of a missing Marine. Next he was to slip back down the slope and whenever he felt safe slowly pull on the rope, gently easing the body toward him. If the body had been booby trapped Charlie would be safe. If not he would be able to get the body closer to us and the stretcher team.
>
> Charlie had been gone for about 3 or 4 minutes when I thought I saw a greenish light on Irene. I raised up on my knees and was staring

at Irene and trying to get Hack's attention when a burp gun opened up on Charlie. Neither Hack nor I saw the muzzle blast, but we both opened fire toward the area where the sound emanated. Charlie got back to us and Hack and I fired again as we began to pull back up the hill. Woody was firing short bursts from his BAR until we got to him then the four of us sprinted up the hill. Several burp guns and at least one machine gun began firing at us as we crested the ridge to safety. The stretcher bearers were already in the draw and the covering fire team met us as we all exited that place.

Later Charlie told us that he tied the rope to a leg, slipped down the hill and gently pulled as he had been instructed. He had no sooner pulled when the rope was violently pulled back. Charlie immediately dropped the rope and ran back to us.

Lavin thinks that there were three more attempts to recover bodies and believes that one was successful in that a single body was recovered. The 2/5 Command Diary reports only one other attempt on 19 August: "At 2000 a detail to recover the remains of the four (4) men killed on 17 August departed the MLR. Within 30 minutes the detail was engaging the enemy in the area near where the bodies were last seen. After a brief fire fight the patrol returned without casualties at 2050."[5]

In addition to defined battles for outposts, activity in front of the MLR remained brisk. In that respect, some end-of-the-month report summaries are revealing. In the 5th Marines alone, there were 109 combat patrols, 240 recon patrols, 185 ambushes, and 815 listening posts manned and defended. As August opened, there were ten established outposts, but, with the loss of Elmer, Hilda, and Irene, that number was reduced to seven.

As August closed, the fringes of Typhoon Karen hit the Jamestown Line and much of the fighting slowed appreciably. Rain was recorded at 9 inches. The Imjin River rose 42 feet, and the Honker and Widgeon Bridges were washed out. Supply roads were badly damaged, and some supply was accomplished only by helicopter lifts. Intelligence reports indicated severe damage to enemy positions. The Marines had fared no better. In most cases, trench lines and bunkers remained intact, but life was miserable for those men, knee deep in water, living in the mud and fighting holes.

CHAPTER 8
PATROLS AND RAIDS

*Agitate the enemy and ascertain the pattern of
his movements. . . . Probe him and learn where
his strength is abundant and where deficient.*
—Sun Tzu, 400–320 B.C.

Outpost Bruce, a particularly critical position, was located east of
Bunker Hill. Later in the war, it would be called Outpost Reno. Bruce
tied in tactically with two adjacent Chinese positions, Hill 155 on the
east and Hill 190 on the northeast. Thus, Bruce broached a defendable
line, which, if occupied by the Chinese, could eventually unite to create
a new and formidable enemy MLR. Like Bunker Hill, Bruce needed to
be held.

During the months ahead, Outpost Bruce would witness severe fighting repeatedly as combatants clashed over and over for possession of this
innocuous pile of dirt on the landscape of North Korea. Yet, while the
Marines stubbornly held, the Chinese, just as stubbornly, continued to
attack. According to Lieutenant Colonel Hicks:

> The CCF often attempted to overrun outpost positions with sheer
> force of numerical superiority. Coming in successive waves, his attacks
> were preceded by heavy concentrations of artillery and mortar fire. In
> an attempt probably calculated to disperse Marine defensive artillery
> fire, simultaneous attacks against several different outposts were made.
> Communist supporting fire was in such close proximity to the CCF
> attackers that a number of casualties were inflicted on Chinese troops.
>
> Sometimes the enemy would stealthily approach and completely
> surround the outposts, hoping to gain his objective by a combination
> of surprise and strength. Usually, however, massive artillery concentra-
> tions were employed for screening enemy movements, and frequently
> he used smoke.[1]

Nowhere is Lieutenant Colonel Hicks's thesis more vividly portrayed than with the Chinese attacks on Bruce and its neighboring outposts. On 4 September, Outpost Gary first became the target of enemy machine-gun fire for an hour preparatory to an assault by an enemy platoon. Then, after a ten-minute firefight, the Chinese suddenly shifted their attack to Outpost Felix and hit it with a reinforced platoon supported by mortars. This battle raged for an hour and a half as the Marines fought back. Then, as suddenly as they had attacked, the Chinese dropped back and left ten dead soldiers. Twenty-five wounded men were left either to surrender or to escape to their own lines.

Outpost Allen was also hit that night. Following an artillery and mortar barrage, two reinforced enemy platoons struck in wave formation, one wave followed by the other. After a two-hour battle, the Chinese withdrew and evacuated their casualties. In their wake, however, were three dead and seven wounded Marines.

The attacks on Felix, Gary, and Allen, however, were merely diversions. At midnight, the Chinese began a major battle for Outpost Bruce and saturated it with a barrage of artillery and mortars. The platoon-sized outpost was attacked from all sides by a battalion of Chinese infantry. Under cover of automatic and small-arms fire, enemy soldiers used satchel charges and bangalore torpedoes in an attempt to destroy forward bunkers and blow gaps in the wire. They sought to gain entrance to the trenches and drive the Marines from the hill.

Replacement men and material were rushed to the outpost as efforts were made to rebuild fortifications. Columns of Korean laborers and Marine reinforcements traveled back and forth between the MLR and Bruce while fire from enemy machine guns and mortars attempted to interrupt their progress. Ultimately, the platoon on the hill was replaced by fresh troops, and more ammunition, medical supplies, and fortifications were brought up. The Marines were determined to hold the position. The following night, history repeated itself when, on 5 September, the Chinese stormed Bruce again.

During an hour-long artillery barrage, an estimated 2,500 artillery rounds fell on the Marines. The incoming was so concentrated that, within minutes, most bunkers and trenches were completely destroyed. Then, at 2015, two companies of Chinese infantry stormed the outpost from all sides. The fresh replacement Marines fought them off. At 2130, a second enemy wave assaulted the hill with the same outcome. Twenty minutes later, a third attack wave was repulsed.

Following a four-hour respite, the attack resumed in the early hours of 6 September. Moving forward under a fifteen-minute artillery barrage, two more companies of Chinese surrounded the outpost and began another attack. Chinese determination was matched only by Marine tenacity.

On this last occasion, however, the Chinese commander had misjudged Marine firepower. Division supporting arms had assembled a massive retaliation from the MLR and beyond. Eight sections of regimental .30- and .50-caliber machine guns and mortars targeted the area around Bruce. Marine tanks on line awaited the attack. An artillery time-on-target firing was brought to bear on the enemy troops massed around the outpost. The destruction was devastating, and the Chinese were driven off. They could not attack through that collective rain of exploding fire and steel.

The men of Item Company, 3/5, on Outpost Bruce had stood fast through a fifty-one hour siege. Although the original platoon had been replaced several times, there were never more than forty men on the hill at one time. Yet, each group of forty men fought off assaults by the hundreds.

During those hours, the Marines on Outpost Bruce met and exceeded their test of courage. Twenty-eight of them died, and seventy were wounded; history does not record the number that survived without wounds. Nor is it known how many casualties the enemy sustained. Heavily outnumbered, the Marines from Item Company, 3/5, fought back with all they had. Some found even more to give. Pfc. Alford ("Al") McLaughlin was one of those.

EARNING THE MEDAL

By Korean War standards, Al McLaughlin was an "old man." At twenty-four, he was on his second hitch in the Marine Corps, a hash-mark private first class. Marine promotions came slowly during the period following WW II. Trained as a military policeman, McLaughlin could have had it pretty easy, maybe in a guard company somewhere stateside or in Japan. But, like so many other Marines, he volunteered for combat. He even volunteered for the 5th Marines in an effort to be with his brother in How Company. McLaughlin did not quite get to How Company. That would have been too lucky, but he made it to Item Company in the same battalion.

On Outpost Bruce, McLaughlin volunteered again. He was a machine gunner on a light 30 and had been on Bruce for a week. When it came time to rotate back to the MLR and let someone else suffer the deprivations of an outpost, McLaughlin requested to remain. He was an excellent machine gunner—he knew the guns, the targets, the fields of fire, and the places where the enemy lurked. A natural, some called him, for his uncanny sense of accuracy. His request to remain on Bruce was granted.

McLaughlin was there on 4 September 1952, the night the Chinese came. With another machine gunner and two loaders, McLaughlin waited in the bunker for the incoming fire to let up. He knew full well that when it did, the Chinese would come up the hill after them.

The incoming lifted. It was replaced by grenades and the screams and noise of an attack. Chinese soldiers, spurred forward by the echo of bugles and colored flares arcing through the evening blackness, began climbing the hill. McLaughlin and the three other Marines left their bunker on the run. Both gunners manned their guns. They dusted the mechanisms and ensured that the belted ammunition was properly fed and ready. Around them, riflemen took up firing positions. Hand grenades and ammunition clips were at the ready for quick access.

Running through their own mortar barrage, the first wave of Chinese came into view. "Here they come," yelled McLaughlin, and come they did. In well-disciplined ranks, firing, yelling, and running, the Chinese stormed Outpost Bruce. Soon, they were within range, and the Marines opened fire. McLaughlin's gun coughed a steady staccato as he skillfully swung the barrel and fired in short bursts to avoid overheating the barrel. He could see soldiers falling, but no sooner did one go down than another took his place. The advance continued forward, toward the ridge and its defenders.

The fight continued for more than an hour. Around the barking machine guns, riflemen fired and threw hand grenades, but still the Chinese came. They kept coming as they used manpower to absorb firepower and tried to overwhelm the outpost with the sheer weight of their numbers. By midnight, they were succeeding. Several groups of Chinese fought their way to the rear and flanks of the defenders. Soon, their bullets were striking exposed Marines as defenses eroded.

Then, the gunner on the other machine gun dropped, his weapon falling silent. Exposed now from all sides, no one moved to replace the gunner—it was certain suicide—no one, that is except McLaughlin. He knew that the key to their continued defense was two functioning machine guns. He had to put the other gun back into action. Again, McLaughlin volunteered. Running across the shrapnel and bullet-strewn hilltop, he fell on his belly behind the idle gun and got it back into action. Less than 50 yards away, a squad of Chinese fell as a burst of machine-gun fire cut through it. McLaughlin continued firing until the barrel of the gun began emitting a faint red glow because it was so hot.

Next, he recrossed the hill to his original position and began firing the other gun. Feeding the ammunition himself, McLaughlin fired until that gun began to overheat. Then, he ran back to the second gun and resumed firing it.

In the meantime, box-me-in fire fell around the surrounded outpost. A hail of Marine mortar fire fell among the charging Chinese, but some still advanced. Shooting and throwing hand grenades, they were seemingly unconcerned that their companions were falling around them. There were more Chinese than mortar rounds. The assault continued.

McLaughlin, the "old man" from Alabama, continued crossing and recrossing Outpost Bruce as he alternately kept the machine guns in operation. Whenever enemy soldiers crept close to him, he paused long enough to fire his pistol or a carbine. His closest friend, Cpl. Martin Petkovsek, picked up a carbine and began picking off Chinese that were closing in on McLaughlin. During lulls in the fighting, another man, Private Eckman, squatted down and began reloading magazines and machine-gun belts. As fast as Eckman loaded them, he fed belts to McLaughlin, who continued to spray the slope with deadly .30-caliber fire.

Finally, the Chinese dropped back. During this lull in the battle, McLaughlin changed barrels on his guns and checked his ammunition. He knew that the fighting was not over. After tending to his guns, he treated the wounded and encouraged the dozen or so men still on their feet.

At 0230, bugles sounded, whistles blew, and signal flares shot through the early morning darkness. Out of it, through their own mortar fire, the Chinese appeared to resume the attack. They charged up all sides of the hill like a Roman legion or a Mongol horde. The Marines were surrounded and could do little more than shoot back at the wall of advancing Chinese. Their bullets were like bee stings, pinpricks against a solid wall of humanity.

McLaughlin repeated his earlier tactic of alternately manning both machine guns and trying to let each cool while he fired the other. Then, the inevitable happened. After thousands of rounds, a barrel overheated and warped. The gun was out of action.

Pressed from three sides the Marines on Bruce were slowly losing ground to overwhelming numbers. Again, McLaughlin volunteered. To gain a better field of fire, he lifted the remaining gun from its tripod and climbed out of the trench. Exposed on the rim of his emplacement, he knelt and sprayed .30-caliber bullets at the rapidly closing enemy. Some of the attackers were so close that he shot them in midair as they lunged at him.

Then, a mortar round erupted a few yards behind him. Hot shards of shrapnel peppered his side and he fell backward into the trench. Bleeding and injured, but not out of the fight, McLaughlin crawled out of the trench and returned to his gun. On the ridgeline, again exposed to the advancing Chinese, McLaughlin first knelt and then stood upright. Cradling his machine-gun in the crook of his left arm, he raked bullets back and forth across the enemy ranks. The gun barrel became so hot that it began to glow red. Burning through his field jacket, the barrel seared the flesh of McLaughlin's left forearm. Switching to the cradle of his right arm, he continued to fire and soon burned that arm as well. All the time, McLaughlin was yelling encouragement to those around him and swearing at the Chinese. Then, unbelievably, he began tapping out "Shave and a Haircut, Two Bits" with the trigger. He appeared to be actually enjoying himself, or perhaps he had gone mad.

Finally, the gun overheated and had to be discarded. Still fighting, McLaughlin picked up an abandoned carbine and fired until its magazine was exhausted. Then, he grabbed hand grenades from a dead Chinese soldier and began throwing them. His firing had a telling effect on the enemy, and they fell back. The attack weakened, and the Chinese survivors began to withdraw.

The battle ended. Bruce had held, and, by some quirk of fate, Al McLaughlin had survived. He had accounted for exactly 150 enemy dead and an estimated 50 wounded. When a corpsman reached him, he was burnt and bleeding. Each arm was seared nearly to the bone.

On 27 October 1953, newly promoted Cpl. Alford McLaughlin was awarded the Medal of Honor by President Eisenhower. Corporal McLaughlin, originally from the town of Leeds, Alabama, remained in the Marine Corps and attained the rank of master sergeant. He retired in 1972 and died on 14 January 1977.[2]

BUNKER HILL REVISITED

The action that began in August continued. In particular, Bunker Hill, its existence a continuing threat to the Chinese, was repeatedly attacked. The enemy did not want the Marines on that hill and was willing to spill gallons of blood to get it back. The Marines accommodated him, but they lost much of their own blood in the process.

As September began, Easy Company, 2/1, was defending Bunker Hill under control of the 3d Battalion, 1st Marines. George Company, 3/1, was defending OP-2 but would soon to be on Bunker. It was time for another round of musical chairs.

On Wednesday, 3 September, the Division Reconnaissance Company sent sixteen men to George Company for a relief party to Bunker Hill. The following day, How Company began to relieve George Company on OP-2, and, by 5 September, it was in place.

At 0100, 5 September, at the height of the attack on Outpost Bruce, an enemy battalion, supported by concentrations of mortar and artillery, assaulted Bunker Hill. From the MLR, tanks with searchlights illuminated three hundred enemy troops storming the left flank of the outpost using pyrotechnics to control their movements. Friendly forces surrounded the hill with artillery and mortar box-me-in concentrations. Easy Company reported that the enemy walked into the initial attack apparently confident that his preparatory fires had neutralized the position, but they had not. The attack was accomplished in eight assault waves. After each wave, the enemy stopped to reorganize and then returned to the fight. One Marine, in particular, did his best to see that the waves of Chinese never reached his position.

Pfc. Jon Adams, a machine gunner with Weapons Company, 2/1, was set up on a vulnerable but important position on the hill. After the initial barrage of incoming fire, Adams moved his light machine gun. Ignoring the shrapnel from bursting artillery, he set it up on the forward slope of the hill in a better position to repulse the inevitable enemy infantry assault. Calmly, he waited until the first three waves were within accurate range of his gun and then opened fire. Spraying the onrushing enemy with bullets, he succeeded in stemming the main assault but was wounded in the process.

Adams moved his gun to another, more advantageous position in time to renew his fire on the second assault and repulsed it as well. Moving to a third position, he threw a belt of ammunition over his shoulder and picked up the hot gun with his bare hands. Ignoring the pain of his burning flesh, he fired the weapon from his hip until he was temporarily blinded by an exploding concussion grenade. As partial sight returned, Adams recovered his machine gun and delivered more fire to the enemy. Finally, critically wounded by shrapnel, he collapsed. Single-handedly, Adams accounted for fifty-eight dead and wounded enemy soldiers. He was awarded the Navy Cross.

HM3 Edward Benfold, a Navy corpsman with Easy Company, 2/1, killed only two enemy soldiers, but he earned a Medal of Honor for his actions. Killing was not his job.

During the attack on Bunker Hill, Doc Benfold was everywhere as he worked in the open and tended to wounded and dying Marines. When his platoon area was attacked from both the front and rear, he moved forward to an exposed ridgeline and observed two wounded Marines lying in a large crater. As he approached the men, he saw an enemy soldier throw two hand grenades into the crater while two more Chinese charged the position. Leaping into the crater, Benfold retrieved the grenades and, holding one in each hand, clambered out of the hole to rush the enemy. Hurling himself at the two soldiers, he pushed the grenades against their chests. In saving the lives of the two Marines, Benfold killed two enemy soldiers but forfeited his own life.[3] Years later, on 31 March 1996, the USS *Benfold* (DDG 65) was commissioned at San Diego, California. Attending the commissioning were many former Marines from Easy Company, 1st Marines, who were survivors of Bunker Hill.

Finally, after two hours of fighting, the Chinese broke contact on Bunker Hill and withdrew from the battle. Temporarily, at least, the battle was over. Casualties for the period were moderate, ninety Chinese dead and two hundred fifty wounded. Four enemy were taken prisoner but two died of wounds. Easy Company lost ten killed and twenty-eight wounded.

At 0301 6 September, George Company, 3/1, departed the MLR to begin relief of Easy Company on Bunker Hill. Setting up on Bunker Hill, the men of George Company surveyed their surroundings. Other Marines before them had built, dug, defended, rebuilt, and died on that hill. Now it was their turn. It did not appear to be a very valuable piece of dirt, especially when one looked around. Cpl. Peter Beauchamp, with the 1st Platoon, found his squad posted on the right flank of Bunker Hill that day. He offered the following description:

> Bunker Hill reminded me of a garbage dump: It was littered with debris, stretchers, C-ration boxes and cans, barbed and communication wire, Chinese bodies still armed with American M-1 rifles and bangalore torpedoes. There were large corrugated metal culvert pipes which were used to protect equipment and the wounded from shrapnel until nightfall, when they could be evacuated. It was impossible to move about in the daylight without attracting incoming mortar fire.
>
> Our sleeping bunkers were very small. The one I was in was approximately 3 feet high, less than 4 feet wide and 5 or 6 feet deep. There were four of us in the bunker, and you had to sleep half sitting and hunched up when all four were inside. The uncovered fighting hole on the forward slope, which I believe I shared with Pfc. Rolin Massey, had a sound powered telephone, with which I could call in

artillery on Chinese positions, about 100 yards in front of us. Every now and then a Chinese soldier would pop up, spray our area with a burp gun and then duck down in his trench or hole.

The Chinese mortars were so close that I could see the flashes from the tubes when they fired. The flashes were coming from three different mortars. They must have been in fixed positions (maybe buried in the ground so that only a direct hit could knock them out) because I could pretty well tell where the round was going to hit based on which of the mortars fired. I called in artillery to try to knock out the mortars. When the first round hit, it really shook the whole area. I asked, "What the hell was that?" I expected to be told that it was a 16 inch shell from a battlewagon. Instead, I was told by the person on the other end of the soundpower that it was an 8 inch shell from an army artillery battery.[4]

RELIEVING THE LINE

East of Bunker Hill, on the division's right, the 5th Marines began to rotate off-line on Sunday, 7 September. They were being replaced by the 7th Marines. The far right sector of the line, next to the British, was assigned to the 1st Battalion. The 2d Battalion assumed responsibility for the left sector next to the 1st Marines. The 3d Battalion took the regimental reserve assignment.

Lieutenant Watson, with the 7th Marines, remembers relieving units of the 5th Marines who had been manning the line for the past two months:

> . . . It was a bright, clear afternoon. Then, and I will swear to this, we actually got wind of the 5th Marines before they came into view, around the bend in the road. We smelled them! I am sure we must have been as rank as they when we came off the line on 1 August, but it was a remarkable experience. We made some ugly remarks about our unwashed comrades, but it was in fun, and I doubt we could have insulted them anyway, in their joy to be off the line. They were thinking of hot food, showers and sleep just as we had. Fortunately there was no Bunker Hill in their immediate future, but in a few weeks, the battle for our outposts began, and both regiments would take some fearsome losses. None of us knew that at the time.[5]

Unfortunately, the relief of men and units on line did not always go as smoothly. First, there were the Chinese, who rarely missed an opportunity to strike while confusion was rampant. Second, and often worse, there was the unexpected.

On Outpost Felix, a platoon from Dog Company, 2/5, was to be relieved when their plans went awry. Lieutenant Matthias called it "the worst day of my life":

> The relief force, accompanied by several of my men from the MLR, arrived at the main gate of our outpost; suddenly our outpost, designed for about a dozen men, had double that number. We were crowded and much coming and going began to occur. Somehow, the gooks became aware of this and incoming began to come in real hard.
>
> The bunkers were full of Marines. I was in one of the forward bunkers when I became conscious of some yelling and crying, "Lieutenant, come quick, we have some real trouble back here." I left the bunker and made my way around to the rear of the largest bunker which was used for our command post and supply bunker. It was strong but the original builder made one major error. The door leading into the bunker faced the trench where the trench line made a sharp corner. Consequently, instead of facing to the rear, the door faced partially to the front. A high-angle shell had hit in this doorway while the bunker was full of Marines.
>
> . . . The sounds indicated that there were people still living and they needed help. One of my sergeants arrived and I said, "Let's go and get it over with."
>
> The bunker was pitch dark. We had no lights initially. I moved toward the voice that was begging for help, grabbed the Marine that was lying on top of the wounded man and tried to move him. My hands were suddenly blood covered and there was no response from the body I had grabbed. We were able to drag the body to the entrance where more Marines were able to pull him out. Then we moved the living Marine to a stretcher outside and went back to check for more living men. I crawled from one body to the next trying to find a pulse or hear some breathing. We found a couple more who were still alive and dragged them to the entrance and the waiting stretcher. It was impossible to crawl even a few feet and not touch a dismembered body part. Blood was everywhere. I managed to get to the farthest part of the bunker and found a Marine just sitting there very peacefully. I could not find any signs of a major problem—no lost body parts or open wounds. Still, I knew he was dead. As I nudged him, he collapsed. It was then I felt the small hole in the side of his temple.
>
> . . . Seven Marines were killed in that one horrible accident. Two of them were my troops and the others from the replacement platoon. I did not go back into the bunker. It was up to my sergeant to supervise the grisly removal of bodies and body parts.[6]

By 8 September, the division's right sector was in the hands of the 7th Marines. Defending seven outposts and the far right of the MLR, the Marines should have had their hands full, but the Chinese apparently had run out of steam, at least for a time, or perhaps they were saving ammunition until the following month. Consequently, the 7th Marines sat and waited for something to happen. It would, but not this month.

On 10 September, two minor engagements were fought near Outposts Felix and Gary and another in the vicinity of Irene, the former outpost lost in August. The Felix engagement consisted of an Able, 1/7, squad led by Lt. Stan Rauh. The patrol engaged an enemy platoon in front of the outpost. Rauh was wounded that night and remembered it clearly:

> Again at dusk, I took a reinforced squad patrol out to "make contact." At this time we were manning positions behind outpost Felix which was manned by a Company A 1/7 platoon very ably led by 2nd Lt. Dick [Richard] Stone. Stone was a Mustang and a good friend of mine. My patrol passed through Outpost Felix and was well forward of it when we spotted an occupied Chinese bunker. As we maneuvered toward it and brought fire to bear, we immediately received mortar, grenades and automatic weapons fire. Several Marines were wounded.
>
> In that we were receiving fire from several sides, I felt it best to have the walking wounded go back to Felix ASAP. I put "Panama" Harris in charge of them and ordered him to head back to the OP. The firefight continued and I, too, was hit by a grenade. A few minutes after Panama had taken off with the wounded, I heard the loud singing of the Marine's Hymn being boisterously sung by the wounded men. It was obvious to me that Panama and his group were drawing attention to themselves to ease the pressure on their fellow Marines who were at that moment heavily engaged with the enemy.[7]

The patrol cost Able Company one dead and six wounded that night while the Chinese lost ten killed and twelve wounded. Lieutenant Rauh recovered from his wounds in the Naval Hospital at Yokosuka, Japan, and returned to Able, 1/7, in time to be wounded again on the Hook in late October.

The following night, 11 September, an Able Company patrol met the enemy again on hills near Outpost Elmer. A combat patrol en route to Elmer was diverted on the way by enemy troops south of its objective. Combat patrols frequently went awry. Sometimes it was tragic and, on other occasions, laughable, but more often than not, patrols did not work out as planned.

Each day cost the Marines a man or two. When death was not caused by direct contact, it was the result of random incoming fire, or a mine, or an occasional sniper's bullet. There were no major attacks in this area, only constant small actions. Waiting for a "big push" was nerve-racking.

TANKS ON THE HILL

Then, there were the tanks. Armored vehicles were not often popular with the infantry, for good reason. They were like magnets for incoming fire, not just little mortar shots but large, powerful rounds that struck and shook the ground and destroyed a tank or entire bunkers.

Tanks are not subtle machines. They are large, noisy, and disturbing. In various places along a ridgeline were tank slots, bulldozed breaks in the line usually on the crest of a hill above the MLR. Daily, at one place or another, a tank would clank, crawl, and groan its way to the top of a hill and enter a slot. There it would sit, in plain view of the enemy, arrogantly threatening, and challenge him to do something about it as its gun swung ominously around—pointing toward the enemy, seeking a target.

The 90-mm gun on an M-46 tank was one of the deadliest weapons in Korea. Originally designed as an antiaircraft piece, it was a long range, flat trajectory gun of exceptional accuracy. The 90-mm tank gun had ballistics identical to an M-1 rifle, except the "bullet" was much larger. Rather than measuring 0.3 inch in diameter, as does a typical .30-06, its diameter was more than 3½ inches, greater by a factor of ten. It also exploded on impact.

With twenty-power telescopic gun sights, tankers on the hilltops used their 90s as enormous sniper rifles. Anything Chinese was fair game. Enemy tanks and trucks were the preferred targets but were seldom seen. Weapon emplacements, bunkers, and trenches were the more common subjects of a gunner's marksmanship, especially if they were occupied by enemy soldiers.

Frequently, at one place or another, a Marine M-46 gun tank crawled its way to the top of a hill and disturbed the peace, everyone's peace. To say that tank fire itself was noisy would be an understatement. It was horrible. The back blast alone could knock a person off his feet. Fire and smoke belched from the muzzle so far that sandbags 15 feet in front of it often ignited. Thick, acrid smoke, mixed with dust, obscured vision everywhere in the vicinity, and the pungent smell of cordite assaulted the nose. Fractions of a second later, the hit registered on an enemy position, perhaps several thousand yards away. Those inside the tank and others outside saw little until the smoke and dust cleared. Then, they might perceive a caved-in bunker or smoking bodies, always an awesome sight.

For Marines in the trenches and bunkers, it was gratifying but only for a moment. They knew what would follow. As predictable as a law of physics, there was a reaction. Chinese heavy mortars or artillery began seeking out the tank, and, as the vehicle was stationary on a hill in plain sight, it was a sitting duck for enemy observers. The Chinese met the challenge as they tried to zero in on the tank.

The contest was one of speed and accuracy. Who could fire off the most rounds at the other before the tank backed off the hill? At the outset, as the tank prepared to fire, so did the Chinese. Soon, the MLR was covered with incoming artillery and mortar fire. Small mortar rounds had no effect whatever on a tank, and the enemy knew it; it used the largest and most powerful weapons in its arsenal—120-mm mortars and 76-mm, 105-mm, and Soviet 122-mm artillery, all seeking to put the tank out of action.

To avoid being hit, tankers developed the tactic of sitting on the MLR, firing a few rounds, and then retiring to another slot to repeat the process. Hopefully, Chinese marksmen would not be able to adjust their fire rapidly enough to hit them.

This tactic suited the tankers just fine but left no option for infantrymen living in holes nearby. They could hardly pack up and move. The infantrymen then caught all of the incoming fire meant for the tanks. Sandbagged and timbered bunkers were not enough against heavy artillery. Or, as a former rifleman said, "The tanks would fire two or three rounds, then turn around and haul ass. By this time, the enemy would have pinpointed the location and us grunts that were left caught all sorts of incoming."[8]

One fortunate Marine described the sensation of experiencing a near miss from one of those large tank-killer rounds:

> . . . I was sitting on the dirt bench in my bunker, a lighted candle on the packing crate I used for a table, reading something. . . . My helmet was on my head, but the strap hung loose, when I heard it coming down. It was not a 61 mm mortar, nor an 82 mm. It was large and the sound grew louder as it descended from the night sky, increasing almost to a roar, and just before it hit, I looked up and just listened, helplessly, a 120mm mortar round. I knew it would be close, and if it hit my bunker roof, or the edge of it, I would die. The roar of its descent then merged with its thunderous detonation. "Wha-room!" My helmet, the candle, the wooden crate, the book, and me, all were

lifted up into the air by the force of the explosion, which occurred just feet away from the flimsy cover over my head. The candle turned a slow loop in the air and went out. The force of the concussion jarred me. I came down half on top of the crate, and fell to the dirt floor awkwardly. My helmet hit me on the shoulder. I sat in black darkness, in disarray, shaken. I needed a few seconds to be composed. I thought someone must have died. The air in my bunker was full of choking dust. Jesus, what a thing. I got up and found my helmet in the dark, snapped it on, and went out into the trench to see the damage. To my surprise, there were no casualties, and no real damage. The round landed between the wall of my bunker and the main trench as it curved around the hill. There was a large hole there, and you could smell the exploded powder. A Marine looked out of a bunker and said, with some disapproval, "Je-sus Christ." Then he withdrew. Indeed, I thought. I walked around the trench. My pulse was racing. I breathed rapidly. Finally, I calmed down. The fright was worse than anything. I wondered, do the odds really shorten every time a close one misses you?[9]

Large artillery made tankers nervous as well. Though tough, a tank is vulnerable. A single hit, if properly placed, could quickly put one out of business. The following quote from the September Tank Battalion Command Diary illustrates what kind of damage a tank can sustain when a Chinese gunner gets lucky:

On 27 September one (1) M-46 (A-14) received a direct hit by a 105mm shell on the gunners periscope. The scope was completely destroyed and driven into the turret interior through the periscope recess resulting in the death of the gunner. The top of the turret was buckled and a gap approximately 2½ to 3 inches appeared around the front of the tank commanders cupola. The damage suffered required that the tank be surveyed [replaced].[10]

A week previously, on 20 September, a flame tank (F-31) sustained a direct hit from a 122-mm artillery shell while engaged in a tank–infantry action with the KMC. The drive sprocket, final drive, and main gun (105 howitzer) were destroyed. The tank was beyond repair and had to be replaced as well. Luckily, there were no casualties.

Fortunately, the Chinese seemed to have a limited supply of those large artillery rounds. They did not fire them in great abundance, only at tanks or during a large push, such as the battle of Bunker Hill a few weeks earlier.

RECONNAISSANCE

Deducing an enemy's intentions always has been a problem in warfare, and it was no less so in Korea. UN efforts to create an intelligence network were never very effective, although its intelligence people tried and, in isolated cases, were moderately successful. Enemy prisoners were helpful in identifying opposing units and assessing their strength, and aerial photos helped to identify potential targets, trench networks, bunkers, and sometimes gun emplacements. This intelligence aided in the pursuit of the war generally, but seldom was it of timely value to the company or battalion commander on the ground who was defending the MLR.

The ground commander needed to know the lay of the land and places of enemy strength and weakness. Where was the enemy dug in? Where were the mines, booby traps, and machine guns? He wanted to know the likely routes of approach to and from enemy strong points. In short, he needed accurate and timely reconnaissance information about the areas in which his men would be fighting.

Part of the 1st Marine Division's table of organization and equipment (TO&E) was a specially selected group of reconnaissance specialists, the division's Reconnaissance Company, a part of Headquarters Battalion. These Marines, many of whom trained at the Army's Intelligence School at Fort Riley, Kansas, called themselves "The Eyes and Ears of the Division," which, in fact, they were.

This small company (a total of fewer than two hundred officers and men) patrolled no-man's-land and set up ambushes to capture prisoners, an endeavor that was consistently unsuccessful. Yet, with equal consistency, the Marines tried. They engaged in two- and four-man layouts, sometimes lasting for days, to gather information on enemy activity. And, like regular infantry, they simply patrolled and sought useful intelligence where they could find it. The recon Marines were experts at moving quietly, at stalking. Many of the men, rejecting steel helmets, preferred to wear lighter cloth utility caps. Many wore tennis shoes rather then boots so they could move quietly and feel the terrain before placing their weight fully on the ground. Each carried his choice of a fully automatic weapons—M-2 carbine, M-3 .45-caliber grease gun, or Thompson submachine gun. Some carried personal side arms sent from home and fused half pound blocks of TNT rather than using grenades. The TNT acted as a concussion grenade to stun the enemy and enable his capture.

Although always cautious, the men of recon company were comfortable prowling about in no-man's-land and performing a stealth task that most rational infantrymen preferred to avoid. More than comfortable, they thrived on it. Reconnaissance was what they did. Chuck Burrill, then a private first class, relates his typical day with the Reconnaissance Company:

> Our usual routine was to sleep in the early part of the day, rise, shower and eat. [Men from the division's Reconnaissance Company lived in the rear.] The word would be passed as to our night's objective, and who would go.
>
> Before going on patrol, we would draw automatic weapons from the company armory. I usually took a carbine because of its high rate of fire, unless it looked like rain. In bad weather I chose a grease gun. While having a slower rate of fire, the grease gun was less likely to jam in rain and snow. The BAR and Thompson were just too heavy to let me move fast and quietly.
>
> Prior to leaving, our patrol leader went over a map of the area. He told us our objective, where we were going, the route we would take and how we would get back. He gave us the password for the day, and the countersign. Units defending the line were alerted as to the area we would be in, our time of departure and our route of return.
>
> In operations with men from line companies, we would often hear the comment, "You guys must be nuts. I wouldn't do what you do for a million bucks." We looked on it as a matter of knowledge and the trust we had in each other as a result of training. Every man knew his job and could be depended upon.[11]

Compared to a rifle company, the Reconnaissance Company might be viewed as a little different. The men lived in tents well behind the lines, rather than in bunkers. Daily, they had hot showers and three meals of hot food. Generally, their sleep was uninterrupted.

On the down side, recon patrols were out nearly every night. The men had no months in reserve alternating with time on the line. Although well rested and clean, they were frequently in front of the MLR. Sergeant Arthur Lipper III wrote, "Those poor bastards on line. Fifty percent watch till 0100 and then 100% watch. I felt guilty when we come in through the line, I was going back to a warm, dry tent, hot chow and no worry."[12]

On his return to headquarters, the patrol leader was expected to turn in a comprehensive written report describing observations of terrain and patterns of enemy activity. The contents of these reports were analyzed by Division G-2 (Intelligence) and summarized for the division commander.

The flaw in this system was that the Reconnaissance Company was spread thinly across the entire division front. A handful of recon Marines could not possibly provide sufficient information to meet the insatiable, but valid, needs of company commanders. In addition to the Division G-2 reports, company commanders required better topical information well before the next night's patrols were sent out.

As a consequence, company commanders found it necessary to send out their own recon patrols. Along with combat and ambush patrols, recon patrols also prowled the hills and paddies of no-man's-land every night. Soon, specialized units began to form. Battalions created their own reconnaissance platoons to seek out and furnish line companies with much of the detailed information that the commanders needed.

Other units also needed the kind of information that only a good reconnaissance patrol could provide. The Tank Battalion was such an example. Within the six-company Tank Battalion organization was a Reconnaissance and Liaison Section provided by the Table of Organization then in effect.[13] This section called for sixteen personnel, including one officer, distributed among the letter companies and Headquarters Company. To achieve better support of infantry operations in front of the MLR, commanders wanted a detailed analysis of terrain and effectiveness of the enemy's prepared defenses against tanks.

Through a joint training effort with the division's Reconnaissance Company, begun in September, the tankers learned how to perform reconnaissance operations forward of the MLR. For the recon men, the training included aspects of terrain appreciation as applied to tank movement, characteristics of enemy antitank defenses, and related subjects. Both units appeared to benefit from the training.

OUTPOST HEDY

Early in September, it was decided that Hill 124, the second knoll on the ridgeline extending to Bunker Hill, should be reinforced as an adjunct to Bunker. Closer to the MLR, Hill 124 would be easier to support and defend and, at the same time, offer vital direct support to Bunker. Before this position could be garrisoned, however, some engineering was required.

There was no subtle way to reach the new outpost because all approaches were under enemy observation. A column of infantry would be slaughtered by incoming fire in daylight or ambushed at night. A tank road would be useful. Tanks might be able to drive the enemy from the troublesome northern slope of Bunker Hill and also transport troops or supplies to the outpost.

Charlie Company, 1st Tank Battalion, was supporting the 1st Marines at this time and was selected for the job. It was augmented by the attached platoon of tanks from the regimental AT (Anti-Tank) Company.

Over a period of several days, a tank–dozer (a gun tank equipped with a bulldozer blade) completed approximately 200 yards of road between the MLR and Hill 124. Except when halted by heavy rains, work proceeded every night from dusk till dawn. As the work had to be accomplished under direct observation of the enemy, a number of precautions were instituted. Smoke was deployed to screen the operation from direct enemy observation, and the dozer was reinforced with timber and sandbags against possible hits from enemy antitank weapons. Two flame tanks burned off undergrowth on either side of the road to prevent enemy infiltrations. All Charlie Company tanks remained on alert to proceed into position. On order from the 1st Marines, they were to repulse night attacks with direct fire and tank fighting lights.[14]

Finally, on 17 September, a twenty-four–hour, squad-sized outpost was created on Hill 124. Shortly thereafter, the hill came to be known as Outpost Hedy. It would be the scene of many engagements until the war's end.

The first effort to dislodge the Marines from Hedy occurred during the early morning hours of 20 September. Following a successful Able Company, 1/1, raid on enemy positions on Bunker Hill's north slope, a Chinese platoon attacked a Fox Company, 2/1, squad on Hedy. Four enemy groups converged on the outpost from three sides, with the main probe at the front. The fighting was brief but vicious. Nearly every Marine on the hill suffered wounds, and enemy casualties were estimated at twenty-two.

During the last days of September, it became almost routine for the Chinese to probe and raid the twin outposts, Bunker Hill and Hedy. None of the assaults ever appeared to be a serious effort to eject the defenders, and the Marines considered them a form of harassment, albeit more personal than artillery.

CHAPTER 9
OUTPOSTS LOST

*The dominant feeling
of the battlefield is loneliness.*
—Sir William Slim: To the officers,
10th Indian Infantry Division,
June 1941

October began in its usual routine way, nearly unnoticed. The weather began to cool and clouds, blown inland from the Yellow Sea, collected over the hills. Within a week, it would be raining and, by month's end, snowing. For men living in the dirt and under canvas, the misery would worsen. On night patrols, field jackets and gloves were in evidence. Wet socks, the nemesis of every infantryman, were seen drying in every conceivable nook and cranny of every sandbagged tent, bunker, fighting hole, and barbed-wire entanglement. No respecter of rank or privilege, dampness permeated CPs, rear areas, and outposts alike. The men slept with their weapons to keep the weapons warm and oiled them down when they awoke. The temperature on 10 October was 38°; on the 17th, it was down to 30°; and, by the 26th, it had dropped to a low of 28°. Three days later, it snowed. The men were not looking forward to winter.

In rear areas, supply sergeants began the process of collecting and issuing cold-weather gear—winter sleeping bags, stoves and kerosene for fuel, wool glove inserts, long cotton underdrawers, parkas, wool sweaters, boots, and the very fashionable "Mongolian piss-cutter," now a bit of Korean War nostalgia. This was a warm cotton cap lined with wool pile and equipped with earflaps that often were worn folded on top, which made the wearer look like a Mongolian warrior from the steppes of the frozen Gobi desert. Its odd title was derived from an obscene nickname given to the standard Marine garrison cap worn with the green or khaki uniform of the day—but not in Korea.

Having taken over the division's right sector the previous month, the 7th Marines remained in place during October. This sector had been relatively quiet, which allowed the men to enjoy a slight respite from fighting. As expected, however, the quiet soon came to an end.

For security purposes, Regimental Headquarters changed the names of all outposts in its sector. Outpost Allen became Carson, Outpost Bruce was changed to Reno, and Outpost Clarence to Vegas. The names of Outposts Felix and Jill were changed to Detroit and Seattle, respectively, and Outpost Donald became Berlin. Later in the month, Outpost Gary became Frisco, and new Outposts Verdun and Warsaw were created to guard the far right section of the MLR. Thus, as October opened, the 7th Marines were defending nine outposts and the MLR. It soon became apparent that this was too much territory to man in the usual way.

Warsaw, garrisoned by a platoon of forty-five, and Seattle with only a reinforced fire team of five men were particularly critical positions. Together, they guarded the northernmost piece of the MLR known as the Hook. The Hook was a ridge extending out from the MLR, north toward the Chinese. On either side of the Hook, the MLR cut sharply back to create the hook-shaped salient facing north. Outposts Warsaw and Seattle guarded enemy approaches to the Hook. The existence of these outposts was vital to the continued survival of the Hook, a fact as obvious to the Chinese as to the Marines.

WARSAW

At 1836, 2 October, the enemy began to bombard the Hook and its various outposts. By 1900, all land lines connecting platoons, companies, and the battalion had been severed. Chinese troops followed the bombardment and attacked Seattle and Warsaw. Twenty minutes later, the commander of Item Company, 3/7, requested artillery VT over Warsaw. His platoon had been overrun by a reinforced enemy company. At 1945, thirteen of the original forty-five men on Warsaw returned to the MLR. They reported that an enemy company was in possession of the outpost and the remaining Marines were unaccounted for.

Four of the men who escaped from Warsaw that night owe their lives to a young Marine from Fresno, California. Eighteen-year-old Pfc. Jack Kelso was barely out of boot camp. He had been in the Marine Corps for less than a year and in Korea for only a few months. On 13 August, just two months earlier, Kelso had earned a Purple Heart and a Silver Star on Bunker Hill. This night on Warsaw, Kelso watched his platoon leader and sergeant fall dead as the enemy stormed the trench line. He was caught in a bunker with four other men when an enemy soldier in the trench threw a hand grenade inside. Faster than it took to think about it, Kelso scooped up the grenade, ran outside, and hurled it back. The grenade exploded as it left his hand and severely wounded him. Returning to the comparative safety of the bunker, Kelso remained there for a few seconds while the Chinese brought the position under small-arms fire. Suddenly, he ran outside and began to return fire. He called for his companions to make a run for it while he covered. As the four men fled down the trench and off the hill, Kelso remained behind and exchanged fire with the enemy to cover their departure. He was soon cut down by enemy small arms. Private First Class Kelso was posthumously awarded the Medal of Honor.

One of the four Marines in that bunker was Sgt. Keith Yarnell, Kelso's squad leader. Later, Yarnell wrote:

> Jack Kelso was the bravest man I have ever met. At the time he was 18 years old. He did so many brave things like going after wounded Marines completely away from the MLR. When they called for volunteers, Kelso was always ready to go. I know that Kelso had to make 10 trips across open ground to get wounded Marines. I know this to be true because I was in the trenches with him when he volunteered. On Outpost Warsaw he gave his life for me and three other Marines. . . . What is written about Kelso and his deeds are absolutely true. He deserved the Medal of Honor.[1]

The same night at 1950, Outpost Seattle was also overrun. A squad of Chinese soldiers attacked the hill and killed four of the five Marine defenders. The fifth Marine escaped to the MLR and left the hill to the Chinese. In little more than two hours the Marines had lost two outposts. Now they had to retake them.

Elements of the 1st Battalion, 7th Marines, then in regimental reserve, were sent forward to augment the 3d Battalion. First to arrive was a reinforced platoon from Charlie Company, which was immediately sent forward to reinforce Item Company. Soon, the remaining platoons arrived, and the entire Charlie Company was to join Item Company in a counterattack. At 0107 on 3 October, Item and Charlie Companies stormed Warsaw. The result was anticlimactic. All of the Chinese troops had withdrawn.

Atop the hill, the Marines recovered the four bodies of the original defenders and then discovered six wounded Marines who had been hiding in bunkers. The survivors indicated that when the outpost was overrun, they had feigned death in the bunker while Chinese soldiers searched the position for prisoners or Marines to kill. A count of men disclosed that eighteen were still missing. Outpost Warsaw was again in Marine hands. Seattle, however, would take greater effort.

SEATTLE

At 0340 that morning, two Item Company squads left the MLR to retake Seattle. Fifteen minutes later, they were under enemy artillery fire and were soon engaged in a stiff firefight. The Chinese had not abandoned Seattle, and they were willing to fight for it. The two-squad attack was inadequate to retake Seattle, however, and, after suffering six casualties, the Marines were ordered to withdraw to the MLR.

That evening, they tried again. At 1818, two more Item Company squads attacked Seattle. Under cover of smoke, the Marines stormed the hillside and engaged in a fierce exchange of grenades and small-arms fire as Chinese troops attempted to surround them. Meanwhile, a squad from Able Company, 1/7, (attached to 3/7) left the MLR to reinforce the counterattack. By 2048, the Item and Able squads had joined but not in time to prevent the enemy from flanking them. They called for artillery fire on Seattle, which enabled them to evacuate one dead and two wounded Marines to the MLR. When the artillery lifted, the counterattack began anew. At 2305, the Marines reported no forward progress, and they were ordered to withdraw. The enemy was left holding the hill with an estimated two platoons.

DETROIT

Concurrent with the initial bombardment of Seattle and Warsaw on 2 October, enemy artillery also struck Outposts Detroit and Frisco. Neither outpost was attacked at that time, but incoming fire was so intense that the Marines on those hills believed that an attack was imminent. Lieutenant Watson (George Company, 3/7) was outpost commander on Detroit that night, and he included the following account in his memoir:

> Detroit, when the artillery and mortar fire began, was a place I did not want to be, but we functioned. Hearing the radio transmissions, all outposts under fire, infantry attacking Seattle and Warsaw, I presumed the worst. It was dark, and the moon was not up. Outside, in

the increasing intensity of mortar fire, including the big ones, the 120 mm, it was dangerous to your health. I decided if they were coming to make it expensive for them. I asked our artillery FO to "box me in" with VT fuses. . . .

In our case, combined with the Chinese barrage, we were getting an unmerciful shelling, the rounds bursting relentlessly, slamming the earth, concussion in the air above us, around us, the earth shaking, and hot shrapnel raining down like tornado-driven hail. It is hard to believe we did not take a direct hit on any bunkers, nor even a round directly in the trench. I had got the troops under the flimsy cover of their shelters and all we could do was to sit and hope nothing hit us. The simple term "fear" does not apply. It was absolute fear, or terror, yet I was in control, but actually shaking with fear. How many minutes all of this continued, I do not know, but when our guns stopped and the earth and air stopped their convulsive shaking, the Chinese guns had stopped too. It was quiet on Detroit. I sat and breathed slowly, trying to get composed again. The radio told of the fighting on Seattle and Warsaw, and their loss. I went out into the trench, my realm, went around it, talked to the men, very young men I will remind you. Had the barrage been a diversion? Did they mean to hit us? Had our fire broken up the attack, or had the four deuces [Marine 4.2-inch mortars] the night before disrupted their plans? I do not know. We were still alive. I'm not sure what I thought. . . .

I can say one thing for all of us who were on Detroit that week, we were a tough fucking bunch of Marines. None of the men were over nineteen years of age. I was twenty-two. There was never a word of complaint from them. None broke or whimpered. No one will ever convince me that any such group of young men ever took any more punishment, especially mental punishment, than we did that week on Detroit, confined, isolated really, in such a small place, stressed by unending fear, hunger, fatigue, and a sense of being sacrificial lambs, yet we still functioned rationally until our relief came. And I have this thought. I do not believe the stress I experienced on Detroit, or anyplace else on the Imjin line [Jamestown Line], exceeded the worst moments of my first days at Parris Island. And that, Sir, is what that awful place in South Carolina is all about.

The rest of the night was quiet around Detroit, while we were losing men on Seattle and Warsaw, and more men tried to recover the positions. We were, quite literally, expending more men to recover the places of pawns. There is no other way to assess it, and that seems unwise to me. No one asked me at the time, naturally, but if the outposts represented positions of such vital importance to the security of the Division, or of the Imjin line, then someone, a long time ago, should have selected better and more defensible terrain upon which to establish them, and then prepared them in such a way as to make them capable of withstanding heavy artillery and mortar barrages. This was not the case and I have always considered it a command failure at the highest level. By the time the 7th Marines occupied the Hook sector in late September, it was too late to make the outposts more defensible, or to develop other positions. The mistake then was in counter-attacking, and expending so many men in the fruitless bargain, to recover outposts which, as the Chinese had just demonstrated, could be overrun by relatively small numbers of men taking advantage of darkness and their superiority in mortars and artillery. Why did we want them back? To repeat the agony?[2]

One might agree or not, but Lieutenant Watson had a point of view that deserves expression. It is a view derived from the experience of being there. It was earned.

During the night of 3–4 October, the Chinese did not move against Detroit or Frisco but remained busy with Seattle and Warsaw. On the night of 4 October, Lieutenant Watson's reinforced squad of twenty-one men was relieved from Detroit and replaced by another group led by 2d Lt. Henry ("Monk") Conway. In two more days, most of this group would be dead, Conway captured, and Detroit lost to the enemy. Watson's agony was only beginning.

On Seattle and Warsaw, the Chinese had shown an aggressiveness that had to be countered. On 5 October, worried that the aggressiveness might lead to the enemy breaking through the line, the 1st Battalion, 7th Marines, was taken from regimental reserve and given defensive positions on the MLR. Each of the other battalions compressed their areas of control to make room. The 1st Battalion assumed responsibility for the area containing Warsaw, Seattle, and the Hook, and the 3d Battalion shifted to the left.

The 7th Marine Regiment was now functioning with all three battalions on line and no reserves. This situation was made to order for the Chinese. With a thinly held Jamestown Line, even thinner outposts, and virtually no reserves, it would not take much for the Chinese to effect a breakthrough.

On 6 October, the enemy made his move. According to the October Command Diary of the 7th Marines, "Beginning at 1830, under cover of heavy mortar and artillery fire, an estimated enemy reinforced battalion in a coordinated effort made contact with the COP's across the regimental front and made contact with the MLR in two instances."[3] At 1935, Warsaw was hit; at 1940 Detroit was attacked, followed by Frisco twenty minutes later. At 1945, Reno was attacked. The Chinese made assaults on the MLR at 1920 and at 2000 and, at 2010, on Outpost Carson. Thus, within an hour, the entire regiment was either fully engaged or momentarily expecting an attack.

FRISCO AND DETROIT

The fight for Outposts Frisco and Detroit was particularly vicious and ultimately resulted in their loss. Both outposts were small. Each was held by two reinforced Marine squads, something less than thirty men.

Archival data relating to the fighting on these positions are skimpy at best. Only from accounts of the men who were there does one get the idea that maybe something went wrong. It appears that the Marines did not fight as a unit and put up a coordinated defense. Rather, they fought as individuals, every man for himself. Possibly the attack came too swiftly, and, in the case of Frisco, it occurred during a critical relief of forces. Whatever happened, or failed to happen, was not good.

Frisco

Late in the afternoon of 6 October, a routine relief detail assembled on the MLR to replace the platoon on Frisco. It was a normally scheduled replacement, the platoon on Frisco having been there for some time.

The relief detail consisted of a How Company platoon reinforced with a machine-gun squad. The platoon leader was Lieutenant Pundit, and Cpl. Ray Tittle led the machine gunners. Sgt. Robert Thornton and Sergeant Stevens combined their depleted squads to form a full squad led by Thornton.

Leaving the gate (gates were breaks in wire to permit passage of men) at 1900, the platoon proceeded quickly down the forward slope of the MLR, crossed the valley, and climbed to the outpost. Sergeant Thornton deployed his men by posting one with each person to be relieved. Numerically, the defense on Frisco was immediately doubled, although effectiveness was not. None of the new men was oriented as to fields of fire, positions of the enemy, or defense tactics for his position.

At 1940, the Chinese attacked in large numbers.

The attack was fast and furious. Striking when it did, with two separate platoons on the position, caused the Marines to be disorganized and confused. Too many men were on that tiny piece of real estate. Platoon members of one platoon did not know those of the other platoon. Little coordination existed and even less visible leadership. Frisco was not one of the Marine Corps' finest hours.

There was speculation that the enemy had probably tunneled within 50–75 yards of the outpost, enabling the Chinese to begin their assault without being seen until the last minute.[4] As a consequence, men hiding in bunkers, as they waited out the storm of falling artillery, could not respond to their fighting positions quickly enough to ward off the attack.

The assault came from three sides. Within fifteen minutes, Chinese soldiers were in the trenches, and the enemy controlled the hill. Twelve Marines with a radio were trapped in the command post bunker, and they called for VT fire to keep the enemy away from their position. Sergeant Thornton was making his relief at the time. He described what happened when the Chinese came:

> Before I could report to the lieutenant, the Chinese hit our lines at our most vulnerable moment and mass confusion ensued. During the first half hour, I assembled as many men as I could find, about fifteen. I told them who I was and we proceeded to defend ourselves. It wasn't long before we thought we were the only ones out of seventy or eighty men who were still alive, so we simply grouped together and fired at anyone who moved.
>
> We were getting a lot of mortars, probes and grenades. The barrages would last for about ten minutes, followed by a lull of probably fifteen minutes, then they would start again. The Regiment must have thought we had lost the outpost because we started to get VT from our own artillery. As a result, we were getting hit by the Marines and Chinese at the same time.
>
> About 2030 I crawled out of my bunker to relieve myself in an ammo can. I threw the ammo can over the trench towards what sounded like an army of Chinese. Then, as I was crawling back to the bunker, a piece of an artillery round hit close, throwing me in the air and wounding me in the leg and buttocks. . . .
>
> Discovering I was not dead, I recalled most of my first aid training, but could only focus on shock and bleeding. While administering to myself in the bunker, I looked up and saw a Chinese soldier crawling on the parapet. Yelling to Marines on top of the bunker I told them to shoot, but because he was half way into the bunker, they could only shoot his rear. One of the men rushed into the bunker with a BAR and pushed him down the hill with about ten rounds. Then I told them to search the body. It was a Chinese corpsman with a full bag of pre-salved bandages. The men used it on my wounds. Within ten minutes I looked like a wrapped mummy. . . .
>
> . . . After a long barrage of incoming, I crawled out of the bunker again, looking for some Marines. The gunpowder haze was just lift-

ing, and there wasn't a soul to be found. I went down the trench line trying to find a weapon. After crawling about twenty feet, I saw two men wearing bullet proof vests, but without helmets. They jumped over the trench line and got in front of me with burp guns. Thinking they might be Puerto Rican members of our platoon, I told them I was Sgt. Thornton. This did not impress them and three more guns were pressed into my back with words like, "surrender, surrender, don't shoot, move." Since I couldn't speak Chinese any better than I could Spanish, I was still hoping they were Puerto Ricans.

They weren't. It was then I realized I was captured.

We walked about forty feet around a corner of the trench line when another artillery barrage began. Seeing a bayonet on the ground, I dove for it, yelling, "Charge." In the incoming, everyone ran in different directions. Best of all, no one followed me.

I made it back to the bunker area but decided to keep going to try and find someone, anyone. About thirty feet past my bunker, I spotted a Marine on a machine gun, it was Pfc. Vincente Carlos-Perez who was one of my fire team leaders. I asked him where everyone was, and he pointed to a partially blown away bunker a few feet away. He said all of the wounded were in there. Perez was not inside the bunker because he couldn't walk; one leg was gone and the other badly mangled.

I stayed with Perez at the machine gun for a while until we were hit with another VT barrage. Raising my arm to shield my face, shrapnel hit my left elbow and left knee. When I pulled my arm off the sandbag, it felt like my hand had fallen off. I grabbed my hand and it felt like the elbow fell off. My immediate conclusion was that I was lucky, the arm was only broken in two places. Just to make sure, I pulled very easy on the arm to see if it would fall off, it didn't so I found a piece of comm wire and tied my hand around my neck.

I went inside the bunker with the wounded but after a few minutes decided not to stay. I felt I would likely bleed to death before help arrived. If it came at all.

Returning to the trench I found two men I knew. Pfc. Ramos from Hawaii and Pfc. Capps from South Carolina, and a third, unknown Marine. We found a rifle and gave it to the unknown Marine with orders to guard the bunker full of wounded, while the three of us went for help.

I found a grenade, and Capps had his BAR, but I don't know if Ramos was armed. Nonetheless, we started out for the MLR, probably a half mile away. We went about ten yards when a mortar came in, hitting Ramos in the stomach. We thought he was dead, so Capps and I kept going up the trench line toward the CP, where we believed the trail to the MLR began.

The trench was so full of bodies that we were basically walking on the skyline. We came over a mound and 20 feet in front of us sat about ten Chinese soldiers smoking cigarettes. I yelled at Capps to shoot them. He dropped to one knee, pulled the trigger and all the world could hear one loud click! Either his BAR jammed or it wasn't loaded, it made no difference. Fear of getting captured again made me keep the grenade. I yelled my favorite order, "Charge," and the Chinese dove for cover as Capps and I ran down the side of the hill as fast as we could.

. . . [We] walked until we found a right angle trail that was likely to take us back to the MLR. At this point I decided I could go no further. I threw away my helmet, kept the grenade, and told Capps to keep going for help.

After Capps left, I heard footsteps, as the Marines and Chinese used the same trails due to the mine fields, I didn't know which it might be. So I got up and walked a few more feet until I was back on the MLR. At the wire as I was being cared for I told Lt [John J.] Bissell about the bunker full of wounded Marines remaining on Frisco. Then I was carried off to a med station for evacuation.

I lost my elbow that day and spent a lot of time in various military hospitals before being medically retired from the Marines. Later I learned that Pfc. Ramos, who we left on the trail, had not been killed, but was captured and remained a prisoner of the Chinese till the war ended.[5]

By 0115, now 7 October, two rifle squads from How Company attempted to counterattack Frisco and rescue the Marines trapped in the bunker reported by Thornton. The squads were repulsed with heavy casualties from enemy artillery and mortar fire. Among those in the attack were Lieutenant Bissell, Pvt. Louis A. Pumphrey, Pfc. Preston Woodard, Pfc. Witt, and Pfc. Woods. No sooner had they arrived on Frisco when Lieutenant Bissell was cut down by fire from multiple burp guns. Woodard, Pumphrey, Witt, and Woods returned fire and caught the enemy soldiers while they took cover in the battered trenches. The four Marines set up an effective base of fire that temporarily drove back the Chinese troops. The enemy retaliated with a barrage of mortar fire that killed Woods and Witt.

Woodard and Pumphrey were now alone, nearly out of ammunition, bleeding from wounds, and dangerously positioned in a collapsed trench affording them little to no protection. They remained on the hill until their ammunition ran out. At this opportunity, Chinese troops swarmed the position and captured them.

The next effort to retake Outpost Frisco was an assault by a compos-
ite platoon from How and Item Companies at 0300. The Marines met
resistance from small arms, machine guns, and grenades. While replying
in kind, the platoon sustained many casualties and, by 0405, was forced
to retire.

At 0510, an Item Company platoon made a third attempt to retake
Frisco. Dawn had broken, and the men were able to see what was happening and where. More important, Marine air was able to support the
attack with an effective air strike. After a one-hour firefight, the Marines
reached the trench line.

After Frisco was secured, communications wireman Don McClure,
who had heard the fighting, was troubleshooting wire breaks behind
the MLR. When he was recalled to How Company to lay a new line to
Frisco, he was not prepared for what he found there:

> ...My wireman partner, Cpl. [Sherman] Vangsness, had been sent
> out to Frisco earlier with another platoon.
>
> As I approached the MLR behind Frisco, I walked into an almost
> surrealistic setting. I remember the smoke and people sitting on top of
> the bunkers, some with their shirts off, some with and some without
> helmets, or vests. Most seemed to be in some kind of trance. I vividly
> remember the eerie calm and silence. The entire area was cluttered
> with equipment, vests, 782 gear [web gear, canteens, etc.] helmets, and
> other debris. One man was crying and hysterically screaming while
> two or three other men tried to console him. As the sun rose through
> the smoke, the quiet confusion was a sight I'll never forget.
>
> Within fifty yards of the Company CP and the main body of troops
> (about twenty-five or thirty men), I came upon four men carrying a
> wounded man on a stretcher. Another man walked alongside carrying
> some gear including an IV [intravenous] plasma bag; it was my partner,
> Cpl. Vangsness. The poor guy looked fifty years old. His face was white
> as paper. His eyes were red and sunk back in his head. He, like the
> stretcher bearers, was sweating profusely and shaking; he seemed
> almost incoherent. He had no helmet and was barely able to shuffle
> along. I walked right up to him, but he didn't recognize me. Calling
> his name, I got his attention. He tried to explain what happened the
> night before but had a 1,000 yard stare and was very confused. I told
> him to go along with the stretcher; I would finish laying the line and
> catch up with him later.
>
> Soon as I had communications restored between Frisco and the
> MLR, I located Vangsness and we began to talk. He told me that Frisco
> was like "hell on earth." It had been total confusion, yelling, screaming,
> small arms fire, grenades and incoming.[6]

Vangsness had been one of twelve men trapped in the CP bunker for two days on Frisco. And, although possession of Outpost Frisco was left with the Marines on the morning of 7 October, it was subsequently ordered abandoned at 1804 the same day. Reasons for the abandonment were not given.

Detroit

Simultaneously with fighting on Frisco, George Company squads on Detroit came under artillery attack followed by an enemy assault in over-whelming numbers. At 2030, as the artillery lifted, a company of infantry attacked the twenty-two Marines on the hill. The Chinese troops quickly overwhelmed the small garrison, which fell back to its bunkers and called for VT. Enemy troops had gained the forward trench line, but the rain of shrapnel from the VT drove them off. Regrouping, the Chinese returned at 2100 and were again able to attain the main trench line. Fifteen minutes later, the Marines on Detroit called for more VT. Soon after this last call went out, communication with Detroit was broken.

From the MLR, two squads were sent to reinforce Detroit, but they were stopped by mortar and artillery bombardments. Once again, Marine artillery fired on Detroit but with little effect, because the Chinese troops were able to take cover in the trenches and bunkers of the outpost. They could not advance, but neither would they retreat. The garrison on Detroit now appeared to be half friendly and half enemy. During the night, attempts were made to reestablish radio contact with the men on the outpost, and, on one occasion, battalion radio operators reported hearing Chinese language on the outpost frequency. Two wounded Marines had escaped from Detroit, but the rest were unaccounted for. Battalion Headquarters needed to know who held the hill.

At 0505, a twenty-two man relief patrol from George Company was dispatched to Detroit to determine who owned it. The patrol was led by Lieutenant Watson, who had been outpost commander two days before. His platoon was now manning a sector of the MLR near Detroit gate. Watson was offered the opportunity to volunteer. He recalled:

> I called the Company CP. Lt. McNamara, the Executive Officer, was on the line. "Mac," I said, "what's happening?" Of course, I knew. "No response from Detroit," he said. "We have to find out." He meant me, naturally. "Take a squad reinforced and find out who has it."
>
> That is a thirteen-man rifle squad, and two light machine guns, four men to a gun. Twenty-one men and me. Why so many? To reoccupy the position, naturally. I was frightened anew. What in the fuck did they

have in mind? I knew what had happened on Detroit. A massive barrage of mortar and artillery fire had reduced that puny trench and the toy bunkers to rubble. Lt. [Henry] Conway and his men were dead, or wounded, or in such deep shock they didn't know what day it was. It wasn't just a case of faulty radio. . . .

Standing there in that high place in the trench, I asked Mac a very direct question. The first time I started thinking like a lawyer, as I have remarked many times since. "What are my orders?" I said. "If I meet resistance, do I attack or withdraw?" He said calmly, "You withdraw."

At last, a small piece of wisdom. This pawn, and the men it represented, would not be reclaimed, not by blood anyway.

. . . I got with the squad leader before we went through the wire. I explained the mission. I wanted the men spread out. If we took fire, small arms or mortars, or worse, I didn't want one round doing a lot of damage. I made it clear we would not assault. If we took fire, we would withdraw. But here I made a mistake. I should have made it clear our withdrawal would be orderly, phased, not just "get your ass gone." It didn't make a lot of difference as it turned out, but I was embarrassed and angered by the way things went in that regard. I forgot these young men were not combat experienced. . . .

We went through the wire at good intervals, and across a deep ditch just beyond it on a large, square piece of wood, about the size of a railroad tie. The point fire team in a big diamond formation, the squad leader behind, then me. By a good interval, I mean a lot of yards. It was so bright. I had visions of a Chinese blocking force ready to spring an ambush as we approached the base of Detroit where there was still some vegetation. We were on an open piece of ground, hard, and flat. The term "grazing fire" came to mind. There was no cover or concealment. None. A single automatic weapon could have done us immense harm. But obviously the Chinese were focusing on Detroit for the moment. They had detailed no one to intercept the counter attack force, or else our defensive barrage during their attack had broken up their ambush scheme before we got there. That, in fact, is what happened.

. . . It took us ten or fifteen minutes to get across the open ground. Then I saw what may have happened to the ambush detail, if that had been their purpose.

At the base of the hill where we turned to start up a long slope, about 300 yards from the trench, we found the remains of many Chinese soldiers. I didn't go off into the vegetation on either side of the trail to look for more bodies. I'm sure there were more, many more probably. Here there was a dead man, stretched out in the moonlight, apparently unmarked, and then there were pieces of men. I noticed particularly a set of red, dripping human ribs, sitting upright, the rest of the man gone. Their covering barrage, or our counter barrage, had caught them, either as they encircled the hill to swarm it, or as they set up to wait for us. Either way, they went to the next life, brutally hacked to pieces by shrapnel. Of course, physical form is irrelevant after death.

It was too quiet and I was keenly aware of an ambush, but we had a mission. The command diary for that evening said that our little force was driven off by intense artillery fire. So much for that piece of fiction, authored perhaps by the same man who wrote my Bronze Star citation for what ensued. If not the same man, he was equally creative, and ignorant.

As we started up the slope of Detroit, a steep grade, we spread out more, the lead fire team staggered in a skirmish line, the squad leader on the left behind them. I was on the right. One fire team strung out along the brush on our left, the other one the right. Machine gun section between the flanks. And so we went slowly up Detroit, looking at the shadows on either side, but always ahead, straining to see what lay ahead. The hill grew steeper and more so as we came in sight of the crest. The stillness was a presence of its own, the moon so white. I saw my shadow on the ground.

The slope of Detroit was bare, shell craters, one superimposed on the other, worse than I remembered. Lt. Conway had called for VT on position when he sensed the attack, as I had done three nights before. The Chinese barrage had been intense, as well, big caliber shells. A place of sacrifice.

. . . Then the lead fire team, the Sergeant and I, were within twenty yards of the trench and we could see that the bunkers were broken, akilter. The trenches were mostly reduced to rubble, a shallow ditch, and it was here the terrain did us an odd favor. The slope took a steeper incline just there, the last few yards to the crumbled trench, so precipitously that someone firing down on us would find us in a sort of hollow, a protected zone. They would have to stand up literally and fire down at us. They let us get to there, out of fear, stupidity, or maybe they were in shock too, from their guns and ours. Or they may have been green troops unsure of what to do. I don't know, but it was their doom. My grenade sergeant at Parris Island, the one who did not curse, would have been proud of me.

Both machine guns started firing at once and as soon as I heard them, I yelled out loud to the men, "Get back. Get out of here." And I flung myself down flat on the ground. The mission then was done. They had let us come in close, but they had erred. The guns were light machine guns, I judged from the sound of them, not their standard burp guns. They had a higher pitch to them, firing in rapid bursts. I didn't know what was happening to anyone else, although as I learned later, they were obeying orders, withdrawing very rapidly, without any regard for their comrades who were up with me. Oddly, I did not feel a sense of haste. I scanned the trench ahead of me. To the right of a destroyed bunker, the muzzle flash of one of the guns was very clear, truly not more than twenty yards away up that steep slope. The moon was huge and bright behind me.

I got my knees under me and took the grenade out of my left hand jacket pocket, bent over with my head about touching the ground. It was in this position, I learned later, that a round of machine gun fire struck me between the shoulder blades, penetrated the jacket, ricocheted off my flak vest, and out of the jacket again. Ready, pull pin, throw! I threw the grenade vigorously, on a nice trajectory, not too high, and it was a good throw. There was so much moonlight I could follow the grenade through the air, right to the hole in which the man was standing, a remnant of our trench. The grenade landed right beside the hole, on the edge of it, and rolled in at his feet. The muzzle of his gun was still flashing when the grenade roared upward in a burst of light, tearing him in shredded parts. I gave him not a second thought. My flank was secure.

But still the chatter of another gun, same sound, to my left. I got my rifle, got up, crouching, and started moving laterally about the hill, looking up and trying to find the gun while running on that cratered slope. I stepped down hard on my left ankle, full weight on it, and felt it creeling, first to the left, then back again, and the heat rushed through it. I pitched forward, sprawling. I knew it was hurt, sprained I thought. In fact, it was broken, the low-topped "boondocker" shoe we wore gave no protection for such an incident. I got up, hobbled a few steps, and saw the gun spitting bullets. I went flat on the ground again. The gunner was not firing in short bursts, he had the trigger down. The gun was located in the notch in the trench where we had entered the position, just about between the bunker I had occupied and the one straight across the trench from it. There was a cover or "roof" over the trench right there as well.

Then an odd thing occurred which made me think later, when I had time to consider it, that one of their people was not thinking very well at that point in time. He fired a rocket launcher, something like a 3.5 inch bazooka we used against tanks or bunkers. But he fired it at the general direction of the MLR, not down the hill at our people. I doubt it was a signal device, so what did he have in mind? The machine gun is still firing, so there were two of them. Then a couple of hand grenades burst in front of me, one of them not more than ten feet from my face. I am looking directly at the explosion, an orange light, and the shrapnel should have found me, but a young Marine, PFC. Mounds, stepped between the grenade and me at that very instant, taking all the metal in the calves of his legs. I did not get a piece of it. He passed by me. I have my second grenade in my hand, on my knees again, and I threw again, another vigorous throw. Too hard, I thought, but maybe not. It may have hit the cover above their heads and dropped down between them, or it could have taken the gunner right in the face. The gun was still flashing as the grenade roared, leaving me alone in silence on that burial place. There was not a sound. I lay there on my rifle, looking at the shadows in the ruins above me, searching for a sign that I must fight some more. Nothing. After a few seconds I knew, simply as one knows a thing intuitively, that the Chinese soldiers were dead. They represented no danger to me. I could leave. And so I did. . . .

Limping, very slowly, I went down that long, steep hill. It was quiet except for my own sounds, foot steps on the pummeled ground, my own grunts of pain, a gasp if it was sharp, carrying my rifle with bayonet fixed in my right hand, watching my step in the moonlight. My troops were gone. I don't know what I thought in those few minutes, just getting down, but not concerned about Chinese. They were spent certainly. Not many had survived the assault. They took at least one prisoner off and left a few people to engage us. Marine prisoners. I don't like the idea, still, but our posture there invited the event. . . .

At the bottom of the hill, I passed by the butchered men, reached the dry, hard ground and turned right toward the MLR. Private Mounds was standing there, his weight more on one leg, the other bent like a hurt animal would do, favoring the injured limb. I had no doubt of what I should do. I went over to him straight away, changed my grip on the rifle so it was pointing down, and then brought it up, and then down again hard, like a spear, driving the bayonet into the ground several inches, deep enough that it stood there. It is odd, I could not just throw down my rifle. As far as I know, it is still there, in that same place, my private monument to the Imjin War. Then I bent down and put my right arm between his legs and got him on my right shoulder, a fireman's carry. Something else I learned at Parris Island. Thus, we started toward the MLR, slow, painful steps for me. I could hear my breath, and his soft sounds of pain, both his legs full of grenade fragments, his blood on my jacket now. I have it still, a priceless thing. I don't know how long it took me to cover those 600 yards to the ditch in front of our wire. No matter. Young bodies can endure so much. We got to the cross tie over the ditch and I knew I couldn't walk across it alone, much less with him on my shoulders. I sort of sat down and he rolled gently off me to the ground, groaning. Once more, as so many times before, I was soaked with sweat, even in the cool night air. The moon was still brilliant in the blue-black sky.

"Marines" I called out. "Lt. Watson here. We need help! I have a wounded man!" Fuck, I was a wounded man.[7]

Detroit Postscript

In researching material for this book, the author considered the story of Lieutenant Watson's patrol to Detroit as quoted above, to be one of the finer narratives of personal experience written about the outpost war. Then a sequel, written by Lt. Henry ("Monk") Conway, surfaced. A few years ago, Monk had occasion to read Watson's account, as quoted here, and wrote him a letter in response. The bulk of that letter follows:

Dear Bill,

After the shelling you took on that outpost on October 2 and 3 along with Frisco, Seattle and Warsaw, Van Zuyen called me to his CP on October 5 and said that he was going to send me with a reinforced squad from my platoon to relieve the squad from your platoon. By this time I was aware of how dangerous Detroit was and so, without invitation, I reached below his bunk, on which I was sitting, seized the ever present bottle and without objection on his part, took a long pull and returned to my platoon to make ready.

I was scared stiff going out there but was confident, after the shelling and probes we took at Bunker Hill, that we would measure up to anything that was likely to be thrown at us. Unlike you, until it happened, I never anticipated the enormous magnitude of the artillery assault that befell us.

... About 7 PM on October 6 we began to receive regular shelling. Now it was no longer intermittent but steady; one after the other. At this time a Puerto Rican Marine went berserk in the CP and had to be subdued. He was put on the cot and he began to babble in Spanish. From the rhythm I took it to be prayers. We needed them because just at that moment the shelling, now multiple and consistent, thundered down. It seemed to last forever. . . .

The effect of that shelling was calamitous. Apart from those wounded and killed, the bunkers, such as they were, broke down but even more disastrous, the dirt from the sandbags and the roof of the bunker covered the extra ammunition we had stored in the CP. We were in dusty chaos.

Not long after the barrage lifted the cry went up, "Here they come." I shouted "Everybody out." We took our stand in the trench at the point where the path and the CP met. At that time and at that place, we were a fighting force of seven. I do not know what happened to the other fifteen men, but I had no time to rally any more because the Chinese were upon us.

We took them as they came up to the trench at the CP and the path. I saw countless heads coming at me, bobbing and weaving. They wore khakis with red borders on their collars. When we opened up, they could not have been more than 10 feet away. None of them made it into the trenches, but they did not fall as we shot into them; they faded away. I remember one, a handsome Chinese about my age. I fired into him with my carbine on full automatic. He did not drop but his arms and body began to jerk about, as if he were a marionette doing a dance, then he went away.

. . . At this time I took two men and led them along the east side to the trench on the north side of the hill to see what was up. As I got further along the curving trench line, all was silent. I then realized that if the Chinese were further down the trench line, I was hell bound along with the two men behind me. I returned to our original stand at the CP.

Upon returning I saw a tall, jug eared, olive skin BAR man, whose name I cannot remember, standing in the trenches. I heard him say, in a conversational tone, "Hey, that one blew my hand right off." The next thing I remember I was out of the trenches, standing on top of the hill and the BAR man, by cradling the rifle in what was what was left of his left arm, was firing down our trench line from east to west. I never saw him again.

Tharp, the radio man, with his pack on his back was standing next to the BAR man firing down the path as it came by the CP. I called for him to request VT on our position. At this time I did not care that we might be killed by our own incoming. Most of the men were already dead and the rest, including me, would soon join them. . . .

The next thing I remember is crouching down along side the flame thrower operator who was badly wounded in the arm. He was at the entrance to the bunker between the CP and the machine gun bunker facing the MLR. We used it for our ammo dump. He was trying to tie a thick rubber strip around his arm to stop the blood. I finished the job for him and we tried to get the flame thrower working. He turned the nozzle and I struck matches to light it. It sputtered a couple of times and went out. He then gave me an M1 and a bandoleer to replace my carbine which was now out of ammo. We were completely ruined. I called out, "It's everyman for himself" and began running down the trench, this time from east to west.

I passed several burning bodies, heard rifle fire, and then it happened. A hook on my boot caught the communication wire on the floor and sides of the trench and I went down. I thought I was going to die and was sure that bullets would start ripping into me. Then, a most strange thing happened; I had a vision of a beautiful, black haired, fair skinned woman who resembled no one I ever knew. The apparition quickly passed when a Marine using the bunker facing the MLR west of the "ammo dump" called to me.

I made the mistake and went into the bunker.

It was occupied by the man who called out. He was lying along the west side of the bunker and Zolo, a machine gunner, was at the aperture. I was against the east side with my head at the bunker entrance. We were trapped. One Marine was taking pot shots down the trench line. I heard the VT explode above but it did not have the desired effect. Not long afterward the gooks blew a hole in the west side of the bunker, and shortly thereafter a grenade came spinning through the hole. I can see it now, the fuse spitting its shower of sparks. It was going to land between us.

I drew myself up on my right side into the fetal position trying to get all of me inside my helmet. When the grenade exploded, my face felt as if it had been torn away from my head. My hands went to my face, and I could feel and taste globs of flesh and blood all over my face. I then lost all control over myself and began screaming, "My face, My face," and rolled around the floor. Not long afterward I realized my face was not blown away (only a piece the size of a dime under the right eye was gone). I had been struck by body parts from the Marine opposite me. Zolo was breathing very slow and low with a croaking uneven sound and then it stopped. It was then that I yelled, "Surrender! Surrender!" I threw my M1 out of the bunker, looked up and saw a gook pointing a burp gun at me.

When I left the bunker, several Chinese took me to the top of the hill. The irony of my euphoria in being alive did not penetrate my dazed state, but standing there I heard machine guns open up. I thought they were our guns and that the counter attack had started. Not until I read your account, Bill, did I realize that it was the gooks shooting at you on your way up the path. I remember thinking, "What a Hollywood finish." But as you came up the path, I was being dragged down the north side of the hill by various members of the Chinese People's Volunteers. Three others were captured; all four of us were wounded. Two returned to the MLR and as you know, seventeen died.

That's my story. Until this moment I have been unable to reveal all of that tale to anyone. I tell it to you by way of personal purgation and because, after reading your chapter on Detroit, I know that we share a passionate interest in that obscure battle of 6 October 1952. I've had a difficult time keeping those events from taking over my life. I have thought of that battle every day since it was fought and have been very hard on myself because of the loss and my surrender. Even though I know that we stood our ground and fought the good fight, I still cannot rid myself of the image of an all too eager killer too cowardly to take the death his enemy has offered and which, in their opinion, he deserved.

But hope springs eternal. Recently I determined to make peace with myself. Your book has helped me immensely but after 41 years of war, peace comes slowly. It has been difficult for me to realize I was vulnerable and that I was unable to endure the unendurable. Still it is comforting for me to finally realize I was not Achilles, the god like, but tried to be Hector, the citizen-soldier. Ours was but to do or die. We tried both. I salute you.

Very truly yours, Monk [8]

Lieutenant Conway spent eleven months in Chinese prison camps. He was released in September 1953.

AMBUSHING THE AMBUSH

The night of 4 October was overcast and chilly. The temperature hovered around 40 degrees. At 2030, fifteen men from the division's Reconnaissance Company, including two from Tank Recon, departed the MLR from Easy Company, 2/1's, sector abutting the neutral corridor. The objective of the patrol was Hill 90 (formerly called OP White when it was part of the old OPLR). Currently up for grabs, the hill was owned by any side that occupied it.

Intelligence sources indicated that a Chinese squad was setting up a tank-killer team on the hill. Here, the Chinese would be able to overlook a road and firing positions in front of the MLR frequently used by tanks when they supported infantry encroachments into no-man's-land. It was a fine spot to ambush a tank.

On this night, the Marines were to circle the hill and approach the enemy from the north at his rear. The intent was to ambush the ambush. Once the patrol was in position, a tank, acting as a decoy, would leave the MLR and begin an approach down the road toward Hill 90. While the enemy's attention was fixed on the approaching tank but before it got within range, the recon patrol was to attack. As usual, the unforeseen occurred.

The patrol took its time getting to the base of Hill 90; the men were quiet and methodical and walked stealthily. They kept OP Marilyn between them and the objective for as long as they could. Then, they struck off and circled the rear of Hill 90. It took them four hours to reach the base of the hill, a distance of approximately 2 miles.

The Chinese discovered the column as it worked its way uphill and fired a 3.5-inch rocket into its flank, which wounded two men. With no supporting arms, the point of the patrol was pinned down. Pfc. Howard Davenport wrote:

> We were truly outgunned with an estimated 50 Chinks on the hill. I was with George Samaha on my right and Paul Hess was to my left and behind. Suddenly, John Allen was hit in the face and chest. He died instantly. One of the tankers [McNamara] was hit about the same time and his arm was just hanging on.
>
> Samaha and I had been John Wayneing it up the hill, firing as we went. Until Allen got hit, then I lost all my courage, as did Samaha. We just stopped and hugged the deck. Bill Clark was firing a BAR. He kept yelling that Allen was dead, and laid down a continuous stream of fire toward the Chinese. He was magnificent.
>
> The patrol held on for over an hour. All of us with the exception of Hess, Lt. Williams, Guidry and one other were hit. Finally, we gathered our wounded and dead and left the hill with the enemy in pursuit. I had a choice of carrying Allen or covering the rear. I carried him for some time, but felt that as I was only slightly wounded, I might be more useful covering the rear. I changed positions, and the men passed their ammo and weapons back to me.
>
> We came down the hill and cut sharply west toward the no fire zone that ran just west of OP-2. We set up a defense on a bridge at the edge of the Neutral Zone and the Chinks stopped their chase. We placed Allen and others on jeeps that had responded to our call. We then called the roll and found that Joey Shockley was missing. We went to a line company CP and had coffee. Lt. Williams said we had to go back for Shockley and asked for volunteers. He looked right into my eyes as I took a drink of coffee and said, "Thanks Davenport, I knew you would go." Then the others volunteered. The strange part of this was that I didn't volunteer. I must have looked a certain way and the lieutenant thought I did. Later he would comment that when I volunteered, the others simply followed suit. I told him many times over that I never volunteered, but he would always say what courage I had to spark the group to volunteer. To this day I don't know if he was kidding me or really believed that I volunteered that night.
>
> We went out to recover Shockley accompanied by a group of infantry from the MLR [Easy Company, 2/1] augmenting our depleted team. This time we rode on tanks to within 200-300 yards of Hill 90. All of us were cold, and our boots were wet from fording a stream previously. Aboard the tank I sat behind the turret warming my boots on the muffler cover. The warmth felt great. My buddy Hess didn't

[fare] too well. He was riding on the side of the turret, and every time we brushed by a tree limb it knocked him off. After the third time I suggested that he ride along side me so I could care for him (a continuing joke between us). Doing so, he, too, began warming his boots on the tank muffler. When we jumped from the tank, we discovered our error. The tank muffler had heated the soles of our boots so that we couldn't walk on them. An enormous hot foot. All we could do was jump around in an odd looking dance till our boots cooled sufficiently to walk on. We must have looked ridiculous.

As dawn broke we all moved up the hill in a skirmish line, maybe thirty of us. My fire team consisted of Paul Hess of Coryon, Indiana, Jim Willis of Lafe, Arkansas, George Samaha of Norwalk, Ohio, and myself. The first thing we encountered was barbed wire with an enemy bunker about twenty yards beyond. Trying to cross the wire, I became entangled and slowed. I was sort of hoping that the guys would get ahead of me, but they waited till I got clear. Now I found myself in a direct line with the front of the bunker, up a slope of 60 degrees. My three heroic buddies called out that they would cover me as I threw a grenade.

I struggled to remove the pin as the crimp was tight. Finally I managed to free it on the front sight of my grease gun. I called out again for my brave warriors to "cover me" and tossed the grenade underhanded since the aperture was so small. The hill was so steep that as soon as I tossed the grenade, I lost balance and fell flat. I began sliding down the hill. Rocks, dirt and quite possibly the grenade, following me as I slid. It was gratifying to hear a dull thump as the grenade exploded inside the bunker.

Moving up we were faced with another bunker in the identical situation, directly in front of yours truly. We went through the same "cover me," and "cover me" again—as I struggled with the pin. Again, I tossed the grenade underhanded and slipped and fell downhill amid tumbling rocks and dirt.

We encountered a third bunker identical to the others, surrounded by loose rock and up a steep slope. I was still in front and noted that the aperture was larger on this one. I found great pleasure in announcing to the guys that I was fresh out of hand grenades. Hess called for me to use one of his and tossed me an old rusted grenade that appeared to have been left over from WW I. I was actually afraid to pull the pin. I told the team that I was not going to use Hess's defective grenade. To my astonishment, Hess suggested that we charge the bunker firing our weapons. He even said that he would accompany me. This we did and discovered to our surprise that the enemy had covered the aperture with a tarp. Had we thrown a grenade, it surely would have deflected back to us. Finding the bunkers abandoned we reached the top of the hill only to find that Bill Clark had beat us there. It was now full daylight.

We searched the hill and could not find Joey Shockley or evidence of wounds. He never was found. Most of us felt that he was dead, and the Chinks had taken his body. Or, that he was wounded and they killed him. We left the hill cold, wet, sad, and hungry. But we left with a pride that we had gone back to look. We had done our best to recover one of our own.

We later heard propaganda loudspeakers on the line calling for us to surrender so that we could play football with Shockley. From this we still didn't know he was alive until Operation Big Switch [the prisoner exchange beginning 5 Augist 1953].

(Shockley and I shared the same birthday, December 25th, and I sent him a card on Christmas in 1953. We corresponded some, but he was bitter, and would say that we left him out there. I tried to explain the confusion that night, but he didn't seem to get over it. He stopped writing after a few letters.)[9]

In one of his many letters home, Lieutenant Colonel Williamson referred to the performance of his two recon men that night:

> Two of my men were out with a small group on patrol the night before last when they were hit by a platoon of the enemy. These men had just received reconnaissance training, and this was the first time they'd fought. Sgt. Getman charged up the hill and cut down about six with his Tommy gun. The other man, McNamara, was hit in the arm by a bazooka round. Despite his wounds, he grabbed another wounded man and dragged him off down the hill. There followed a cowboy and Indian battle for almost half a mile through the darkness, as the outnumbered Marines, dragging their wounded, withdrew, pausing momentarily to blast at the pursuing foe. McNamara was again hit in the same arm by machine gun fire. He continued to fire with his good arm. I didn't get to see him, but hear that he'll probably lose his arm.[10]

The decision to create and train a tank recon team had proved to be a good one. The men would have to pay their dues in no-man's-land, and, for some, it would be too much. Yet, like Davenport, there were always young men willing to volunteer.

Because nearly the entire 7th Regiment was now on line, with only Charlie Company left in reserve, the division's Reconnaissance Company was operationally attached to that regiment. On 7 October, it moved to the regimental reserve area and immediately began conducting patrols forward of the MLR.

At 1915 on 7 October, ten men from the recon company, led by 2d Lt. Lee Cook, left the MLR to set up an ambush screen in front of Outpost Warsaw. Cook recalled:

> We hadn't moved 100 yards down the path toward Warsaw when incoming from 120mm mortars knocked us silly. In seconds half the patrol was killed and the rest of us wounded. The gooks hit all the outposts and Marine positions at exactly the same time. It appeared to be an all out attack to take the outposts. They fired burp guns from the lower slopes around Warsaw and the Hook. Those of us that could move continued on toward the outpost.
>
> On Warsaw I was led to the CP and found that the officer in charge and all of their NCO's were either wounded or dead. I told their company commander by radio of the situation as best I could and advised that I and my men would stay on the outpost.[11]

Lieutenant Cook took command of Warsaw. The remnants of his patrol integrated among the defenders on the hill and together they fought through the night to hold the outpost. By dawn, the attack died out and Warsaw held. As the firing and confusion waned, Cook was able to remove his wounded and dead to the MLR.

The battalion reported eight killed and twenty-one wounded on Warsaw that night. Of that number, five of the dead and five of the wounded were from the ten-man reconnaissance patrol. Lieutenant Cook was among the wounded.

RELIEF OF THE 1ST MARINES

The division's center sector, the area between the 7th Marines and the KMCs, was still defended by the 1st and 2d Battalions of the 1st Marines, as it had been in September. Forward of the MLR, the battalions controlled eight outposts, from the company-sized bastion of OP-2 on the left to the squad on tiny Stromboli on the right.

For the 1st Marines, enemy activity was minimal that first week. Fighting was generally confined to small patrol engagements in no-man's-land and harassing incoming fire to the MLR. Outposts fought off occasional probes, but the enemy made no serious effort to drive off the Marines.

At 1835 on 6 October, Dog Company reported that Outpost Hedy was being attacked by an unknown number of enemy. A firefight ensued and was terminated at 1910 when the Chinese withdrew. They had been probing for weaknesses. At 2005, the outpost came under attack and was soon surrounded. VT fire was requested but not delivered because of the vagueness of the situation. Simultaneously, the attackers directed their attention up the ridge to Bunker Hill, and, at 2045, a platoon from George Company, the battalion reserve, was committed to support the line. The platoon leader took one squad to reinforce Hedy, and the fighting continued.

Five minutes after midnight on 7 October, the Marines on Hedy reported that the enemy had taken the crest of the hill. The remaining two George Company squads were dispatched to drive them off. At 0040, the fight began. Aided by a Marine mortar bombardment, the platoon was able to drive the Chinese from the hill two hours later.

Enemy strength at the time was estimated at fifty-five. Their casualties were eighteen killed, sixteen wounded, and one prisoner. The Marines lost two killed and thirty wounded.

Pfc. Andy ("Brick") Frey, with George, 3/1, was one of the Marines who had moved out from the battalion reserve that night. Reaching Hedy, he was detailed to help evacuate casualties from the hill. He recalled:

Chas and I teamed up with two other Marines and began carrying dead or wounded back to the MLR. Going out to the outpost for a third trip, the four of us moved out at a pretty good clip. Then all hell broke loose. We had started up the ridge toward the trenchline when we began receiving incoming. It literally rained on us and we hit the deck. It kept coming and coming, each round exploding louder, and throwing dirt into the air. It was landing so close that several times I was picked up and thrown to the ground. I was covered with flying dirt, and I really thought it was all over for me. At that moment I know I made my peace with the Lord. Then it stopped. Suddenly, like someone had turned a switch, it was quiet.

I don't know how long I lay there. I was dazed, and my ears were ringing. I couldn't hear very well at all from my right ear. Then I heard Chas yelling to see if I was OK. He told me later that he had been yelling for quite a while, but I was either deaf or unconscious. Seeing me lying there without responding, he thought I had bought the farm. Chas checked the other two men with us and found that they, too, were all right. I don't know how any of us made it.

Continuing up the hill to the OP, we yelled that we were Marines coming in, and we returned safely to the CP bunker. There we found a commotion going on and learned that in our absence, Cpl. Santo had captured himself a prisoner. It seems that Santo had gotten into some hand to hand combat with a Chinese soldier and given the guy a rifle butt to the head, knocking his eye out. Nonetheless it was a prisoner and good for five days R&R in Japan. I understand that Santo also earned a Silver Star that night.[12]

Thus, even while the line was quiet, it really was not. Quiet war is a relative term. Compared to the 7th Marines, the 1st Marines had it quiet that month. Regimental casualty figures for October reflect the degree of "quiet": 32 killed, 3 missing, and 318 wounded.[13] Fortunately for the 1st Marines, it went into reserve on 12 October and remained there until 26 October. On that date, Item and How Companies, 3/1, were moved forward and attached to the 7th Marines. They participated in one of the major engagements of the outpost war—the battle for the Hook.

RETURN OF THE 5TH MARINES

From the date of relief, enemy probes of Charlie Company, 1/5, units on Bunker Hill continued almost nightly. Initially, the attacks took the form of small efforts to break through the perimeter of bunkers and fighting holes on the reverse slope of the hill. Later, the attacks were better coordinated and appeared to be synchronized with ambushes of the nightly supply trains. In all cases, the enemy attacks were repulsed.

A second principal area of action was in the vicinity of OP-2. Here, the Chinese were able to take advantage of the prohibition against firing into the Panmunjom circle and corridor. They carefully set up rockets, mortars, and, in one area, a recoilless rifle just a few feet outside the no-fire zone but inside the O'Daniel Line. (To be on the safe side, Maj. Gen. John O'Daniel prohibited all firing into this area. It was a shame that he did not require the Chinese to adhere to the order, too.) From this position with its one-sided advantage, enemy soldiers were able to fire freely at Marine targets without fear of retaliation, or so they thought.

On 13 October, the Chinese fired at positions on OP-2 with a recoilless rifle set within the O'Daniel Line. It was impossible to return fire without impacting inside the safe zone. Consequently, George Company, 3/5, moved its mortars so that the long axis of their beaten zone fell parallel to the corridor. Forty-five rounds of 60-mm mortar silenced the offending gun, much to the chagrin of the Chinese.

Two, however, could play that game. Shortly after relieving the line, observers on OP-2 discovered that the enemy was using the small Korean town of Kamam-dong, located in no-man's-land near the neutral zone, as a supply point. Apparently, the Chinese felt safe because of the town's close proximity to the no-fire area and the fact that it was still occupied by a few Korean civilians. At 1600 on 13 October, Marines on OP-2 took the town under fire with a 75-mm recoilless rifle. Lt. Col. Andrew Geer described that action in his book:

> ... It was decided to set up a gun [a 75mm recoilless rifle] at the confluence of the neutral corridor and the No Fire Circle. From this position the gun could fire into Kamon-dong and the [supply] trench without danger of violating the sanctity of the corridor—or the circle. At the same time, it would be virtually impossible for the enemy to return the fire without dropping a shell into the circle or onto the corridor.
>
> If the Chinese should send an infantry force to capture the weapon, all that had to be done was to withdraw a few meters into the corridor, wave the attackers farewell or make gestures even more expressive and understood in all languages. . . .
>
> As soon as [Lt. Col. Alexander W.] Gentleman [Battalion Commander, 1/5] and [Lt. Eric] Pedersen [Commander, Recoilless Rifle Platoon] came to a decision, the younger officer guided a gun squad into position. The circle was three yards to the left and the corridor three to the rear. Sgt. William Cox got the gun set in. With studied exactness Pedersen pointed out the targets in relation to the circle. While this was going on, a number of unfriendly civilians and a few in uniform gathered at the edge of the circle to watch the Marines. Disliking what they saw, they shouted, they spat, they threw rocks. Pedersen and his Marines went about the job of getting set in and ignored the hostile spectators.
>
> Cox sighted in on the first house to the right of Kamon-dong. The range was five hundred meters. The first shot had little apparent effect. It disappeared like a drop of water in a dry sponge. The horrendous back blast scattered the irate North Koreans and their anger increased with the sudden fright received. More rocks and insults were hurled at the gun crew. On the second shot a haze of yellow dust blossomed; on the third, the roof fell in and figures were seen pouring from the buildings. Methodically, Cox went about the task of knocking down the mud huts, one by one, from right to left.
>
> The supply of ammunition for the rifle came from an ASP (ammunition supply point) on COP 2. Although ammunition could have been hauled by jeep to within a few yards of the gun by using the corridor, this was against the rules. This meant the carriers in the squad had to man-pack the 75 mm rounds a distance of nine hundred meters.

. . . It was a panting job for the ammunition carriers. PFC. Coleman, six foot three and weighing over two hundred, could shoulder the one hundred eight pound load with more ease and speed than could his mate, PFC. Jose Cordova. For Cordova the weight of the shells was within thirty pounds of his own.

Then Cox hit pay dirt as one of his shots set off an explosion. The village became covered by dust and smoke and the spectators danced with rage. The Marines unshipped the weapon and carried it into the corridor. Kamon-dong, for the time, was finished as a supply point.[14]

The following day, the natives of Kamon-dong set fire to the remaining houses in the town. Chinese soldiers began firing machine guns into villagers who fled to the nearby neutral zone. Marines on OP-2 took the enemy machine guns under fire and stopped the massacre. It was apparent that some of the Korean villagers in Kamon-dong were being used as human shields for an enemy supply point. When the Koreans were no longer advantageous to the Chinese, they began to kill them.

The incident at Kamon-dong provided inspiration for the enlistment of one of the most unusual Marines of the Korean War—a horse. Watching the risks taken by the Marine ammunition carriers at Kamon-dong gave Lieutenant Pedersen the wild idea of using a horse as an ammunition carrier for 1/5's Recoilless Rifle (RR) Platoon. Running the idea past his regimental commander, Pedersen received permission to travel to Seoul and purchase a horse with his personal funds, which he did, thus giving birth to a Marine legend.

Pedersen bought a mare and named her Reckless, after the nickname given to recoilless rifles. She proved to be a huge success and a useful addition to 1/5's RR Platoon.

For the 5th Marines, October passed with numerous small actions—patrol engagements, probes on the outposts, and the constant incoming of harassing fire. George Company on OP-2 reported finding a new Chinese weapon, a 120-mm warhead on a 60-mm mortar shell. When the object landed and failed to detonate, the Marines cautiously examined it. The crude joining of the two missiles potentially offered a deadly but short-range weapon. On Hedy, a flame tank was sent out on the tank road to burn enemy positions on the north slope. It failed because wind conditions were not advantageous. Thus, the outpost war was one of experimentation, as well as attrition. Combatants were willing to try every trick that came to mind. The Marines even tested the absurd notion that helicopters might be useful for moving troops in combat.[15]

ASSAULT ON RENO

In late October, division intelligence anticipated that a buildup of enemy forces would strike Outpost Reno, Carson, or Vegas. As a consequence, prior to 1800 on 26 October, a majority of the supporting arms, artillery, and tanks was directed toward this area. Outpost Reno was further protected by a supplemental platoon dug in at the rear. This position, called Reno Block, guarded the most vulnerable part of Reno and was destined to play a vital role in the fighting to come.

At 1800 on 26 October, an ambush platoon from Easy Company, 2/7, departed for Reno Block. On reaching the hill, the men concealed themselves in prepared positions that had been dug and camouflaged. While they waited, as they had done on previous nights, two companies of Chinese were stealthily circling Reno to attack it from the rear. At midnight, the Marines at Reno Block detected faint noises to their front as enemy troops deployed for the assault. The ambush platoon remained quiet and undetected as the enemy assembled directly in front of them.

Alerting Reno of the presence and location of Chinese troops, the men of the ambush platoon held their fire. When it appeared that the assault was about to begin, they fired. The ambush took the Chinese completely by surprise. When they turned to engage the ambush, the Marines on Reno began shooting. The enemy force was caught in a deadly cross fire and withdrew forty minutes later.

Three hours later, at 0400, another company assaulted Reno from the northeast. This assault also lasted forty minutes before Marine artillery broke it up. Enemy casualties for this encounter were estimated at sixty killed and fifty-six wounded. The Marines kept Reno but lost nine killed and forty-nine wounded.

By month's end, the Chinese had successfully occupied six Marine outposts (three in the KMC sector) and temporarily occupied two others, as well as a portion of the MLR itself. The intensity of the fighting can be indicated by the casualty figures reported in the Division Command Diary. During October 1952, the Marines sustained 186 killed, an additional 18 who later died of wounds, 1,481 wounded, and 113 missing in action. On the Chinese side were 5,233 known and estimated killed. Enemy wounded was estimated at 4,850, and the Marines took 15 prisoners.[16] The ratio approximated three Chinese casualties for each Marine killed, captured, or wounded.

The lesson here appears to be that the Chinese were willing to pay a high price for driving the Marines from a few hills and outposts. To them, it was affordable. Even if the Marines had the manpower, which they did not, would they have been willing to pay as high a price to regain those positions? Would the American people allow a war to continue that cost an estimated 1,800 casualties per month? The question, of course, is rhetorical, but it illustrates the futility of Americans fighting a war of attrition with a foe that is willing to lose more men than they are. Regrettably, the lesson was not learned, and the strategy was repeated fifteen years later in Vietnam.

CHAPTER 10

RETAKING THE HOOK

A swift and vigorous transition to attack . . .
is the most brilliant point of defense.
—Clauswitz, *On War*, 1832

During an interview by Navy Lt. Hebry Searls, Marine Pvt. Robert Crossno related the following:

> There were forty of us at the end of the Hook . . . two of us in this bunker with the light machine gun. By eleven o'clock there were just the two of us left, I guess. There were Chinks twenty feet down the trench. One would pop around the corner and toss a grenade: we'd spot the sparkle in the dark and shoot. Then we'd dive out of the bunker and wait for the explosion, and dive back in afterward. This happened maybe two or three times. The last time the Chink hit the gun, and me too, in the hip and legs. That time we just kept going, crawling down the reverse slope of the ridge. We ran into some Reds in the draw. They were walking around near us, so we lay quiet.
>
> Somehow we got separated there. I lay down in the draw that night, and the next morning crawled near the river and slept under a tree. I was trying to find our lines. That night I slept again. The next morning I crawled back up another hill. Then I found I'd crawled back up the Hook again, but it was OK—the Marines had it back.[1]

The Hook was not an outpost. It was a piece of the MLR, a continuation of rocky trench line, sandbagged bunkers, and fighting holes. It was also one of the few sections of line that could not be fully protected by the outpost defense so successfully used elsewhere. On 26 October 1952, the Hook fell to an overwhelming assault by Chinese forces. A day later, it was regained by the Marines. In the interim, 70 Marines died, nearly 400 were wounded, and 39 were missing, 27 of whom were later confirmed as captured.

Once again, the Chinese demonstrated that when they wanted a position badly enough and were willing to pay the price, they could take it. On 26 and 27 October, it cost the Chinese 532 killed and 216 wounded to take the Hook, but, despite the price, they were unable to hold it.

In October 1952, the six miles of the MLR in the 7th Marines area meandered its way northeast to the boundary with the British Commonwealth Division. The terrain here was a little more rugged than in the west. The hills became higher and steeper until they fell abruptly into the broad valley of the Samichon River.

Known as Point Fox to defenders earlier in the year, the Hook was a vital segment of the Marine MLR. It was also extremely vulnerable. It was more or less astride a ridge that ran directly into Communist lines and was under observation by them from higher ground. The former outpost, Seattle, which the Chinese had seized on 2 October, lay only 500 yards northwest of the Hook.

As poor a military position as the Hook was, the Marines had no alternative but to occupy it. In enemy hands, the consequences would be catastrophic. One observer at the time postulated that Chinese occupation of the Hook "would afford a corridor to outflank our right (NE) flank and reach the Imjin River. This in turn would not only cut us off from the adjacent 1st Commonwealth Division, but would probably render untenable our whole position beyond the Imjin. At the very least, possession of 'The Hook' and adjoining ridge would give the Communists observation of a substantial portion of our rear areas beyond the Imjin, as well as vital crossings of the river."[2]

In the opinion of a major general from the British Commonwealth Division, had the salient been lost, "a withdrawal of 4,000 yards would have been necessary."[3]

THE DEFENSE

The 7th Marine Regiment continued to retain its three battalions on line while holding only a single company in reserve. To augment this meager reserve, the regiment pulled from division resources. The Reconnaissance Company was moved forward and attached to the 7th Marines, where it was deployed as a regular infantry company to back up the line. The regiment had nearly four thousand men, supported by one tank company, and thirty-eight light, medium and heavy pieces of artillery.

Opposing the 7th Marines were two regiments of Chinese infantry numbering about seven thousand men, supported by nine or ten battalions of Chinese artillery—approximately 120 guns. Intelligence reports indicated that 62.5 percent of the enemy's artillery facing the entire

Marine front was directed at one regiment, the 7th Marines. Defending 10,000 yards of line, the proper frontage for a division, the regiment was spread dangerously thin.

In October, the order of battle for the 7th Marines was the 2d Battalion, on the left, responsible for Outposts Carson, Reno, and Vegas; the 3d Battalion, in the center, with Outposts Berlin and East Berlin; and the 1st Battalion, on the right, manning Outposts Ronson, Warsaw, and Verdun. Outpost Ronson had been created on 16 October, after the loss of Seattle, to protect the Hook. Outpost Ronson was not much of a position. Capt. Fred McLaughlin, Commander, Able Company, 1/7, described it best in an interview with the author:

> Ronson was nothing. It was just a little dimple out there on the way to bigger things, but it was about halfway out where we would go and harass Chinese at their mainline positions. We would stash ammunition and supplies there. One of the men came in one night and said he had lost his Ronson lighter out there, that's how it got its name "Ronson."[4]

A significant terrain feature on the Hook was Hill 146, the high ground behind the actual defense positions. From the Main Supply Route (MSR) in the rear, approaching the Hook, the Marines had to climb uphill to Hill 146, pass over or around it, and then descend to trenches on the Hook. Conversely, men departing the Hook for the rear first climbed uphill where they were frequently exposed to enemy observation and fire from the Chinese-held ridgeline beyond.

Captain McLaughlin recognized just how difficult the Hook would be to defend:

> The terrain was very high. Our lines ran way too long. We had to cover two, maybe three times as much line as would normally be assigned to a defensive company. I had the third platoon on the left, almost out in front. They sort of faced a little bit to the west as the Hook was sticking way out there like a big old nose. The right flank drifted on back towards the east at a not so precipitous angle. It was covered by another platoon. Boy, that was a long distance to cover. One platoon, reinforced by FOs mainly, would be out there in front on Outpost Warsaw. So, there you have two platoons covering a two company area with one platoon out in front.
>
> I always felt a little bit leery about the capability of the enemy to sweep the east side of Warsaw and maybe come up on my right flank. They had several patrols out there that we detected, but we had some

pretty alert lads and we managed to shoo them off whenever we detected them. We had such an odd arrangement that we did a number of things to augment our defenses. For example, I don't know if it's common terminology now or not but we had an expression called "Canadian wire." I think it was probably referred to later as random wire, but anyway, it was not like the old World War I wire that you put out with stakes. This was great big ol' bales of round wire that we just threw down the mountain so to speak. It lay there coiled like a serpent ready to grab.

Then the kids decided that they wanted to do something else. Let me digress. I was thirty-two years old, the oldest man in the company. My average Marine was barely twenty years old. I worked that out one day. These kids were young. I'd say that 80 percent of them were eighteen years old. My lieutenants were barely twenty-one. I think the oldest lieutenant I ever had was twenty-four or twenty-five. A couple of the platoon sergeants or the first sergeants might have been in their late twenties.

. . . I'll never forget one time, there was a lieutenant colonel from division who came up. He wanted to see one of our bunkers in particular. We had several that we had dug into the forward line, enfilade. We wanted to see to the front, so we dug through to where we had an opening that let us see forward. This lieutenant colonel wanted to get in one and see what it was like to look out through the aperture and see enemy lines. He had his helmet and his flak jacket on, and we emphasized that he should be very, very careful and keep low as we crept up through the trench into the bunker.

It was early in the morning, just turning daylight. I was sitting there with him. Of course, I had my helmet and flak jacket on too. We were peeking out the aperture when suddenly a figure appeared on the front slope just to the left of us. It was one of my kids again. All he had on was a pair of dungaree trousers. He was barefoot and barechested, and no helmet. Oblivious to his surroundings, he reached into his fly, hauled it out and took a leak standing there in front of God and everybody. I thought that colonel was just going to die. Oh man, did he have a fit about discipline. I chuckled to myself, thinking that the kid figured that by the time he got out of his hole, took his leak and enjoyed the morning view, he would be back in his hole before the Chinese could get a bead on him.

. . . In late-October, Capt. Paul Byrum and his Charlie Company came and took our positions. According to the defense plan, I had to put one platoon, I believe it was the third, under Lt. [John] Babson, out on Warsaw which left me two platoons, a weapons platoon and headquarters kids in the rear. That was a hard thing for the platoon on Warsaw to have to do, go out there after being on line for months.[5]

Normally, in such an undermanned situation as was presented to the 7th Marines, the book says that you cover the weaker, unoccupied portions of your defense by firepower. In that way, the enemy has his hands full holding his own positions in proper repair and strength. On the Hook, however, the Chinese had fire superiority, largely because of the parsimonious allocation of ammunition from U.S. stockpiles.

As a result, not only were the Marines outnumbered and outgunned, but they were short of ammunition. Consumption of ammunition earlier in the month had exceeded expectations. Consequently, for the last eleven days of October, strict allowances of artillery ammunition had been established by U.S. Army Command. Reacting to general comments among Marine infantry regiments concerning the effects of ammunition rationing and in the face of repeated official denials by Eighth Army Command, a Marine officer made inquiries and determined that supplies of sufficient ammunition were indeed being denied to the 1st Marine Division. In an "informal report," he summarized what he had learned, excerpts of which follow:

> The fact is, extremely stringent restrictions were and are in force within the division. This was a matter of such general complaint along the line (and by battalion commanders and staffs) that I obtained from the 3rd Bn, 7th Marines (next Battalion in line to the 1st), a few figures on these restrictions for current periods. During the period 20 Oct.–31 Oct., these were:
>
> 81mm Mortar: 71 rds/day
> 105mm How (HE): 400 rds/day, 7th Mar frontage.
> 155mm How (HE): 75 rds/day, 7th Mar frontage.
>
> Frontage of this typical battalion was *3500* yards, typical in this situation but unheard of by the book. . . . The effect of these restrictions was to reduce firing to the most urgent missions only, or for large bodies of enemy. The complaint was that the enemy could show himself almost at will without receiving fire, that it was impossible either to harass or neutralize his continual fortification activity, let alone embark on systematic destructive fires of the kind he [the enemy] was carrying out.[6]

Although not mentioned in the above report, hand grenades were in short supply and also rationed. Ammunition shortages were so severe that infantry companies on line resorted to indirect fire with machine guns (long-distance overhead fire directed by an observer, like artillery), a technique that had been tactically obsolete since World War I. This was practically the only available method for the Marines to return fire or to prevent a continuing buildup of the enemy's fortifications. Its effectiveness for either purpose was questionable.

An example of the effects of artillery rationing may be derived from the following communication exchange reported by 1st Lt. Walt Mahoney, an artillery forward observer with the 11th Marines:

> While I was FO on Bunker Hill, I saw 5 enemy troops moving down a trench line off to the right and behind Bunker Hill. I rang up the sound powered phone to the Fire Direction Center [FDC] and the following conversation occurred:
> FO: "This is Fox Oboe Charlie—Fire Mission."
> FDC: "Send your mission Fox Oboe Charlie."
> FO: "Azimuth 0225 Coordinates 3425–4500, Five enemy troops in the open—will adjust."
> FDC: "Roger, Wait."
> FDC: "Fox Oboe Charlie——we have to abort the mission! Due to ammo shortage, we need at least ten enemy troops. Over."
> FO: (Pause) "Five more troops have just appeared. We now have ten troops. Over."
> FDC: "Fox Oboe Charlie—mission will be fired."
> FDC: "On the way."
> The fire was adjusted to hit the area where the five troops were spotted. It's hard to believe that you can fight a war on a budget.[7]

Contrasting with the skimpy ammunition allocation in the Marine camp is the following remark attributed to a Chinese division commander opposing the Hook: "In the present we had emplaced 120 guns to each kilometer of front line so that in a rapid fire bombardment of 25 minutes more than 20,000 rounds of ammunition could be hurled against enemy positions. If the fire used in supporting attacks and in repulsing enemy counter-attacks was taken into account the total would reach 70,000 rounds."[8] On 24 October alone, 1,200 rounds of Chinese artillery fell on the Hook.

Lt. Col. Robert Debs Heinl, Jr., was a Marine Corps historian temporarily attached to the 7th Marines. His duty was to observe and report on the war. Being present during the fighting on 26 and 27 October, he practiced his craft by observing, taking notes, and preparing memoranda about his findings. His document, written contemporaneous with the action on the Hook, lends a great deal of credibility to the facts reported elsewhere. His description of conditions on the Hook that resulted from heavy preliminary shelling by Chinese forces is informative:

Throughout 26 October, I "walked the lines" of the 7th Marines, on the customary observer tour. We did not go forward to the Hook, because of the intensification of hostile fire (76mm direct mainly) against that position throughout the day. The battalion commander, while in that area with Brigadier [A. H. G.] Ricketts (British), had been knocked down by the blast of a near miss. Fires were deliberate destruction precision missions; he prohibited observers from visiting the Hook, and gave us a vivid description of the condition of the defenses there: broken caved in trenches, certain bunkers pinpointed and destroyed, and defensive wire largely cut or demolished. Until five days before, he related, they had been in good shape but were now poor, as a result of systematic destructive firing each day. It reminded me (as a naval gunfire officer) very much of our deliberate, pre D-day bombardment before a landing attack, and I told him so.[9]

Intelligence data, it seems, were a little slow in filtering their way down the chain of command. The previous evening, for example, Colonel Heinl had attended a briefing at Division Headquarters for the commanding general. There, the G-2 officer had commented on the intensification of enemy fire near the Hook and that unverified POW information suggested that an attack was planned for 26 or 27 October. Colonel Heinl reported that, by lunch the following day, Lt. Col. Leo Dulacki, 1/7 battalion commander, had not yet been informed of those intentions. The increase in shelling, however, alerted all personnel that something was afoot. There was little that could be done. The 7th Marines were fully committed.

THE BATTLE BEGINS

On 23 October, Chinese intentions began to come into focus as the tempo of artillery fire began to concentrate on the Hook and on Outposts Warsaw and Ronson. As noted previously, the destruction of defenses exceeded the men's ability to rebuild. Nightly, the Marines and two hundred KSCs redug the trench line, restrung barbed wire, and rebuilt deteriorated defenses. Still, they fell behind. The Chinese had more bombs than the Marines had shovels.

As best they could, the Marines fought back. Short on artillery ammunition, they fired what they could—hundreds of shells versus thousands of Chinese shells. An air strike bombed, strafed, and napalmed opposing enemy positions. Tanks fired missions at targets directed by infantry observers. Then, on 24 and 25 October, artillery allotments were eased somewhat, and a two-day artillery duel developed. In the middle of this destruction was the infantry, working on defenses at night and being shelled during the day. Unknown to the Marines, however, the battle, in addition to the shelling, had started much earlier. The Chinese infantry had begun its move days before.

With the weather a clear and crisp 28 degrees, the 3d Battalion, 357th Regiment, of the Chinese Army moved toward the Hook. The forward element, two companies with two days' rations for each man, was within a mile of the Marine MLR. At daylight, the men halted, concealed themselves in the terrain, and waited for nightfall. During the day, two air strikes were called on Chinese positions in the vicinity, but the entire enemy battalion lay undetected, camouflaged in the landscape. Stoically, the soldiers waited for their artillery to prepare the way. That evening, they struck.

Three days of shelling on the Hook, Ronson, and Warsaw had taken a heavy toll. Trenches that had been 6 feet deep were now leveled. Bunkers and gun emplacements had collapsed. Little was left of the defenses.

FIRST THE OUTPOSTS

At dusk on 26 October, the Chinese began their attack. Charlie Company Marines on Outpost Ronson were the first to experience the assault. At 1810, fifty or more Chinese were sighted advancing on the outpost in two groups, one from the east and the other from the west. Heavy mortar and artillery fire to the outpost preceded their advance. The Marines responded with automatic weapons and artillery but were soon overwhelmed. It was simply a matter of too little too late. In less than twenty minutes, the outpost was overrun. Ronson's little squad went down fighting a company of Chinese. Nothing further was heard from the squad, and history does not record if any of the men escaped.

At 1850, Outpost Warsaw was hit, also in overwhelming force. Garrisoned by a reinforced platoon, Warsaw was a tougher nut to crack. The platoon commander, Lt. John Babson of Able Company, called for box-me-in fire, which temporarily slowed the advance but failed to halt it. At 1907, while a relief platoon was being readied to reinforce Warsaw, a radio message came through. The defenders were using bayonets, pistols, hand grenades, and both ends of their rifles to fight off the enemy. Three minutes later, they transmitted, "We're being overrun." At 1944, another message came through requesting VT. The men on Warsaw were calling for air bursts over their own position. This was the last message from Warsaw, and it, too, was assumed lost.

On the remote chance that Marines remained in bunkers and to further neutralize the hill, artillery VT was continued through the night. One 7th Marine Regiment document states simply, "Three survivors from the outpost were recovered."[10] One must assume the accuracy of the report, although it did not elaborate on the circumstances.

THEN THE HOOK

While desperate fighting raged over the two outposts, a major Chinese attack materialized on the MLR. A veritable avalanche of explosives and steel began to saturate trenches on the Hook. According to Lieutenant Colonel Hicks, "Some 34,000 rounds of CCF artillery were used to soften the position before seizure, and when the enemy assault came, there were few left able to resist."[11]

It became apparent that the Hook, then defended by Charlie Company, 1/7, was the enemy's main objective. Capt. Paul Byrum, company commander, reported:

> About 1815 Sunday, I got a call from an outpost. "We're getting clobbered with artillery," they said, "there are Chinese all over the skyline." [This was probably Ronson.] My sergeant and I went along the ridgeline to check on it. There was too much mortar fire coming in. We split up . . . he was killed just afterward. I was buried four times with dirt from near misses.[12]

The Chinese struck the Hook at 1900 with the attacking forces simultaneously assaulting all sides of the salient. It was a well-coordinated, three-pronged attack by a battalion of Chinese opposed initially by a company of Marines. By 1938, enemy troops had reached the main trench line, and, within minutes, a second wave followed. As Chinese soldiers gained a foothold on the Hook, laborers followed them with ammunition, food, and construction material for bunkers and trenches. The Chinese had come to stay.

Pfc. James Yarborough was part of a light machine-gun crew on the Hook when the Chinese attacked under a curtain of falling artillery. During an interview the following day, he related:

> They were coming over the ridge, gangs of them. Just like they say in the papers, they were yelling and blowing horns. They had a horn that sounded like a milk cow. We couldn't get our guns to work, and we had only two grenades. I threw one and my buddy had the pin pulled and was ready to throw the other when he got hit. I threw it. The Chinese were coming down the trench back of our bunker.

We went through the firing hole before they got to the door of the bunker. The hole was so small I could just barely get through. Then I was scared to move and lay close to the bunker because they'd have seen me if I'd made a break.

They started digging around inside and moving sandbags. In about half an hour one of them touched me through the hole while he was moving sandbags. I guess it scared him as much as me, because nobody fired at me when I ran. I hit the wire in about twenty-five yards and dropped again.

I lay there and watched the bunker about two and a half hours. My buddy was still close to it. Finally they came out and it looked as if they were going to shoot him. I still had my carbine and I fired to scatter them. Somehow I got through the wire. My buddy, he got away too.[13]

As enemy soldiers gained the trenches, an FO team of four artillery-men from the 11th Marines became trapped. The team included 2d Lt. Sherrod Skinner, Jr., the FO; Cpl. Franklin Roy, the radio operator; and Pfc. Vance Worster, the wireman. During the assault, Skinner continued to direct artillery fire on the enemy until his communications went out. The artillerymen left the protection of the bunker and fought with the infantry. The lieutenant organized a defensive perimeter and directed machine-gun fire into the enemy. Leaving cover to replenish the depleted supply of grenades and ammunition, Skinner was twice wounded, but he continued to direct the infantry defense until a shortage of ammunition and an overwhelming number of enemy soldiers forced him and his men back into the bunker. Worster and Roy took up positions at the door. They continued the fight with their sharpshooting at enemy soldiers in the trench and killed twelve Chinese before they ran out of ammunition. Trapped in the bunker, they feigned death as Chinese soldiers entered the bunker and searched their bodies.

When they left the bunker, the Chinese threw grenades inside it as a final gesture. Skinner rolled over on one and absorbed the entire blast with his body. The other grenade seriously wounded Worster in the legs. Roy remained with Worster until the early hours of dawn and then left to seek aid.

Unarmed, Roy was wounded twice as enemy soldiers fired at him from an observation bunker. Attaining the top of the position, Roy came upon an open box of hand grenades. He threw grenades into enemy trenches until the box was empty. Simultaneously, he managed to work his way up the hill to the Charlie Company line, where he disclosed the situation existing in the bunker. It was hours before the Marines could fight their way back to the bunker. Skinner and Worster were both dead.[14] Corporal Roy and Private First Class Worster were each awarded the Navy Cross. Lieutenant Skinner was awarded the Medal of Honor.

The momentum of the first assault on the Hook enabled the enemy to gain the trenches and push forward to the crest of the ridge. The outnumbered Marines of Charlie Company were forced back.

BEHIND THE SCENES

When the fighting for the Hook first began, Lieutenant Colonel Heinl was having dinner at the regimental command post some distance away. At 1800, the regimental staff heard the artillery in the distance. Soon, a report indicated that enemy fire on Ronson, Warsaw, and the Hook had intensified. This was followed immediately by a report that Chinese attack forces were seen moving on the outposts. Heinl wrote:

> By this time (1840), the regimental CO [commanding officer] was fully alive to the potential seriousness of the situation, had lifted restrictions on defensive fires, had alerted the regiment's meager reserve, and had directed his Ordnance Officer to start moving such local ammunition reserves forward to the 1st Battalion as the regiment possessed. Shortly afterward, I was present when the division G-3 [operations officer] called for a report (which was given by the R-X) [regimental executive officer] and told the latter that all ammunition restrictions were lifted. Subsequently, about 20 minutes later, Maj. Gen. [Edwin A.] Pollock also called and likewise emphasized that the regiment could have all ammunition it wanted. Meanwhile, the tempo of the incoming on the Hook itself increased heavily. . . . About this time the regimental Ordnance Officer telephoned twice to report that the division dumps would not release ammunition to him (81mm) which he had trucks down to pick up. In order to maintain the forward flow to sustain the defense, R-X, 7th Marines called G-3, and obtained their reiteration that restrictions were off, and promise to get this word to the dumps.
>
> The reserve available for immediate commitment was scanty, Company "A", 7th Marines (really the battalion reserve, but held out under regimental control because three battalions were in line), less one platoon that was already on Warsaw. The regimental commander ordered one of the two remaining rifle platoons committed to back up the north face of the Hook, which, as Warsaw was overrun, was coming under heavy enemy attack. This platoon, I later learned, actually went into line on the left of the Hook, where it was in fact needed, and did useful service throughout the night. The 3d Bn, 1st Marines (from

division reserve) was now ordered to displace from bivouac to the vicinity of the 7th Marines' CP, but still under division control. . . .

By midnight, it was apparent that a serious situation confronted the 7th Marines. This was clearly reflected in the faces and demeanor of the regimental commander and executive officer. Enemy fire was unceasing and his attack continued. . . .

. . . Informal estimates of enemy strength against the Hook suggested the participation by more than one (probably two) enemy battalions. This attack was falling almost entirely on Company C, 7th Marines.[15]

COUNTERATTACK

Charlie Company had been successfully pushed out of position. Earlier that night, a platoon from Able Company had been preparing to relieve Warsaw when the MLR was overrun. This platoon joined the remainder of Charlie Company, located on the crest of the hill, which was firing down on the Chinese on the Hook. Together, they were holding the advance but not driving it back.

It was now the early morning of the 27th. The enemy was successfully established on a small sector of the MLR. The Hook, or at least a portion of it, had fallen. The problem became one of evicting the Chinese, a situation made more difficult because they immediately dug in.

The immediate reserve available to retake the Hook was Captain McLaughlin 's Able Company, which, only days before, had been relieved from the position. Now, it was returning. Captain McLaughlin indicated the following:

> We had not been in the rear for more than forty-eight hours, if that much, when I got the call. The word was to saddle up and get ready to counterattack because the Chinese had taken the Hook. I couldn't believe that they took that thing because we had knocked them off several times before and it was not that hard. Babson was out there on Warsaw. I was still in the rear but I got in contact with him immediately. He said it was bad, really bad. He said Chinese were crawling all over the top of the place and he asked for VT on his own position. I gave him five minutes to get his men under cover and let go with everything we could find as far as supporting arms were concerned. I know we took out a bunch of Chinese, but it didn't help all that much.
>
> Ultimately they took Warsaw. Babson was killed and unfortunately so were his platoon sergeant and many, many others. I had about twenty minutes to prepare a plan of attack. I sent Lieutenant Stan Rauh over to the left flank. His mission was simply to dig in tight and throw out all the fire he could, to draw their attention and hopefully

convince them that we were coming up the left side. I took the remainder of the company. I don't think I had 150 men, but we went up the right side in the middle of the night and swept through the old CP.

We went up on the high ground and started a concerted advance down toward the Hook. I was able to bring in artillery, 81s and 60s, and even got a 4.5 ripple during that period of two to three hours, enough to keep them down and to hold them in place. They didn't get any further than just the Hook. I might add that from what I heard later, from questioning several prisoners we took, 15-year-old kids, that no one knew the plan of attack except the officers. Once they got on the Hook, most of their officers were casualties and the troops didn't know what to do next. They just milled. So we had a whole bunch of Chinese kids with literally a Chinese fire drill.[16]

The plan for recapturing the Hook was dangerous. An attack would have to be straight down the ridge into their old positions, fully exposed to enemy observation and firepower. The Marines would have to contend with defenders in their former trenches and bunkers and with Chinese supporting arms from adjacent hills, including Seattle.

Before daylight, Lieutenant Rauh led the first counterattack with his 2d Platoon of Able, 1/7. Only the day before, Rauh had rejoined his platoon after a stay in the Naval Hospital, Yokosuka, where he had recovered from wounds received in September. In a letter to the author, Rauh recalled the following:

I was called to the Bn CP tent and told by the S-3, Major Jim Short, to "seal off the Hook." I didn't know where "The Hook" was. After a very brief orientation and learning from my new platoon sergeant, Nels Lovemark, that he could get us there we took off with minimal preparation.

The situation on the Hook was reportedly worsening by the moment—it was obvious from the sound of incoming. As we moved up the supply route toward the Hook we were taking lots of incoming—both mortar and artillery.

At one point my radio was shattered, and I attempted to use a nearby tank's infantry phone to order a new radio. The tank was firing over the rear of its hull where the phone is located, and each time I neared the phone he'd crank off a round. The back blast was anything but pleasant. I backed off and had a BAR man blast the tank to get its attention. I got to the phone and a radio was sent up.

A short while later a Willie Peter (WP) round landed nearby and both Sgt. Lovemark and I were hit, he more seriously than I. Hit in the face, Lovemark was evacuated. My WP wounds were mostly to the hands. The WP was so hot it fused the bolt of my carbine to the receiver. Incoming continued. The WP adhered to my hands like glue and continued to burn. Water was unobtainable there so I had several troops urinate on my hands while several others made urine-mud to pack on my hands to cut off the oxygen. My Marines were great and most of the time maintained a superb sense of humor. I heard one young lad yell to the troops in the rear, "Hey, you guys—come up and piss on the lieutenant!" After that I was confident they'd follow me to hell and back. Soon a corpsman (bless them) came up and applied zinc oxide to my wounds.

We continued the march to the Hook through increasing incoming. On reaching the Company C command bunker, Capt. Byrum advised that he had several wounded in the mortar pit and would I go get them? I replied that I would if he'd have a lieutenant who was in the bunker lead me. The captain agreed and assigned Lt. Martin Givot the task.[17]

Two small groups of Marines had been caught by the Chinese encirclement and were surrounded. There, in one of the mortar pits, they had dug in to fight off the enemy and await rescue.

Rauh organized several fire teams of men from his platoon, and, guided by Givot, they fought their way to the trapped men. When they received word that two wounded Marines were pinned down nearby and could not escape, the rescue group counterattacked to the men's position and successfully brought them out. (The next morning, Lieutenant Givot, while attached to How Company, successfully led a counterattack to recapture an enemy-held position. Mortally wounded during the fighting, he was posthumously awarded the Navy Cross.)

As elements of Able Company reinforced Charlie Company, Pfc. Enrique Romero-Nieves distinguished himself when he attacked the enemy as the Marines dug in. In the face of heavy fire, Romero-Nieves directed the emplacement of a machine gun within 75 yards of the enemy. Then, armed only with grenades, he charged a bunker. In midstride, he was hit and knocked to the ground. His left arm rendered useless, he regained his feet and continued to advance. Unable to pull the pin of the grenade with his wounded left hand, he managed to extract the pin by hooking it in his belt buckle and throwing the grenade into the bunker. It killed six Chinese. Romero-Nieves survived and was awarded the Navy Cross.

Rauh's letter continued:

Communications on the hook were terrible due to the incoming, the terrain and the general confusion of battle. At one point I was talking to battalion by radio not three feet away from and facing my radioman when a grenade landed on his chest killing him—I didn't get touched—only severely jarred. A few moments later a mortar fragment tore the flesh off above my knee.

My men continued in a bold effort to run the well armed Chinamen off the hill. Grenades were flying everywhere. I received a grenade wound to the right ankle. Early on the 27th I received orders to pull back. As I passed the word I saw one of my men—a great Marine, a few feet away from an abandoned BAR. I told him to pick up the BAR and pull back. He said, "I can't lieutenant, I'm hit—I'm hit!" I replied, "Grab the BAR and move out you SOB, everyone's hit." I was helped down the hill. This young Marine, a black man, got off the hill by himself—with the BAR. As I was being placed in a vehicle for evacuation, I noticed him being tended to by the Corpsman. He had lost his entire foot.[18]

With the easing of ammunition restrictions, Marine artillery from the 11th Marines continued to saturate Warsaw in an effort to deny benefits of that position to the enemy. The artillery also blasted other enemy targets designated by forward observers. Air strikes attacked the area at 2113 and again two hours later, with each strike unloading 1,300 pounds of ordnance. Tanks also joined the act. Although the terrain was too mountainous for movement, Able Company tanks took up stationary positions and fired 350 rounds of 90-mm at targets of opportunity. In exchange, they received nearly 500 rounds of Chinese artillery and mortar of all sizes.

This battle, however, was an infantry show. Planes, tanks, and artillery all helped to kill Chinese, but not the ones on the Hook. The enemy was securely dug in, and the longer he remained the more difficult it would be. Marine infantry was the only way and they had to move swiftly.

The 3d Battalion of 1st Marines was moved forward from division reserves to an assembly area behind the 7th Marines. Meanwhile, Able Company, on the crest during the early morning of 27 October, had temporarily blocked the Chinese advance south from the Hook, but it did not have the strength to push them back. How Company, 3/7, received orders to pass through the ranks of Able Company and counterattack.

By 0545, Chinese troops controlled more than a mile of trench line and were consolidating their gains from the Hook toward the crest of Hill 146, the dominating high ground behind the Hook. The enemy had not yet attained Hill 146 but left little doubt that it would be the objective of their next push.

Leaving the Able Company position, How Company worked its way northeast toward the ridgeline of Hill 146. It attained the ridge in two hours and began the counterattack at 0800.

2d Lt. George O'Brian led How Company and raced across an exposed saddle from Hill 146 toward the Hook. Continuing through bullets and shrapnel as he neared an enemy position, he was wounded in the arm. Regaining his feet, O'Brian waved his men forward and continued to spearhead the attack. He paused once to aid a wounded Marine.

One of the men of How Company in another platoon recalled with pride his view of Lieutenant O'Brian:

> . . . They had a Texas lieutenant named O'Brian, whose platoon was slated to spearhead the drive.
>
> Jeez, on the way up, five gooks jumped out of nowhere and went for O'Brian. The guy must have had tremendous reflexes, because he dropped all five. He was also wounded, but did this stop him? Hell, no! He continued to lead his platoon. He must have been a hell of an officer.[19]

O'Brian and his platoon fought for nearly four hours until they could advance no farther. Establishing a defense perimeter to prepare for an enemy counterattack, he continued to attend to his men until relief of the position was effected by another unit. He then took the position of rear guard to ensure that none of his men was left behind. He survived the Hook, his wounds healed, and he was awarded the Medal of Honor.

Instrumental in preventing enemy reinforcements from adding to the overburdened How Company, Marine close air support bombed and napalmed Chinese reinforcements streaming from Seattle. At 0900, an air attack struck the former Marine outpost of Irene with 3 tons of bombs and 2 tons of napalm. Thirty minutes later, another strike bombed and strafed groups of Chinese soldiers running toward the Hook.

Despite the support, How Company's counterattack stalled, as did Able Company's before it. How Company had pushed the enemy back 200 yards but could make no further progress. Resources of the 7th Marines were exhausted; there were no more troops. It would now be up to the 3d Battalion, 1st Marines, from the division reserve that had been moved forward earlier. The task of replacing How Company fell to Item Company, 3/1.

At 1350 on 27 October, the 1st Platoon, Item Company, 3/1, led the assault. As the skirmish line advanced, enemy soldiers fired from protected positions around the perimeter of the Hook. Chinese artillery matched that of the Marines as shelling increased. At 1344, another air strike attacked enemy troops near Frisco that were moving to reinforce the Hook. A flight of four Marine Corsairs each dropped a ton of bombs on Chinese soldiers.

Under this umbrella of falling ordnance, noise, smoke, and bullets, the men of Item Company crawled to within 100 yards of the trenches. It was now 1635. Chinese artillery was bombarding not only the advancing Marines but was impacting as far to the rear as the regimental CP. Enemy troops were still clinging to remnants of defenses on the Hook. By 1700, a few Marines were in the trenches where others soon joined them.

West of the Item Company counterattack, Baker Company, 1/7, also moved forward to close the pincers, and, by 1930, one platoon had nearly closed with Item, 3/1. The Marine advance was slow but relentless. The cold and moonless night made it more difficult. Shell holes pockmarked the landscape; landmarks were gone. Nothing was the same as it had been twenty-four hours earlier.

At 0019 on 28 October, Baker Company assaulted the Hook from the west. With rifles and grenades, the Marines tried to reach enemy troops dug into the abandoned trenches. After a ninety-minute firefight, they had failed. The Marines were again driven back by small-arms fire, hand grenades, and Chinese supporting fire from the outposts.

Pulling back, the Marines called for artillery and mortars on targets observed during their assault. Precise concentrations were called, and approach routes from Ronson and Warsaw were saturated with shells. With this preparation, Baker Company tried again at 0340. Advancing against still heavy resistance, the Marines gained first a foothold and then the entire trench line. By 0600, the Hook was again in Marine hands.

Thirty minutes later, squad-sized patrols dispatched to OPs Ronson and Warsaw reported that the enemy had also fled those positions, and they had been reoccupied by 7th Marine units.

After the battle, Captain McLaughlin wanted to take out a detail in an effort to recover bodies. His observations attest to the ferocity of the fighting on the Hook:

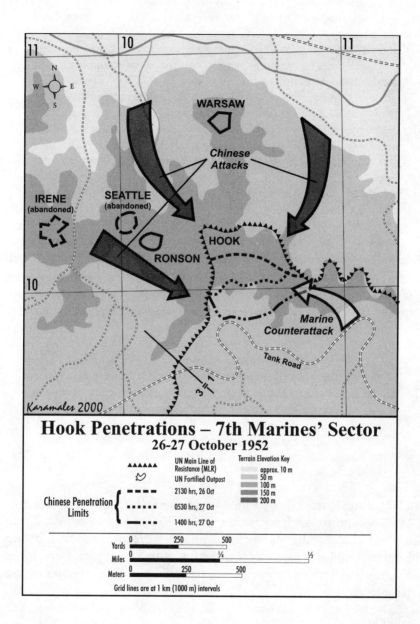

Hook Penetrations – 7th Marines' Sector
26-27 October 1952

▲▲▲▲▲▲   UN Main Line of
           Resistance (MLR)

〜♡   UN Fortified Outpost

Chinese Penetration {   – – –   2130 hrs, 26 Oct
Limits   • • •   0530 hrs, 27 Oct

                 – • – •   1400 hrs, 27 Oct

Terrain Elevation Key
approx. 10 m
50 m
100 m
150 m
200 m

Yards   0   250   500

Miles   0   ¼   ½

Meters   0   250   500

Grid lines are at 1 km (1000 m) intervals

I got permission to go forward the next day to lead a search party to recover bodies. We had a lot missing and I felt that they might be in the area, possibly buried. I do remember walking down a trench line and felt something kind of squishy beneath my feet, and we dug in there and found a weapons platoon commander from another company. His body was there. I went around an abandoned trench line at one point and there was a face looking at me from the side of the hill. It was just like it was painted on the side of the hill. It was a Chinese trooper who had been blown into the side of the hill, just the face. We dug these people out. I don't know exactly how many. It seems to me that over a period from 0800 in the morning until 1500 in the afternoon, we probably located 40–50. Most of them were Chinese, but we did recover quite a number of American boys who had given their lives up there on that awful hill that day.[20]

It was clear that enemy forces had planned to drive the Marines from the Hook and occupy it themselves. Although they occupied the point for a few hours, they could not prevail. The major reason that they accomplished even that was the lack of Marine firepower caused by the ammunition restrictions in effect during the previous weeks—the critical buildup period. Lieutenant Colonel Heinl reported:

> ... [I]n the opinion of those I talked with, a vigorous use of firepower on the scale to which we have become accustomed (and of which we boast) would have prevented the Chinese either from his "creeping" approach to our MLR through gradually picking off small outposts, or from preparing for his attack in the systematic way he did. In other words, the use of firepower as a preventative against decisive enemy action, by preventing his buildup, by holding down his own firepower, etc.[21]

Compared with other fighting in Korea, the battle for the Hook was brief, only thirty-six hours, but it was one of the most intensive. It was the first time that the Marine MLR had been breached and held for any length of time. The battle for the Hook was made most significant by its critical location. It simply could not be yielded to the enemy, no matter what the cost.

The Marines on line traded bodies for bombs to retake and hold the Hook because of the ammunition shortage in Korea. In November, Gen. Mark Clark wrote to Secretary of Defense Robert Lovett to deplore the October shortfall. Clark acknowledged that the authorized ninety-day supply of ammunition would have been adequate had it been met. Paraphrasing Clark's message, historian Water G. Hermes wrote:

> The trouble, Clark went on, was that many of the items [ammunition allotments] were below the ninety day level and that the shipments scheduled for the remainder of the year would not make up the deficits. Since a high rate of artillery fire resulted in lower friendly casualties, he deplored the need to reduce the allocations of 155-mm howitzer ammunition from 15 to 9.4 rounds [per tube] per day.[22]

Later, in 1953, Congress held hearings to investigate ammunition supplies and shortages in the Far East.

AFTER THE BATTLE

Still, the fighting was not over. Ronson and Warsaw continued to attract Chinese probes through the early part of November. Despite this minor activity, however, the Hook remained trouble free.

On 3 November, elements of the British Commonwealth Division began relieving the 1st Battalion, 7th Marines. The Marine sector of responsibility finally had been shortened, and the British were given responsibility for defending the Hook. At 0220, Company D of the 1st Black Watch assumed responsibility for Outpost Warsaw. Three hours later, Company B of the 1st Black Watch took over responsibility for Outpost Ronson.

A serendipitous aspect of the fighting on the Hook was the mutual respect that developed between the 7th Marines and regiments of the British Commonwealth Division. During the fighting on the Hook, elements of both the Black Watch Regiment and the Canadian Princess Patricia Light Infantry had been heavily involved in their own sector, as well as reinforcing the American Marines. Subsequently, both units had been badly mauled by the enemy. A demonstration of the camaraderie born of that struggle is recalled by Lt. Dick Stone with Able, 1/7:

> While at Camp Rose [regimental reserve] on 10 Nov., the Black Watch, which had suffered heavy casualties on the Hook, joined us to celebrate the USMC Birthday and brought along their pipes and drummers for entertainment. The birthday cake was decorated with a map of the Hook and military designations of the two organizations.
> Over the next week a series of social exchanges took place at every level from CO's to privates. When the A/1/7 officers were invited to the Black Watch CO's bunker for dinner, we found it was replete with

regimental silver, crystal and battle flags (they took everything with them to the field). During dinner Colonel Rose, the regimental CO, turned to Captain McLaughlin [A/1/7] and asked in a heavy brogue, "Da ya lakta hearrr the pipes?" Capt. Mac replied, "Very much sir, especially when the sound comes drifting across the moors." Other conversation ensued for about thirty minutes, then stopped as the burr of a bagpipe was heard from afar. It seems a lone piper had been sent out to a knoll in no-man's-land to play for Capt. Mac's pleasure.[23]

The shift of line responsibility in November that gave the Hook to the British permitted the 7th Marines, once again, to defend the Jamestown Line with two battalions. The 1st Battalion, terribly exhausted from its defense of the Hook, was taken off line and assigned to regimental reserve for a well-deserved rest. The month of November proved to be comparatively light. With few exceptions, fighting consisted of small enemy probes, often unsupported by artillery, and patrol clashes in no-man's-land. The Chinese war machine again demonstrated its inability to sustain a major attack continuously for more than a few days.

The enemy was noticeably less active, and there was a significant decrease in its use of artillery. Late in the month, for example, in a company-sized raid on an enemy outpost, elements of 2/1 were repulsed only with mortar and automatic weapons fire. The Marine assault received no artillery fire.

Had the enormous quantity of ammunition consumed in fighting for the Hook exhausted Chinese stockpiles? Or was the enemy saving up and preparing for a winter push when the rivers were frozen and could be more easily crossed? Such were the thoughts of G-2, the officers and men of Division Headquarters who were paid to ponder such possibilities.

On 15 November, the 1st Marine Regiment began relief of the 7th Marines. It was time for a change; the 7th Regiment had been on line since early September.

The British had no better luck with the Chinese than had the Marines. On 19 November, a battalion-sized enemy force attacked the Hook and was driven off only after Canadian reinforcements arrived. Between 1900 and 0430, the British fought hard to defend the position. With the support of Marine and U.S. Army artillery, they held the Hook. More than one hundred Chinese soldiers died in that battle.

Throughout the remainder of the war, the Hook salient continued to be a troublesome spot on the UN line. On 30 January 1953, the U.S. Army 2d Infantry Division replaced the British on line.

Armies changed, but the Hook remained.

CHAPTER 11

BIDING TIME

In front of Outpost Kate, among the paddies and low hills of no-man's-land, was a small Chinese-held outpost called the Boot. So named because of its shape on a topographic map, the Boot was approximately 2,000 yards in front of the MLR. A small hill, it commanded one of the assault and patrol approaches to Yoke, the well-fortified enemy stronghold.

On 8 November, twelve Dog Company tanks crossed the MLR and carried the war to the enemy. The tanks closed on the Boot, where they destroyed bunkers, gun emplacements, and trench line. The tankers counted ten enemy killed and estimated that nine more were killed or wounded. One tank took a direct hit, but the crew escaped without injury. The purpose of the tank attack was to soften defenses on the Boot and weaken it, thus enabling subsequent patrols and infantry raids to Yoke.

Two days later, an Able Company, 1/5, patrol, in an effort to capture prisoners, surprised an enemy listening post on the forward slope of the Boot. The Chinese discovered the four Marines during their approach and fired at them. Unable to take prisoners, the Marines returned fire, killed two enemy, and wounded another. During the ensuing firefight, the patrol sustained one casualty. Under a base of fire established by the remaining squad members, the casualty was successfully evacuated. To the delight of men watching the action from nearby outposts, two squads of Chinese, attempting to encircle the withdrawing Marines, mistook each other's identity and engaged in a firefight.

Throughout the 1st Marine Division sector, later that day, customary Marine Corps Birthday ceremonies were conducted in every unit capable of safely doing so. The 1/5 Command Diary entry, following a report of the earlier skirmish on the Boot, was typical of many such celebrations. It stated: "On this 177th anniversary of the founding of the U.S. Marine Corps, the appropriate chapter in the Marine Corps Manual, the Commandant's Birthday Message, and congratulatory messages from other commanders in the theater were published at the battalion CP and all company messhalls in conjunction with cake cutting ceremonies."[1] The ceremony illustrates that even during wartime, the Marine Corps continues to emphasize the traditions that contribute to its esprit de corps and uniqueness among fighting forces.

The following day, 11 November, Operation Greek II took place. This was a 2/5 combat raid on Hill 104 north of Outpost Ava. At 2005, a reinforced platoon from Easy Company left the MLR. When an assault squad engaged an enemy company that was well dug in, it was pinned down with casualties. Two more squads, responding to its call for aid, also sustained casualties. Finally, the platoon disengaged and returned to Ava. Total casualties were six dead and seventeen wounded.

BUNKER BUILDING ON HEDY

Elsewhere on the 5th Marines front, Outpost Hedy was still a problem and growing worse. Because of Hedy's location, Chinese creeping tactics were particularly dangerous. Each day, the Marines noticed that enemy trenches north of the outpost were being slowly extended. Shielded from supporting arms by the terrain, there was little the Marines could do to stop the slowly advancing enemy, who soon would be close enough to launch an attack. For the men on Hedy, it must have been much like watching the Romans in 72 A.D. slowly building a ramp to Masada.

Outpost Hedy was situated on an extension of a ridge jutting out 325 yards from the MLR. A further continuation of the ridgeline from Hedy ended at Bunker Hill. Because of the enemy's proximity to the ridge and the ability to observe it, the Marines were having extreme difficulty in building and maintaining adequate fortifications. In September, a tank road had been built to the outpost so that tanks could get closer to Chinese positions on the north slope. The road was completed but to little avail. Once atop the hill, the tanks were unable to depress their guns sufficiently to hit the enemy below.

The Command Diary of the 1st Tank Battalion noted: "The need for a strong bunker on this OP was imperative since constant enemy mortar and artillery fire had inflicted considerable damage to the existing bunkers. There was little possibility of constructing additional bunkers on the hill because of the volume and accuracy of fire."[2]

Early in November, planners from 1/5 met with people from Dog Company tanks to develop an unusual scheme. A tank-dozer[3] would drive to Hedy on the tank road and scoop out a hole for a bunker that had been prefabricated earlier in a safe position behind the lines. Then, a tank retriever, carrying the bunker suspended on its boom, would drive to the outpost and set the structure in place. Following the retriever, the dozer would return and push earth around the bunker. Result—instant bunker.

The plan was risky. To see what they were doing, the tankers would have to operate unbuttoned in broad daylight as the enemy watched and tried to stop them. And try they did; the Chinese fired everything they had at them. Along with discouragement from the enemy, the weather, terrain, and mechanical difficulties piled up against the Marines. They attempted the feat four days in a row before finally succeeding. For a while, the tankers thought that Murphy's Law would prevail.

On the tankers' first attempt, heavy rains covered the area and the operation had to be postponed because of a lack of visibility. On the second day, the tank-dozer engine would not start. The hydraulic system that controlled the blade failed on day three, and, while returning to the MLR, the tank threw a track. Exposed to more shelling, the tank crew had to stop, dismount, and reinstall the track.

The fourth try was charmed. On the morning of 16 November, tank-dozer D-43 lumbered across the ridge to Outpost Hedy. Alerted by the previous three-day effort, the Chinese began to fire their artillery when the tank left the MLR, but the Marines were ready. At 1000, four Corsairs swooped down on Hills 70, 66, 66A, and 66B to bomb and strafe enemy artillery positions that could fire on Hedy. Simultaneously, five Dog Company tanks from the 1st and 3d Platoons fired their 90-mm and machine guns at the enemy. From the MLR, automatic weapons and rifles covered the tanks as they worked, keeping enemy suicide squads away.

Arriving at the chosen spot on the reverse slope of Hedy, the tank-dozer began its dig. At a depth of 4 feet, it met solid rock, and the men were forced to try a different location. Elsewhere, they found rock at 5–6 feet. Apparently, they were not going to find a better place, so the Marines decided to install the bunker at that site. Under continuous incoming fire, the tank-dozer finished off a hole 11 feet wide and returned to the MLR. The digging operation had taken about thirty minutes.

It was time to install the bunker in the hole. The bunker was constructed of foot-thick wood timbers and roofed with two layers of sandbags. It was 6 feet wide, 6 long, and 5 feet deep, and it weighed about 2 tons.

Shortly after 1100, a tank retriever left the MLR with the wooden monstrosity dangling from its extended boom. At 1130, the retriever gently lowered the bunker into the bulldozed hole while two crewmen hung out of their open hatches and controlled the sway with attached cables. When the bunker was in place, the crewmen ducked into their hatches and the retriever made tracks for the MLR. This part of the operation covered little more than ten minutes, and the men had been constantly under fire.

Upon return of the retriever, the tank-dozer returned to Hedy and pushed dirt around the installation. Finessing the job took a little longer but was accomplished at 1315. By this time, the enemy was fully aware of what had occurred. In full view of its guns, the Marines had installed a bunker fortification on Hedy without losing a man. During the operation, Chinese cannoneers had fired fifty-five rounds of artillery and ninety-two rounds of 82-mm and 120-mm mortar at the tanks but had failed to stop them. Upon completion of the operation, a loud cheer arose from the MLR. Another pawn had been moved into the king's row of the enemy.[4]

Elsewhere on the Jamestown Line, other Marine tanks were active. Korean Marines were using the services of Able Company, 1st Tank Battalion. Elements of the KMC tank company were slowly being released from training and returned to support their countrymen in the KMC, but, in the meantime, Able Company substituted.

The KMC sector was east of Panmunjom and the dividing neutral corridor near the Sachon River. The area was comparatively open—great for tanks and poor for infantry. Consequently, much of the patrolling was done by armored vehicle during daylight.

TANK PATROL WITH THE KMCS

A small glow in the eastern sky preceded the sun as dawn began to break. Five Marine tanks warmed up their huge twelve-cylinder engines. Exhaust from the twin mufflers on either side of the cumbersome machines blasted flame 2 feet to the rear. The half-light was eerie as men and machines prepared to engage the enemy.

Sgt. Roland Kershey, tank commander of A-31, climbed up the front of his tank and squirmed through the open hatch into the turret. Today, he would be the gunner, sighting and firing the tank's main 90-mm gun and .30-caliber coaxial machine gun. For this patrol, he had temporarily demoted himself to make room for his platoon leader, 2d Lt. Warren Kitterman. Kershey could have stayed behind on this trip as there is no place in a tank for an extra body. Rank has its privilege, however, so Sergeant Kershey bumped a private.

On the road in front of the Able Company CP, the 3d Platoon formed up, tank A-31 joined A-32, A-33, A-34, and A-35 in line. This patrol would be designated Patrol Number 140500Ida, a number derived from the date and time of departure. It was to leave the MLR at 0500, 14 June 1952, to locate and engage enemy forces in the vicinity of Hill 87. Any Communist activity west of the Sachon River would be fair game for the deadly tank guns.

Accompanying the tanks this morning would be a platoon of infantry from the 5th Company, 2d Battalion, Korean Marine Corps Regiment. The Korean Marines would beat the brush in front of the tanks and look for evidence of mines or enemy ambush. As they left the CP, the Korean Marines scrambled aboard the tanks for a ride to the MLR and confirmed a soldier's axiom "that it makes no sense to walk when you can ride."

Reaching the reverse slope of the MLR (the safe side), Lieutenant Kitterman paused to confer with the infantry commander and to deploy the troops in front of the tanks. The Koreans fanned into a skirmish line and disappeared into the dense scrub growth.

Walking with the infantry was Danny, its unofficial but very effective translator, who was one of those fortunes of war. Claiming to be seventeen years old, he appeared to be fourteen—a boy doing a man's job. As a refugee appearing from nowhere, Danny was adopted by the Korean Marines to facilitate communications with their American trainers. With an excellent command of English, Danny deployed into combat armed only with a radio. His role, however, was critical. One misunderstood word could foul up the entire operation and get people killed. On that day, as he moved out with the infantry, he was in radio contact with Kitterman.

Rumbling, squeaking, and clanking behind the Koreans, the tanks followed two dusty ruts that passed for a road. They stopped every 100 yards or so to study the terrain and let the troops regain their lead. Mine clearance teams from the Engineer Battalion had previously checked the area, but that had been days ago. It only takes one night and a few minutes to bury a stack of antitank mines. The men were cautious. Soon Kitterman turned the column off the road to break trail cross-country. With no defined route of travel, there was less danger from mines.

As the patrol traveled deeper into no-man's-land, radio traffic began to increase. Danny, in front with the infantry, talked almost nonstop with Lieutenant Kitterman and Capt. Milt Raphael, Able Company commander. Captain Raphael had positioned himself on high ground at the MLR where he could observe much of the activity. Pfc. Robert Frohn, the displaced gunner of A-31, helped to monitor radio traffic on the big ten-channel tank radio. They began to pick up interference as the enemy attempted to jam radio frequencies. Kitterman, believing that the radio interference indicated that they were being observed, warned Danny to alert the Koreans to be ready for action.

By 0705, the Korean Marines reached the hill where the tanks were to deploy. They were 3 miles in front of the MLR. The tanks soon crested the hill, and, across the Sachon River to their right, the crews could see Chinese troops. The tanks opened fire.

At the end of eighty-six rounds of 90-mm fire, the tanks had destroyed four bunkers, one shelter of unknown use, two firing positions, two lengths of trench line, and an undetermined number of enemy soldiers. Then, incoming fire began.

After nine rounds of 120-mm mortar landed, any one of which could have severely damaged a tank, one of the Marine gunners was able to spot the source. The mortars were being fired from behind Hill 87, in-accessible to the flat trajectory tank guns. Kitterman tried calling for artillery but could not get through on the radio. Danny advised that the Korean Marines had been attacked by two platoons of Chinese and were heavily engaged in a firefight. Finally, Kitterman got through and requested artillery support on targets behind Hill 87. He was told that grid coordinates were insufficient and that the artillery plotters required an azimuth reading.

A magnetic compass does not function inside or even close to a tank because of the mass of steel. In order to shoot an azimuth, Kitterman had to get out of the tank, run forward through incoming mortars toward the firefight, stop, read his compass, and then hightail it back to safety. The azimuth was 247 degrees magnetic. Dashing back to his radio, he transmitted the vital information and awaited the sound of artillery to pass over his head and fall on the target behind Hill 87. Finally, he received an answer: "No artillery support is available at this time."

Now there was no choice; the incoming Chinese mortars would soon hit a tank or the infantry. On the hill, they were all sitting ducks. The patrol had to withdraw. Kitterman ordered the infantry to disengage and fall back behind the tanks. After providing cover fire for the infantry, the tanks were to back off the hill.

As they prepared to leave, tank A-35 would not move. An oil line was clogged, and the vehicle was disabled. The problem was quickly discussed over the radio. One of the other tanks moved in behind A-35, and crewmen hooked up steel cables. Under tow, A-35 was returned to the MLR with no further damage. The Koreans' only casualties were two men with minor wounds.

Measured in terms of strategy, this patrol was a success. It was aggressive in that it brought the war to the enemy. It damaged, albeit temporarily, its fortifications and likely killed and wounded a number of enemy soldiers. The patrol gained intelligence suggesting that the enemy was not employing creeping tactics to cross the Sachon River, thus giving some respite to those on the MLR. The patrol also served a real-life training purpose. Each patrol uses different people and subtly different tactics; the learning is ongoing. Every time a platoon or squad engaged the enemy, lessons were learned and the men improved.[5]

CHINESE MORTARS

A key element of Chinese infantry warfare was the mortar. As any Marine who fought the Korean War will attest, "The Chinese could drop a mortar round in your pocket." Without question, they were excellent mortar men and they should have been. The Chinese invented mortars. The Chinese zeroed in on all approaches to their positions, and their ability to switch mortar targets with accuracy was phenomenal. Offensively, their ability to "walk" mortar rounds to a target was legendary. For men inside a fixed target, such as a machine-gun bunker or a tank, watching mortar rounds fall methodically closer and closer, one after the other, could create feelings of helplessness bordering on terror.

The Chinese were also masters at concealing their mortars. Often, the weapons were fired from deep holes in the ground with the outgoing projectile passing through a small, tunnel-like aperture that concealed the flash and much of the noise. To make matters worse, many of the mortar positions were interconnected by tunnels or concealed trenches. The enemy could fire a few rounds from a given position and then break down the weapon and quickly move to another position to resume firing. Consequently, it was very difficult to locate active mortar emplacements and silence them with counterbattery fire.

ACCIDENTS

Mortars are a relatively simple weapon, but it might be useful to explain that one is fired by dropping a round down the nearly vertical directed muzzle. At the base of the tube the falling round strikes a measured powder charge that fires the projectile back out of the muzzle and lofts it to the target.

Byrne and Pendas, in their chronicle of George Company, 3/1, described a tragic mortar accident on one of its outposts. Three members of a Marine mortar crew died when one of the mortar rounds detonated inside the tube:

> When [S/Sgt. Timothy] Tobin arrived at the site all he could recognize was the base plate and the round ball at the end of the tube. S/Sgt. Wilbur "Red" Jones was in command of the 60mm mortar section and witnessed the devastating explosion. Initially, he was at a loss to explain what had happened. It wasn't until several days later that an investigative team finally determined that a second mortar round had been inserted or partially inserted before the first round had cleared the tube. Jones remembers that the assistant gunner, a young Marine from Puerto Rico, was faster than any assistant gunner in his section and assumed that his quick hands led to the tragic accident.[6]

It is not difficult to imagine the outcome of such an event, particularly with three men clustered around the weapon and a supply of ammunition within arm's reach.

Wartime accidents can be particularly harsh. One accident that came to light is even more gut wrenching than the mortar incident, not because of its suddenness but because of its slowness. Lieutenant Colonel Williamson described the event in a letter to his wife:

> The other day down in the Amtrac sector a Korean got mired while walking in the muddy riverbed while the tide was out. A Marine

answered his calls for help, and he too became mired in the deep sucking mud. Three other Marines rushed out to help and became stuck fast. Somehow the Korean and the first Marine managed to extricate themselves and help was summoned for the others. Boards or logs were laid by them but they too sunk in, and those attempting to pull them out couldn't budge them, they merely sank deeper. By this time the tide was beginning to come in. A helicopter was summoned. It hovered over the desperate men and lowered ropes to attach to their bodies. They tried to pull them straight up and to the side but either way the ropes broke, or failed to budge them. Their position was actually in front of our lines, so little was closely available to help. All effort to rescue the Marines failed, and the tide finally rose high enough to drown them all. The most horrible thing imaginable! I've never heard of anything so ghastly outside of fiction.[7]

The practice of war brings on great numbers of unintended terrible events.

1ST MARINES RETURN TO THE LINE

At 1630 on 21 November, Dog Company, 2/1, then in reserve, passed to control of the 1st Battalion for the purpose of conducting a night raid. Objectives of the raid were enemy positions on Hills 150–153 north of Outpost Vegas.

The raiding force consisted of Dog Company reinforced by 2/1's 81-mm mortar and heavy machine-gun platoons. Dog Company's 1st Platoon would be deployed as a base of fire on the forward slope of Vegas, with the mortars and heavy machine guns set up on the outpost itself.

At 1600, four aircraft hit the enemy position on the hill with six hundred gallons of napalm, three thousand pounds of high explosives, and more than three thousand rounds of 20-mm cannon fire. At dusk, two squads of Marines left the MLR to set up and protect the right and left flanks of the approach route. Four hours later, another squad was dispatched to scout the actual approach. Then, at 0350 on 22 October, the two-platoon assault group pushed off. Advancing in column they approached the hill as stealthily as two platoons (approximately eighty men) of fully equipped Marines could manage. At 0430, the Chinese discovered them and fired ten rounds of 60-mm mortar. The mortars seemed to initiate a volley of fifteen to twenty-five concussion grenades from a trench line on the forward slope of Hill 153. Following the fusillade of mortar and grenades, one melodramatic Chinese soldier called out, "Die, Marine," and the entire trench line burst into small-arms fire directed at the assaulting Marines. An estimated seventy-five defenders on the hill were armed with the usual assortment of rifles, burp guns, and hand grenades. These men were supported by seven light machine guns, eight heavy Maxim machine guns, and mortars.

The intensity of defense rendered the assault nearly impossible. Both platoons of Marines were stopped dead in their tracks on the frozen ground. After calling for a preplanned artillery preparation, which was delivered three times, they resumed the assault, albeit with less enthusiasm.

Men of the 2d Platoon managed to reach the trench line, where they hurled satchel charges at two machine guns and destroyed another gun with a 3.5-inch rocket launcher. By this time, however, casualties were too great to allow the platoon to continue, and it withdrew.

Meanwhile, the 3d Platoon, ascending the hill shortly after the 2d Platoon, became pinned down behind a projection of rock halfway up the slope. The men were unable to render any effective support to the lead platoon.

At 0526, the raiding party was ordered to withdraw, and the 2d Platoon successfully retired under a smoke concentration. The pinned-down 3d Platoon acted as rear guard until the 2d Platoon was clear. Then, under cover of the smoke, it too withdrew. Contact with the enemy was broken at 0622.

Enemy casualties from this engagement were 8 counted KIA, 20 estimated killed and 20 estimated wounded. Dog Company casualties totalled 93 Marines. Two were killed and 89 wounded; 55 of the wounded were evacuated. Two men were carried as MIA until 0930 the following morning when one of them reported to the MLR. The 23 November Command Diary entry revealed, "The man had been wounded during the Company "D" raid and remained on the battlefield after the company had withdrawn. The following morning he wandered into the Company "I" lines on the MLR. The man is reclassified as WIANE [wounded in action not evacuated]."[8]

For the Marines on line it was a life of bleeding, shooting, and exploding ordnance, seemingly with no end in sight.

CHAPTER 12

YEAR'S END

Greater love hath no man than this,
that a man lay down his life for his friends.
—John 15:13, King James Version

On 8 December 1952, Sgt. Lloyd Smalley, Reconnaissance Company, 1st Marine Division, earned a Navy Cross. His citation reads:

> When a numerically superior enemy force effected a partial penetration of his squad's position far forward of the main line of resistance, Sergeant Smalley skillfully directed the fire and efforts of his small group of men in repelling the attack, inflicting heavy casualties and forcing the enemy to withdraw.
>
> During a temporary lull in the battle, he quickly moved about the area to locate and rescue his wounded comrades and, while working his way to a sector extremely close to the enemy, discovered a severely wounded Marine in urgent need of medical treatment. While subjected to intense hostile automatic weapons and hand grenade fire, he proceeded to remove the stricken man to the comparative safety of the squad's position. Although sustaining two severe and painful wounds while engaged in this action, he succeeded in gaining the friendly position with his comrade before he was again struck by enemy fire and fell, mortally wounded.[1]

Cutting through the hyperbole of anonymous citation writers, the reader clearly understands that Sergeant Smalley risked his life and lost, thus enabling one of his men to live. That man was Pfc. Howard Davenport, barely twenty years old.

In the Headquarters Battalion Command Diary of December 1952, this patrol was officially reported as "Reconnaissance Company Patrol Number 91." Like many such reports, it is agonizingly brief, barely an outline. By contrast, Davenport's memory of that night in 1952 remains extraordinarily vivid and far more enlightening. He recalled:

> The patrol had its beginning on Hill 59, an observation post with BC [powerful binocular] scopes, bunkers and FO's. This key terrain was southwest, by perhaps a half mile, of Outpost Nan, also called OP-1. We had gone to the outpost just before sunset on December 6th and had observed smoke coming from cooking fires behind Hill 37, occupied by an enemy battalion. We observed a bunker with four Chinese on top having their "C-Rations." When I say "behind" I mean that this bunker was deep behind enemy lines. It was well beyond Hill 37, which itself was a good distance from our lines. Our thoughts were that the four men felt safe, hidden as they were, behind their own outpost. They might become careless. We thought that under cover of darkness, we might be able to slip out there and capture one of them.
>
> The following night, December 7, I was with a patrol of eight men that left Hill 59 via a narrow dirt road that carried us through two abandoned villages. We had the strong impression that we were observed and found it difficult to get to the bunker by this route. We felt, however, that the enemy was not in force in this area but that listening posts could be near the villages. After spending four hours checking out the vicinity, we returned to our lines with plans to go out the next night. We believed that by following an intermittent stream we could approach to within 300 yards of the bunker.
>
> We left on December 8th in platoon strength. Our squad included Sgt. Smalley, the squad leader, George Samaha, Jim Willis, Pedro Aviles and others. One squad from the platoon was dropped off about three-quarters of the way out to secure our flank and act as a rescue group if we were hit. As we left the stream bed, another squad was dropped off to directly support the snatch team.
>
> Our squad continued walking. We followed a dike to a fork of dikes leading to a rice paddy. All the dikes were about three feet high. They surrounded a paddy about 50 yards square and rejoined at the fork. Eight of us set up a base of fire at the fork. The "snatch team," led by Lt. Lee Cook, began walking the seventy-five yards to the bunker where they would try to [effect] the capture. The eight of us were arranged in a circle on the dikes, facing outboard. Aviles had a BAR and was about ten feet to my left.
>
> I should mention here that this area was in front of the KMC main line of resistance. Major [Dermott H.] MacDonnell, our company commander, was on the MLR with the KMC's. If we had not [effected] the snatch by 2200 the KMC were to jump off to push the Chinese battalion off the hill. Then as the enemy retreated we would try to grab a prisoner.

There was snow and ice on the ground and the temperature was around zero degrees. It was cold. About 2150 we saw a column of men coming down the very dikes that we had traveled. About thirty yards from us, the dike veered ninety degrees and we counted about thirty of them. They were talking and singing low as they approached. We thought at first that they could be KMC's that hadn't got the word. When they entered the dike that we were on, I slid off to the side outside the paddy. Then we saw that they had shiny black helmets and their weapons were slung with the barrel pointing down—Burp Guns! They must have been returning from a patrol to our lines and were walking directly into the rear of our four man snatch team. We knew then that we were trapped, and so was the snatch team unless we did something to stop them.

I motioned for Aviles to turn his BAR in their direction. As they walked on the dike that I was on, I let two pass and raised to fire. Smalley called out "halt" and the Chinese started hitting the deck. Because of our position only Smalley and I could fire without hitting our own men.

The enemy column had separated me from the rest of the squad. They were on the inside of the dike, the rice paddy side. I had a grease gun[2] and fired down the column until I had emptied my 30 round magazine. One soldier fell over me, throwing up. I had to push him away with my grease gun as I fired. The Chinese were now in the smaller outside rice paddy with me. I moved toward Aviles and jumped onto the top of a dike which sloped away from the enemy. Aviles was on my right front but I couldn't see him since he was on the inside of the dike that I was previously on. I reloaded and heard grenades and more firing. Then all was quiet. The fighting had stopped. I thought that I must be the only one left alive.

The Chinese began to come toward me to treat their wounded. There were groans and throwing up everywhere. I could see them bend down and hear clothes tear as they administered to their casualties. I decided that I was far from any of our men and felt that all were dead anyway. Dear God that was a lost feeling.

I could hear more enemy troops coming from behind and to my left, extra drums for their Burp Guns bouncing on their hips as they ran. I decided to play dead.

As more Chinese arrived they grew bolder and began walking around looking for our dead and wounded. Then I heard movement in the snow and ice and listened as they discovered Aviles. They took him prisoner and moved off. There was nothing I could do.

Two enemy soldiers came over to the dike that I was on and looked over my head. I watched them with my grease gun pointed up, at their faces. They were within two feet of me and didn't look down. Soon they returned with another man. They were coming to get me. I placed a grenade in my left hand with a finger through the ring and readied my grease gun. The soldiers stepped up onto the dike and two of them opened up with their burp guns. I don't believe the third one got to me, or at least initially.

Snow and dirt flew around me and I felt the hits. I must have fired. They dropped a grenade in my face and the explosion mushroomed upward. Had I been in a raised position I would have received the full impact. I had a hollow sound in my head and heard sirens. I thought that I was dead until I moved my tongue, tasted blood and felt my lower teeth missing. I tried to roll on my left arm and felt the pain. I rolled onto my right side and called out quietly "I'm hit."

I wasn't alone! Smalley and the rest of the squad must have moved toward a cut in the dike earlier. Smalley called out, "Take it easy kid, I'm coming after you." From past experience I knew to tell them how badly I was hit so I said, "I'm hit in the arm, head and face and . . . I am blind." I told Smalley to keep talking and I would crawl to him, that the Chinks were all over me.

I heard George Samaha cry out that they were on top of me trying to pick me up. He called for me to stay low as he was firing. The Chinese soldiers dropped me. I couldn't crawl on my stomach because of the wounds so I rolled over on my back and kicked off the body of one of the soldiers that had fallen on top of me. He had been hit by Samaha's fire.

Smalley kept talking as he crawled toward me. He said, "Why don't they fire, they are on top of us." We met head to head and he pulled me toward a cut near the dike. I was on my back and he on his stomach. Getting through the cut he turned loose and I rolled into the arms of the other guys. Jim Willis said something like, "We knew you could make it." I replied, "Yes, thanks to Smalley." Willis said that I had come in alone. I told them that Smalley had released my hand suddenly, he must have been hit. Willis went out about five yards and pulled Smalley in beside me.

Smalley asked how badly I was hit and I told him that the worst thing was that I was blind. He said that he was hit in the throat and paralyzed. Our corpsman straddled me and began checking both of us over. I told him to work on Smalley first. (I must have seen that in a movie.) Then I mustered up the words and said to Smalley, who was about two feet away with our heads side by side, "Thanks for saving my life, it took guts." His answer was that he "had to do it" and now he could relax. He died minutes later and no one told me.

Lt. Lee Cook and the snatch team, soon as they heard the firing, fell back to where we were. We decided that I could walk out with someone guiding me but Smalley would have to be carried. I wanted my grease gun but Samaha said, "We'll do the firing, you count the dead for us." The squad formed a circle around Smalley and me and we came out firing. Samaha would drop to fire and I would sit on his knee.

I had tape over my eyes to hold my right eye in since it was lying on my cheek. I had lost so much blood that my legs would give out and the men had to carry me. This was more uncomfortable than trying to walk. I could never describe our coming out of there with the Chinese following us. Gunny [T/Sgt.] Jackson E. Tracy told the men to carry me and they replied that I preferred to walk. He told them to hit me on the head with a carbine and carry me. I told the Gunny that if he "was man enough to do it to come ahead." He laughed and said, "He'll be all right." He had been afraid I'd go into shock but after my comments he knew I was OK.

The men from support team came forward and covered our rear as we came out. Another squad met us in the stream bed with a jeep. Smalley and I were loaded on stretchers. Can you believe that a jeep would come out into enemy territory to pick us up? They took us to a forward aid station where I received blood and a shot. A helicopter took me to the battalion aid station for X-rays and more blood. Then another helicopter flew me to Inchon and the hospital ship *Repose*. Smalley was with me on the first chopper, in the other basket. I seem to remember, on the hospital ship a doctor saying, "We have a critical and a DOA [dead on arrival]." I must assume now that the DOA was Smalley.[3]

The DOA was indeed Davenport's squad leader. Smalley was twenty-two years old when he died. Following endless surgeries and hospitalizations, Davenport was ultimately medically retired from the Marine Corps. Davenport never forgot that night and never ceased paying tribute to his sergeant. Every Mother's Day, Lloyd Smalley's mother receives flowers from the former Marine, whose life her son had exchanged for his own.

Aviles also survived. On 5 August 1953, he was returned during the prisoner exchange, Operation Big Switch, after the signing of the truce.

Korea's reputation for severe winters was reaffirmed in December. On the night of 7 December, while Davenport and his recon patrol were sloshing around in rice paddies, the recorded temperature had warmed to a toasty 14 degrees. A few days earlier, the mercury had dropped to 4 degrees, and it had snowed.

The Marines had been issued their cold-weather gear—thermal boots, parkas, long johns, wool mittens, and other items necessary to survive the chill. Molykote, a special cold-weather lubricant, was distributed, and the men were encouraged to use it on their weapons. Standard petroleum-based oils tended to freeze when left out in the weather. Cold-weather triggers were also issued. This somewhat experimental device was attached to the trigger of an M-1 rifle, which enabled the user to fire the weapon with his mittens on. Although they were well intentioned, cold-weather triggers were awkward and did not prove very popular; the Marines ultimately returned to gloves or finger mittens.

In a letter home, Sgt. Arthur Lipper III described his efforts to stay warm during a December screening operation (a tactic where a patrol sets up in front of the line during a change of command on the MLR):

> The 7th is relieving the 5th and [it's] our job to see that no infiltration takes place during the time of unavoidable confusion. It will be mostly a matter of sitting for 4 or 5 hours in the mud and snow and waiting and watching. . . . It will be a long, dull, cold night. My clothing and equipment will be as follows: undershirt, undershorts, sweat shirt, sweat pants, dungarees, green trousers, alpaca vest, waterproof trousers, flack jacket, field jacket with lining, knit headpiece, nylon scarf, gloves, two pocket warmers, 3 frag grenades, carbine, ammo, my .45, knife, thermal boots and parka.[4]

Staying still was particularly difficult in the cold because the men simply became more chilled as time passed. On an ambush, they spent the first two hours in wishing that something would happen and the remainder of the time in hoping that it would not.

AROUND COP-2

Looking north from the aperture in the FO bunker atop Combat Outpost Two, one could clearly see enemy trench lines and bunkers on Hill 67, the Arrowhead. Ninety degrees right, at a position almost due east, the Chinese outpost of Three Fingers was also conspicuous. The valley between the two hills was approximately 1,000 yards wide with a low knobby hill (134) in the center. Surrounded on three sides by rice paddies, 134 had a long low finger of land connecting with the lower slope of Arrowhead.

Like most of the terrain in the vicinity, Hill 134 had been repeatedly pounded by bombs, artillery, mortar shells, tanks, and machine guns. It continued to be occupied by a platoon of Chinese troops that were easily reinforced from the two neighboring outposts.

On 1 December, a Dog Company, 2/5, patrol from COP-2 reported hearing enemy digging and stake pounding on Hill 134. The Marines assumed that the enemy was improving its fortifications and fired artillery and mortar shells into the area with unobserved results. The following night, shortly after 2100, a reinforced squad of Marines from Dog Company departed COP-2 to scout out enemy dispositions on the hill. The Chinese permitted the Marines to approach within twenty yards of their trench on the crest of the hill. Then, they opened up on the patrol's front and right flank with grenades, small arms, and automatic weapons.

A report of the engagement, written by journalist Robert Sherrod, was published in the *Saturday Evening Post* about three months later. No stranger to the Marine Corps, Sherrod is most noted for his reporting of the bloody World War II invasion of Tarawa atoll and for his book *History of Marine Corps Aviation in World War II*. Then in Korea to write about the 1st Battalion, 5th Marines, he noted for his article that considering the size of a battalion (1,000 men) and the monthly casualty rate at the time (22 killed and 260 wounded), that it would be reasonable to expect that "three out of four men in the battalion were likely to become casualties before they get out of Korea."[5] Contrasted with his experiences in WW II, he also observed, "This was the sergeants' and lieutenants' war, far removed from the four- and three-star level. . . . Mostly the patrols were squad-sized commanded by a sergeant, and platoon-sized under a lowly shavetail [second lieutenant]."[6]

Sherrod had a skilled eye for recording the conduct of the war in Korea. He wrote the following about the 2 December patrol on Hill 134:

A few nights before I got there [Korea] a combat patrol had gone out under the command of S/Sgt. Arnold Marsili, a twenty-seven year old Marine from Peckville, Pennsylvania, with six years' experience. This was his second patrol and it consisted of two four-man fire teams, himself, a radioman and one naval medical corpsman, William C. Woods, a Negro from Rockymount, Virginia, who was two days short of his twenty-fourth birthday.

A "tourist" on the trip was 2nd Lt. Hunt Kerrigan, of New York, nicknamed "Tiny" because he is six feet six inches tall and weighs 230 pounds. Kerrigan had just arrived in Korea for his second tour. On his first, as an enlisted man, he had been wounded on April 23, May 29 and June 17, 1951. He went along on Marsili's excursion to get the feel of the new-type war because he was scheduled to lead a platoon on a prisoner-snatching patrol four nights later.

Marsili and his eleven men moved out about eight o'clock, well aware that their path was marked and zeroed in by the communists, and possibly mined. But it was a job to be done. They pushed ahead to find out what enemy outposts were being manned and what the news was. They managed to make about 400 yards across the paddy, and progressed about forty more along the finger of a Chinese-held ridge. Then, from a distance of twenty yards, the enemy—who had been lying doggo [hidden]—opened up with mortars, machine guns and hand grenades. Kerrigan at the time was on one side of the hill with Corpsman Woods, a corporal and a private first class from Latvia who had spent five years in Nazi prisons and whose father, mother and brother are currently being held by the Russians.

After a few minutes, the machine-gun fire turned to their side of the hill and the corporal got a bullet through his leg. Woods carried him down the hill to the paddy, where a twelve inch dike afforded some protection. Meantime, on Marsili's side of the hill "the goonies tried to assault us from the left flank," he said, "but we had a lot of fire power—four Thompsons and four BARs—and we repelled them even with some of the weapons frozen."

Marsili passed the word to pull out. Kerrigan, Woods and the Latvian tugged at the wounded corporal, and in the process the big lieutenant got a slug through his armored vest that pierced his lung. Despite Kerrigan's entreaties to forget about him, Woods stuck with him. ("I wasn't going to do that," Woods told me when I saw him later on board the hospital ship [USS] *Consolation*.) In the process of inching under fire through the icy sludge of the paddy, Woods lost one of his shoes—field shoes are better for patrolling than the heavier thermal boots. The big problem now was to get Kerrigan out of there. Marsili figured that the lieutenant, by soaking up melted ice, weighed nearly 300 pounds. In the meantime, four men were slightly wounded, including Marsili, who turned over command to Sgt. Tom Boylan, now serving his second Korean tour. Three hundred yards remained to be negotiated.

A mortar shell knocked out the radio, so at 12:45 A.M. a runner was sent back to the outpost to fetch help. Two more fire teams were dispatched with a stretcher. Marsili said sixteen men were required to get Kerrigan back to the outpost, but Kerrigan told me later that was nonsense. Not more than six, he said, unless you count everybody who took a turn.

The odd thing about the whole patrol was that Woods, the heroic corpsman, seemed likely to be the biggest loser. His uncovered foot had frozen as he lay beside Kerrigan in the paddy, and the doctors said he probably would lose part of a toe.[7]

The Marines arrived at COP-2 with seven WIAs. Chinese casualties were estimated at four killed and twenty-one wounded.

For Lieutenant Kerrigan, this injury constituted his fifth combat wound in Korea and the basis for his fifth Purple Heart. He was later sent home. For the patrol of 2 December, Kerrigan earned a Silver Star for advancing against enemy fire until he was wounded. Severely injured, he had remained in the area to cover the evacuation of other wounded men.[8]

FIREFIGHT

The combat around COP-2 remained active but somewhat different. Because of the outpost's proximity to the no-fire zone, supporting arms were often inappropriate and much of the fighting became closer, more personal. On 3 December, for example, a lone Marine scout was operating from a listening post in the vicinity of COP-2 called the Molar (because of its molarlike shape on a topographic map) situated about 50 yards from the corridor boundary. Investigating a seemingly abandoned trench line, the Marine heard someone walking and humming a tune. The scout crouched at a turn in the trench. Within seconds, a Chinese soldier appeared and walked nonchalantly around the bend. It was his last walk. The Marine fired three shots and killed him instantly. Afterward, he resumed his watch at the listening post and reported the confrontation when he returned to the outpost that evening.[9]

The following night at 2222, more close-in fighting occurred when a squad patrol from Dog Company, 2/5, engaged two squads of Chinese at the base of COP-2. The point fire team of the patrol was fired on by two enemy soldiers dug into foxholes. As the remainder of the patrol attacked, the Chinese reinforced and the fight was on.

One of the wounded in that action was the patrol leader, 2d Lt. Howard Matthias. Because it was his last experience in Korea, his recollection remains clear and yields details normally omitted from the Command Diary:

> Capt. Judge then informed me that I was to lead a reinforced patrol out much further than before and to expect some contact. In fact the patrol would be an all night patrol and cover a distance of well over two miles, if it was completed. The other two lieutenants exchanged relieved glances. It was my patrol and not theirs. It was suggested that we beef up the patrol with about five extra troops carrying additional weapons. I was not any more concerned than I had been with other patrols.
>
> . . . On days of patrols or raids, the men involved generally had the afternoon off to clean their weapons, take a nap or carry on personal chores like writing letters. I did the same. I remember trying to decide between taking my carbine or a heavier weapon. I decided that we had

plenty of firepower and opted for my lighter carbine. I did decide to carry my .45 in addition to the carbine.

I met the squad at 1700 and went over the patrol. I discussed the route, the order of the patrol and the fact that Sgt. Gwiselda ("Whiz"), would be going along as second in command. No questions out of the ordinary. Over half the patrol had been out with me before.

... As usual, I conducted a quick inspection of the patrol before leaving, and we checked out at 2200. We were heavily dressed and heavily armed. Normally I was the person out front. This night, because of the larger number of men, I assigned another man to precede me. We moved along the assigned route to the first check point and everything went fine.

After checking with headquarters, we continued, but my point man, Parsons, was moving a little too rapidly. The remainder of the patrol was dropping too far behind. I had just caught up with him when two explosions occurred right behind me. A brrrrp noise immediately followed. Two grenades and a burp gun told us that an ambush had separated us from the rest of the squad.

I was faced with a dilemma. We were cut off from the remainder of the men. The radio was back with my sergeant and the rest of the patrol. I also knew the rest of the men would not return fire until they knew where we were.

I decided that our best bet would be to fight our way through them and try to get back to our squad. I whispered instructions to Parsons. I yelled "now" and we each threw a grenade. As soon as they exploded we charged, firing our weapons. I was yelling, "Whiz, bring them up." I later found out that the men either did not hear or understand me. Suddenly I realized I was in among several Chinese troops all in foxholes. They were too shocked to realize what was happening or where we had come from. I remember shooting into one foxhole and charging to another. I tried shooting into this next one and realized that my carbine had jammed. I grabbed this gook and was pulling him out of the foxhole when I realized that shooting was going on next to me. I remember throwing him back into the foxhole and swinging my carbine and hitting him. The feeling of his quilted uniform and startled cry will never be forgotten. I was now in among an undetermined number of enemy with no weapon. I yelled to Parson, "Get over the ridge," and ran toward the small ridge that separated us from our own men. I was now yelling, "Whiz, don't shoot, it's us."

About three steps from the ridgeline (and safety) I was hit. Since I was running away from the enemy, the bullets came from the rear. Strange thoughts and feelings began to occur.

"Fifteen yards, that is a clip you bastard" After all, I had played enough football to know what it feels like to be clipped.

"I can't move my legs." A burning sensation at the top of both legs.

Another explosion. "My God, I hurt everywhere, both legs, arm, neck."

A temporary blackout. "My God I'm dead."

"No I can't be dead, I hurt too damn much."

Still one more shell hits my arm. "My God, now I can't move that arm either."

This had probably taken only a few seconds. My next thoughts were "Where is Parsons" and "If only I can just crawl over the edge, I'll be all right." Unfortunately, Parsons had been killed at that time. I did not know that and had only one thought—get over that ridgeline.

Somehow, with only one arm I did manage to pull myself over the ridge and literally roll to the bottom. I remember the euphoria of rolling down the other side of the ridgeline. I am reminded of experiences as a kid when rolling down a hillside and the happy dizziness that followed. Instead of dizziness, mine was the sensation of joy knowing that I would not be shot again.

I was conscious of several different things. There was firing nearby and considerable movement about me. Chadwick was there with a relief squad and I felt relieved. Somebody, probably a corpsman, was probing all over my body. I was placed on a stretcher and soon jostled at a quick pace back toward COP-2. The pain now became intense. I was conscious of the change of litter bearers quite often. As soon as we began the move uphill I came to the happy realization that I was on my way home. Just before reaching the OP, I realized that Captain Judge was with me. I apologized for fouling up the patrol and getting my man killed. He, along with several of my men, stayed with me right up to the time I was evacuated.

. . . About half way to the aid station a glorious sensation came over me, NO MORE COMBAT, I MADE IT. I was finally on my way home. I had no idea what kind of shape I was in, but by God, I made it.[10]

RAIDING FRISCO

The 3/1 diary entry for 16 December indicates, "At 2123 a 45 man raiding party from George Company engaged 40 to 50 enemy on Hill 13. . . ." The attack employed eight tanks firing from the MLR, artillery concentrations targeting adjacent enemy hills, and heavy machine guns supporting the assault from the MLR. It was a larger raid than most.

Hill 13 was the former Marine outpost of Frisco yielded to the Chinese in October. Predictably, a Chinese-held Frisco had become a thorn in the side of the MLR. Otherwise, why would the Marines have held it in the first place? Frisco remained a danger to patrols in no-man's-land, and the Chinese there continually harassed the MLR with sniper fire.

Pfc. Gene Thomas of George Company, 3/1, described some of the preparations that went into rehearsing for the engagement:

> For several days prior to the raid, my platoon went through numerous dry runs just behind the MLR. Although we practiced conventional squad deployment and assault techniques, we could tell that this mission we were training for was going to be a bit different from most raiding parties.
>
> We practiced with empty MG ammo cans that on the night of the raid would be full of napalm. Someone had devised a way to place a grenade in napalm filled ammo cans so that a modified spoon stuck out on top of the can [a spoon is the trigger lever of a grenade]. Once the pin was pulled, the spoon would fly and the resulting grenade explosion would ignite the napalm. With these improvised and modified satchel charges we would, theoretically, destroy any bunker we encountered.[11]

In preparation for the raid, George Company conducted layout patrols every night beginning on 13 December to observe the terrain and to watch enemy activity. Two of the layouts were led by 2d Lt. Frederick E. Hilliard, who subsequently led the assault platoon on Frisco. He so distinguished himself during that action that he was awarded the Navy Cross.

Private Thomas, also with the assault platoon, described the battle:

> We left our MLR and very shortly dropped one squad off to serve as a base of fire. The remaining two squads continued across a paddy and started climbing to get to a nose and a saddle directly in front of us. When we reached this high ground, another squad set up as an additional base of fire.
>
> By this time our tanks on the MLR had flooded the Chinese outpost with spot lights and fired point blank into their positions. My squad, the assault squad, moved out toward the trench and bunker complex that was about 100 yards ahead of us.
>
> The tanks were firing over our heads as we moved forward, but so far, there was no fire from the Chinese. I thought several times that here I was holding a can full of napalm and tank tracers passing a few feet over my head. I wasn't totally sure what would happen if a stray tracer were to hit the napalm I was carrying, but the thought of it left me a little shaky.
>
> In the confusion of all the tank fire and because the terrain wouldn't allow for a neat skirmish line, the squad was soon spread out in a col-

umn. Somehow my fire team with a Weapons Company flame thrower was in the lead. Suddenly the spot lights were turned off, and the tank fire shifted so as not to hit us.

We crawled to the parapet of the Chinese trenches. The plan at this point was to use the flame thrower to clean out the trenches and then we would hurl our "napalm bombs" into any bunkers we could reach.

The Marine with the flame thrower got to his knees, but for some reason he was unable to get the flame thrower to function. Within seconds, or so it seemed, concussion grenades began to rain on us. We were lying only a few feet from the trench line and totally exposed to hostile fire. We took casualties immediately, including the Marine with the flame thrower.

Confusion and a certain amount of panic set in. We were in an untenable position and had no choice but to get out of there as fast as we could.

We got our wounded out but Pfc. Ray Dowler, the BAR-man from my fire team, was KIA while almost in the enemy's trench line and was left behind in the confusion.[12]

In the chaos of the attack and subsequent withdrawal, twelve Marines were wounded. Lieutenant Hilliard and nine others required evacuation by stretcher. Private First Class Thomas had risked his own life by pulling the seriously wounded man with the flamethrower to safety. For that effort, Thomas was awarded the Silver Star.

Still, the company had a man left on the hill, an error that had to be rectified. Thomas reported what happened next:

At dawn on the second morning after the raid, we could see Dowler tied to a stretcher and placed right in front of us over a shallow trench on an unoccupied nose of the main hill we had made the assault on. We knew we would go after him, and they knew it too.

As soon as it got dark my squad leader, Sgt. Fred Miller, myself and two others from another squad set up a listening post at the base of our hill, about 100 yards in front of the MLR. Somewhere around 2200 hours, we heard noise in the area where they had placed Dowler, so we called in a concentration. After heavy shelling, we waited several hours, crossed the rice paddy and crept up to the trench. We tied com-wire to the stretcher, in case of booby traps, and pulled it about 10 yards down and away. From there we picked him up and half ran, half tumbled back down, across the paddy and up to our own trenches.

Dowler's cold weather boots and parka were missing, but they had stuffed his remaining clothing with Christmas cards and propaganda.[13]

EAST BERLIN

On 19 December, How Company, 3/1, executed a raid on a Chinese trench line north of Outpost East Berlin. This action was somewhat different because it employed the tank fighting light in a new way. The effects were quite unexpected.

At dusk, two reinforced squads left the How Company MLR for enemy positions on Jersey Ridge. By 1915, the squads were within 300 yards of the objective. The patrol leader called for the tank light to illuminate the ridge and for support fire on the target. As tank fire, machine guns, 4.2-inch mortars, and artillery covered the surrounding terrain, the infantry advanced undetected under the beam of the fighting light. At 1930, the patrol leader gave the signal to shift fire from the objective to adjacent hills so that his men could advance. It had been planned to turn off the fighting light as well, but because he had received so little opposition, the leader decided to assault with the light on.

His decision was the right one. Unopposed, two fire teams attained the enemy position, attacked enemy personnel, and burned 200 yards of trench line with previously prepared napalm bombs. After sweeping the hill, the Marines withdrew to leave the objective free for the supporting arms units to resume their pounding. How Company personnel returned to the MLR at 2100 with eleven casualties, five of whom required evacuation.

Use of the tank fighting light kept the Chinese in their trenches. They were still down when the Marines arrived. The enemy soldiers, appearing to be confused and blinded by the illumination, had been unable to detect the advancing infantry under the beam of brilliant light.[14]

ONE LAST RAID

The final raid of 1952 began during the early morning hours of 27 December on a hill called Harlow, nearly 1,100 yards in front of the 2/1 MLR. Harlow was a small knob of land connected to the southern end of the Kumgok hill mass. Situated east of the Chinese stronghold on Ungok, it was easily reinforced by forces located there.

History does not record why Harlow was raided. Perhaps, like Detroit, it constituted a continuing sniper threat, or maybe it was just to keep the enemy off balance. For whatever reason, it did not appear to constitute a serious and continuing threat, as this occasion seems to be the first and only time that Hill Harlow ever appears in Marine combat documents. Speculation aside, a reinforced platoon from Easy Company, 2/1, conducted the raid.

The raiding platoon was divided into three elements. The first element, Group Able, was a demonstration and covering force. Attached to Group Able was a squad from the division's Reconnaissance Company. This squad's mission was to set up an ambush astride the likely enemy reinforcement route from Ungok. Here, the squad could protect Group Able from a flank attack. The Group Able left the MLR for its objective at 0200.

The second element was Group Baker. Also a covering force, it would set up on the southeast approach to Harlow. Its mission was identical to Group Able but in a different place. Group Baker departed the MLR at 0230.

Five minutes later, the third and largest element, the Assault Group, left the MLR to approach Harlow from the west.

Groups Able and Baker arrived at their objectives with no difficulty and, as planned, immediately set up. At 0300, the Assault Group arrived at its second checkpoint. The men advanced west across a rice paddy, turned, and began their ascent up the hill without contacting the enemy. Then, moving farther up the hill, they encountered a heavily laid barbed-wire entanglement. The wire caused the Marines considerable difficulty, but they managed to work through it and came upon a freshly dug trench line. At their approach, a voice shouted in perfect English, "Halt! Who goes there?" The Marines remained mute. The challenger rose to fire his burp gun and was immediately cut down.

Their position thus exposed, the Assault Group was immediately taken under fire by seventy-five enemy troops in two groups. According to the Command Diary of the 2d Battalion, "The platoon leader ordered his force to commence the assault, and it was made at 0337, the objective being reached at 0340. During the action, there was a fire fight with the enemy employing 6 to 9 machine guns, small arms, concussion grenades, fragmentation grenades and, as the action progressed, mortar fire."[15]

Noting that the support fire from Group Able was ineffective against enemy defenses at the trench line, the platoon leader ordered them to cease fire when the assault reached its objective. Then, as they received intensified mortar fire, the platoon leader ordered his platoon sergeant to withdraw with half of the assault group. The sergeant complied, fell back with his men, and, by 0420, had set up in a new defensive position on the hillside. As the platoon had pulled back, the firefight dropped off until all that could be heard were shouting and talking on the hill above them. The language, Chinese or English, was not discernible.

As time passed, the hill became quiet and the fighting ceased. The platoon leader, who had been last seen reorganizing the remainder of his men, did not return. Concerned, the platoon sergeant took two fire teams and returned to the scene of the skirmish. They swept the area to a point at a short distance downhill from the enemy trench line, but results were negative. The platoon commander and eleven men were missing.

Under orders to withdraw, the sergeant joined and assumed command of Group Baker, which retired to the MLR at 0727. Group Able and the Reconnaissance Company had retired at 0655.

Obviously, the raid on Harlow had been a failure. Chinese defenses were strong and the fighting intense. Ten Marines had been wounded. No enemy had been confirmed as killed, but weighing on everyone's mind was the fact that twelve men were missing, apparently captured or killed, and had been carried off by the Chinese.

As dawn broke on the MLR, Easy Company was licking its wounds. When the sun climbed high enough to allow the men to see north, they saw the missing men, lying dead, scattered over Harlow and on the southern slopes of Kumgok. Fox Company was ordered to assemble a combat patrol with the mission of recovering the Marine dead. Again, the patrol was split into two groups, a support and assistance group of fourteen men equipped with stretchers and led by the platoon commander, 1st Platoon, and the main force of twenty-two men led by the platoon commander, 2d Platoon.

The patrol departed the MLR at dusk on the evening of 27 December. The support force trailed the main force by fifteen minutes, and both arrived simultaneously at their respective positions. Halting his men short of the trench line on Harlow, the leader of the main force went ahead with a fire team to reconnoiter. The Command Diary reported:

> As the five men reached the top of the hill, they received three rounds of 60mm mortar and a heavy volume of small arms and automatic weapons fire from the trenchline. The Platoon Commander, 2nd Platoon, and three of the four men with him were immediate casualties. The remaining man, although wounded and stunned by the shell bursts and cut off by enemy small arms, made his way down off the hill and, guiding on a tank searchlight, withdrew to the MLR . . . arriving at 2040. When the first contact was made, illumination was ordered; illumination commenced at 1915 and continued until contact was broken. When "Harlow" was illuminated, the Platoon Sergeant, 2nd Platoon, who had remained behind with the majority of the main group, realizing the situation, attempted to move the main group to the top of the hill to retrieve the bodies of his Platoon Commander and mem-

bers of the fire team. This attempt was resisted by the intense fire of an estimated 50 enemy. Friendly elements returned the fire and called in 4.2" mortars and artillery. During the action the enemy attempted to envelop the group's right flank. After a 25 minute fire fight, most of the Platoon Sergeant's group became casualties.[16]

At 1940, the support group was ordered forward to assist. The men reached the main group and set up a perimeter defense around the casualties. Then, two fire teams attempted to reach the bodies of the casualties from the initial contact. Three attempts were made to reach the top of the hill, and each was driven off by enemy fire. Finally, at 2020, the platoon commander returned to the MLR. All efforts to retrieve the bodies had failed. Fox Company had lost four more missing and thirteen wounded. The day of 27 December 1952 had been very bad for the men of Easy and Fox Companies, 2/1. Evidently, the missing Marines were never recovered, as end-of-the-month statistics for 2/1 revealed sixteen men missing in action.

CHAPTER 13

HARD LESSONS

Study the human side of military history which is not a matter of cold blooded formulas or diagrams. . . .
—Sir A. P. Wavell, Lecture to Officers, Aldershot, c. 1930

In November 1950, through the mountains of eastern Korea, the 1st Marine Division had advanced slowly up the road to its appointment with destiny at the Chosin Reservoir. Maj. Gen. Edward M. Almond, U.S. Army, Commanding General, X Corps, had told them that they might encounter a few "Chinese laundrymen." They had encountered Chinese all right, but there were more than a few and they were not laundrymen. General Almond had gravely underestimated the number, skill, and ability of the Chinese soldier.

Since 1951, the truce talks in Panmunjom had been stalled over the issue of repatriation of prisoners of war. Communists pushed for the forceful return of their soldiers, whether they wanted to return or not. The UN insisted that prisoners be given a choice of returning to their own country or remaining in South Korea as free men. Neither side was willing to move, and negotiations finally came to an impasse.

Brig. Gen. William K. Harrison, U.S. Army, senior UN negotiator, caught the Communists off guard on 8 October 1952 by proposing a recess. He announced: "We are not terminating the armistice negotiations, we are merely recessing them. We are willing to meet with you at any time that you are ready to accept one of our proposals or to make a constructive proposal of your own, in writing, which could lead to an honorary armistice. . . . Since you have offered nothing constructive, we stand in recess."[1]

However, while taking a hard line at the conference table, the UN allowed the battlefield strategy to remain unchanged. No military pressure was to be applied that might persuade the Communists to return to the negotiation table. UN policy acted as though time were on its side. Meanwhile, troops on both sides were dying. China could afford the loss, but the United States and South Korea could not.

In 1952, the U.S. Marines learned once again about the Chinese soldier. On the Jamestown Line, they opposed some of China's best troops, and, although prohibited from pushing them back, the Marines also refused to be pushed back. They learned to fight a war for which they had never trained or imagined possible—a new kind of war, one of defense with political limitations. In this war, possession of territory did not count. Only the killing was important.

INNOVATION

A dubious advantage to a stalemated war was the ability to improvise; to experiment with products, techniques, tactics, and innovation; and to find better ways of destroying or saving lives. In the Marine sector, warfare experiments and innovation efforts were continual. One such innovation, the M-39 armored personnel carrier (APC), had been introduced earlier in the year. In June 1952, the U.S. Army assigned six of these compact and relatively fast, fully tracked vehicles to the Marines for the purpose of rescuing UN delegates from Panmunjom should the need arise. Consequently, the platoon of APCs was placed with the Rescue Task Force, traditionally the mission of the Marine center regiment.

Not an organization to allow an asset to sit idle, the Marine Corps soon found a way to utilize the vehicles until such time as they might be needed for their original purpose, a possible but improbable likelihood. An excerpt from the Tank Battalion Special Report follows:

> Since their arrival in the Division, the APC Platoon has been employed extensively as an evacuation and re-supply vehicle during major operations in the Division sector. These operations included a battalion size raid on Hill Yoke, Bunker Hill and operations on the "Hook." Approximately 1,370 casualties have been evacuated from forward aid stations to helicopter strips over roads impassable to wheeled vehicles.[2]

The APC had been in Korea for some time, but this was the Marines' first experience with it. They came to love it. With its speed and maneuverability, it was nearly impossible to hit with mortar fire. As the war progressed into 1953, the APC was seen more and more in front of the MLR as it raced around to pick up wounded and take them to aid stations. It became an armored ambulance, a combat resupply vehicle, and a versatile off-road truck.

Another innovation that proved practical in Korea was the introduction of tank fighting lights. These 18-inch searchlights mounted on tanks proved most useful during the August fighting on Bunker Hill. By November, however, a number of experiments demonstrated that they had even greater versatility as aids in infantry night fighting.

Originated as an effort to illuminate the battlefield for tank operations at night, the lights were soon used to support infantry raids, to spot targets, and to blind the enemy. Attached to a bracket over the main 90-mm gun, the light was controlled by the gunner. It was discovered, however, that the light did not benefit the tank on which it was mounted; it was too brilliant when one looked directly down the beam. Further, when the gun was fired, muzzle blast and smoke contributed to obscure the target entirely. The tactic that became most effective was to deploy two tanks, one spotting with the light while the other fired on the illuminated targets. This soon developed into a "clatter" method, whereby a pair of tanks alternated between switching the lights on and off and firing their guns. This technique gave the eyes of the enemy no time to adjust. It was reported that enemy soldiers were not only blinded but also became physically ill. With one tank after the other turning on lights, the guns always had a clearly illuminated target. In one action, tanks moved within 200 yards of the enemy without being hit.

The lights were also found useful for marking enemy targets during a night air attack. When attacking ground targets illuminated by spotlight, the planes were less exposed than when attacking by the light of dropped flares. Aircraft could attack in the darkness with comparative immunity from antiaircraft fire. Interviews with prisoners disclosed that they often felt demoralized and helpless when they could not anticipate where the strike would hit.

Some innovations were also well intentioned but failed. On 10 November, members of 2/5 conducted an experiment to increase the effects of napalm bombing on the enemy. Someone in the unit apparently had learned that a 9:1 mixture of napalm, after almost two hours of saturating loosely packed dirt, could be easily ignited by a white phosphorus shell and would burn effectively for several minutes. The idea was to drop napalm bombs with the fuses removed and, after the enemy left the shelters, to ignite the napalm-soaked area with a white phosphorus mortar shell.[3] There is no record of this procedure being implemented, but it sounded ingenious.

Another experiment involved an interesting effort by the 5th Marines to capture prisoners. Some imaginative Marine in the 2d Battalion came up with a bizarre scheme to simulate a firefight and capture enemy soldiers as they came to assist their comrades. The idea was implemented at 0045 on 24 November. Two fire teams of Marines proceeded to a location near Outpost Kate. Each team fired U.S. weapons and Chinese burp guns to simulate a firefight. Chinese speaking interpreters and Marine personnel carried on a dialogue intended to appear that a small patrol of fighting Chinese troops was outnumbered. In the meantime, two more squads of Marines secreted themselves in likely positions to intercept and ambush enemy soldiers responding to reinforce the engagement.

Unfortunately, the Chinese failed to respond. The Marines returned to the MLR with nothing to show for their efforts but dirty weapons. Had the ruse worked, its creator, no doubt, would have become famous; instead, he remains gratefully anonymous.[4]

THE LEARNING CURVE

It is difficult to locate an exact moment in the outpost war when the Marines stopped learning and began practicing. Of course one never really stops learning and neither do organizations, yet there does come a point where the practice of trial and error evolves into learned skills. For the outpost war, the author chose, rather unscientifically, December 1952 as that point. If not precise, it is at least close.

After fighting for and holding the Hook, the Marines realized that the enemy had the manpower to take virtually any position that it wanted. The Marines also learned that overwhelming firepower was the only method in the American arsenal to prevent such a takeover. It was a trade—bullets for people. China was willing to spend men lavishly, whereas the United States was frugal with both ordnance and people.

The Hook validated the strategy of outpost defense. The taking and holding of Outpost Bunker Hill, the other major battle of 1952, created and retained a solid protection against incursions on the MLR. Quite the opposite situation existed with the Hook. It never saw an enemy footfall until Outposts Seattle, Ronson, and Warsaw fell. Naked without outposts, the Hook was lost in a single day.

The failure of the Outpost Line of Resistance (OPLR) earlier in the year was also part of the learning. The OPLR was too extensive and too far forward for the Marines to take advantage of observation and fire-

power from the MLR. Men manning positions on the OPLR were pit-
ted man to man against an enemy that outnumbered them. The OPLR
was a temporary tactic. Fortunately, it was abandoned in a month.

Aggressive patrolling was another lesson learned, at least presumably
so. Although no empirical data exists that validates its actual value, frequent patrolling was helpful in gaining intelligence of enemy activity,
keeping the enemy from creeping closer to friendly lines, and, of course,
causing a few casualties to enemy troops. An important benefit of patrolling was that it kept the Marines alert and in the war, thus avoiding the
lethargy of garrison mentality.

The Korean War was an infantry war. Although planes, tanks, and
artillery participated, the burden of war rested disproportionately on the
back and legs of the foot soldier. On both sides, the infantry carried the
battles; lived in the dirt; and fought with rifles, hand grenades, mortars,
machine guns, and, in many cases, fists and shovels. All too often the
men fought up close—personal contests of individual strength—face to
face and toe to toe.

Little existed in the way of the "high-tech" systems that are now considered essential. About half the time, radios did not work, communication lines were destroyed, maps were inaccurate, and intelligence of
enemy intentions was nearly nonexistent. Despite these obstacles and
more, the Marines usually carried the day. They did not win every battle,
but they did not lose every one either. They held the Jamestown Line in
a firm grasp and did it mostly with guts.

The Marines—the kids—fought with high morale and a discipline
born of training. They were led by young, aggressive officers and knowledgeable NCOs. They fought for each other, their platoons, their fire
teams, their buddies—men with whom they lived, patrolled, and, in
some cases, died.

Still, the war dragged on.

THE FINAL MONTHS, 1953

If 1952 had been a period of learning, 1953 was a period of doing, the
peak of the curve. Outpost tactics had stabilized, and there were more
raids and larger battles. There were also more casualties. The outpost war
was still one of attrition, and the numbers grew. Anyone who believes
that the last months of the Korean War—the "stalemate"—were inactive
has not read history. During a period of eighteen months, the Marines
fought four major battles: Bunker Hill, the Hook, Reno-Carson-Vegas,
and Boulder City, the latter two in 1953.

In addition, the Marines engaged in daily patrols, ambushes, raids, and constant artillery barrages. Anecdotes of their experiences are plentiful. Stories of triumph and error, loss of friends, and loss of life and limb are told in heart-wrenching pathos. Some of the official records are rich in detail and authenticate personal recollections.

The sequel to this volume illuminates the final months of the outpost war. That period saw the loss of more outposts and more men. The story begins with January 1953 and follows the course of the war through to its gruesome conclusion on 27 July 1953. There was terrible fighting on the Nevada Cities positions, where the Marines took "the highest beachhead" in Korea. Finally, on the last day of the war, a major breakthrough on the MLR at Boulder City rivaled fighting on the Hook. It was arguably the deadliest battle of the war.

CASUALTY TABLE

Marine Corps Casualties[1]
Korean War 1950–1953[2]

Date	Killed in Action [KIA][3]	Killed Nonbattle	Wounded in Action [WIA]	Cumulative Total
August–December 1950	1,526	30	6,229	7,785
January–December 1951	960	82	7,924	8,966
January–March 1952	87	19	600	706
Outpost War				
April–December 1952	960	66	6,815	7,841
January–July 1953	729	47	4,470	5,246
Total				
August 1950–July 1953	4,262	244	26,038	30,544

1. Taken from Meid and Yingling, *Marine Operations in Korean,* vol. 5: 575.
2. Abstracted from U.S. Marine Corps Strength in Korea vs Korean Casualties by Month, 25 Jun 1950–27 Jul 1953, based on Korean Operation Report, Statistics BR., HQMC and Log Sheet, 21 August 1967.
3. KIA includes DOW [died of wounds]; captured and died; and missing in action, presumed dead.

HILL AND OUTPOST SITES

Western Korea 1952–1953
Hill, Outpost, and Military Sites:
Grid Numbers and Place Name Cross-Reference

Place Name	Comments
Allen/Carson/Hill 27	See Carson
Ambush Alley (CT068073)	Supply trail to Carson
Arrowhead/Hill 67 (CT063080)	CCF hill N of Carson
Ascom City (Bupyong)	USMC/Supply center
AvA/Stromboli/Hill 48A (CT044059)	USMC OP
Berlin/Donald/Hill 19 (CT082082)	USMC squad + OP
Betty Grable	CCF hill
Black (CT019039)	USMC OP, June 1952, later became MLR
Blue/Hill 88 (BT997026)	USMC OP (June 1952)
Boot/Hill 70A (BT996030)	CCF hill, vicinity OP-2
Boulder City/Hill 119 (CT084078)	USMC MLR
Bronco/Detroit	USMC OP on June 1952
Brooklyn (CT089109)	CCF hill
Bruce/Reno/Hill 25	See Reno
Bulb (CT050067)	E side of Kumgok
Bunker Hill/Hill 122 (CT017046)	USMC platoon OP (est. Sept. 1952)
Camp Brittania (CS259916)	Reg. area, Corps Reserve

Numbers are elevations in meters; for feet, multiply by 3.28.
Map references refer to 1:25,000 AMS Series L851, duplicated in part in the endpapers.

Place Name	Comments
Camp Casey (BT307984)	Reg. area, Corps Reserve
Camp Doughtry (CS103973)	Bn. Reserve area
Camp Indianhead (CT372093)	Reg. area, Corps Reserve
Camp Lee (CT090034)	Bn. Reserve area, Div. Reserve
Camp Matthews (CT079063)	Bn. Reserve area
Camp Meyer (CT047013)	Bn. Reserve area, Div. Reserve
Camp Pope (CT371108)	Bn. area, Corps Reserve
Camp Rose (CS078994)	Bn. area, Div. Reserve
Carson/Allen/Hill 27 (CT064076)	USMC OP, 1 off., 38 men
Chicago/Elmer (CT082094)	See Elmer
Clarence/Vegas/COP 5/Hill 21	See Vegas
Claw/Hill 70 (BT994034)	CCF hill, vicinity Marilyn
COP-1/Nan (BT975012)	USMC 2 squad OP
COP-2/Hill 84 (BT970028)	USMC OP company +
COP-2A/Toothache/Molar (BT965025)	Covered rear of COP-2
COP-3 (BT987043)	USMC OP, abandoned Apr. 1952
COP-4 (CT020050)	Same as Hill 120, abandoned Apr. 1952
COP-4 (CT034057)	Abandoned May 1952
COP-5/Hill 21/Vegas	
COP-6/Hill 104	
COP-7/Hill 201(CT021038)	May 1952, later became MLR
COP-19/Berlin	USMC OP
COP-19A/E. Berlin	USMC OP
COP-21/Vegas	
Corrine/Dagmar (CT039050)	USMC 2 squad OP
Dagmar/Corrine (CT035050)	USMC 2 squad OP
Detroit/Felix/Bronco/Hill 15 (CT087089)	USMC OP, lost 7 Oct.

Place Name	Comments
Digger (CT074078)	USMC OP (possible early name for Vegas)
Dike (CT053071)	CCF position vicinity Ungok
Dinosaur (BT981019)	Hill in no–man's–land
Donald/Berlin	USMC OP (July 1952)
East Berlin/Hill 19A (CT088082)	USMC squad(-) OP, est. 13 Oct. 1952
Elko/Hill 47/Reno Block (CT068075)	USMC OP
Elmer/Chicago/Hill 190 (CT082093)	USMC OP, lost 7 Aug. 1952
Esther/Samoa/Hill 56A (CT029048)	USMC squad OP
Fan (CT013037)	Saddle between Bunker and Hedy
Felix/Detroit/Hill 110	See Detroit
Frisco/Gary	See Gary
Gary/Frisco/Hill 13 (CT090104)	USMC OP, lost 7 Oct. 1952
Gertie	USMC OP, abandoned June 1952
Ginger/Hill 100 (CT022044)	USMC squad OP
Green/Ingrid	See Ingrid
Harlow (CT051065)	CCF hill connected to Kumgok
Hedy/Yellow/Hill 124 (CT014036)	USMC OP, 2 squads
Hedy Gate (CT150032)	Trail to Hedy from MLR
Hilda/Queen (CT091099)	USMC OP, lost 11 Aug. 1952
Honker Bridge (CS067953)	Bridge over Imjin
Hook/Point Fox (CT103104)	Salient on MLR
Horseshoe (BT989031)	Approach to Hill 90
Ingrid/Green/Hill 64A (CT011030)	USMC 2 squad OP
Irene/Rome/Nan/Hill 41 (CT097103)	USMC OP, lost 17 Aug. 1952

Place Name	Comments
Island (BT976028)	Terrain feature vicinity OP-2
Little Frisco (CT088093)	USMC OP
Jersey Ridge (CT084087)	CCF trench line
Jill/Pete/Seattle	See Seattle
Kate/Hill 128 (BT999021)	USMC 2 squad OP
Kirby (CT058067)	Hill vicinity Ungok
Kumgok/Hill 35A (CT050067)	CCF-held OP
Libby Bridge	Across Imjin, formerly X-Ray
Little Rock (CT084086)	CCF-held hill
London	CCF hill
Marilyn/Hill 92 (BT992015)	USMC plt. OP
Molar (BT963028)	Hill vicinity OP2
Nellie	USMC OP abandoned June 1952
New Bunker/Hill 122A	Bunker Hill relocated
New York	CCF hill
No Name Ridge (BT977028)	Hill vicinity OP-2, possibly Gray Rock
Omaha/Hill 161 (CT090108)	CCF hill
Paris	CCF hill
Pentagon (CT013036)	South slope of Hedy
Pete	Name change to Jill (July 1952)
Pheasant (CT113113)	Hill mass vicinity of Hook
Point Fox/see the Hook	
Queen/Hilda	Name change (July 1952)
Red Hill/Hill 33B (CT056068)	
Reno/Yoke/Hill 25/Bruce/Hill 148 (CT064086)	USMC OP approx. 40 men, lost Mar. 1953
Reno Block/Elko/Hill 47 (CT068079)	Reno support. plt. +
Rome (CT096104)	CCF hill

Place Name	Comments
Ronson/Hill 41 (CT101102)	USMC squad OP
Rose Bowl/Stadium (BT958013)	Terrain feature
Royal	USMC OP abandoned June 1952
Samichon River	Boundary between USMC & Br. CW Div.
Samoa/Esther	See Esther
Seattle/Jill (CT100103)	USMC fire team OP, lost 6 Oct. 1952
76 Alley (CT093080)	Road east of East Berlin
Siberia/Hill 58A (CT023048)	USMC squad OP, lost 9 Aug. 1952
Spoonbill Bridge (CS088972)	Bridge across Imjin River
Stadium/Rose Bowl (BT958013)	Terrain feature vicinity OP-1
Star/Hill 132 (BT986017)	Hill vicinity OP-2
Stromboli/Ava/Hill 48A (CT045059)	USMC squad outpost
Three Fingers/Hill 80 (BT985032)	CCF hill, vicinity COP-2
Toms Thumb (CT076082)	Vicinity Vegas
Toothache/COP-2A	
Toryum	Burnt village in right sector, Bn. Boundary
Tumae-Ri Ridge/Hill 40D (CT45073)	CCF–held, vicinity Hill 104
Ungok/Hill 31 (CT059072)	Major CCF hill mass w/3 fingers, 31A, 31B, 31C
Vegas/Clarence/Digger/Hill 21 (CT074078)	OP-5 in Mar. 1952 USMC OP, lost by Turks June 1953
Verdun (CT132095)	USMC OP, abutting British Div.
"W" (CT014037)	Opposite Fan on Hedy/Bunker
Warsaw/Hill 137 (CT104108)	USMC 2 squad OP

Place Name	Comments
White (Hill 90) (BT987024)	OP until lost
Widgeon Bridge (CT151034)	Bridge across Imjin
William/COP-3 (BT987043)	Abandoned, early 1952
X-Ray	USMC OP, abandoned June 1952
X-Ray Bridge (CS096013)	Bridge across Imjin
Yellow	(Early name for Hedy)
Yoke (CT069079)	USMC OP, June 1952 (early name for Reno)
Yoke/Hill 159 (BT001037), 2d hill, same name	CCF hill near corridor
Yongji-Ri (103886)	1st Marine Div. CP

Cross-Reference by Hill Number

Number	Name	Comments
13	Gary/Frisco	See Gary
15	Felix/Detroit	USMC OP
19	Berlin	
19A	East Berlin	
21	Vegas	
21B	(CT071082)	CCF-held
23	(CT072087)	CCF-held
25	Reno/Bruce (CT068079)	
25A	Hill 150 (CT069083)	CCF-held
27	Allen/Carson	
29	(CT063085)	CCF-held
31	KMC OP	
31	Ungok (CT059072)	Major CCF
31A	Part of Ungok (CT058072)	
31B	Part of Ungok (CT061070)	
31C	Part of Ungok (CT059070)	
33	KMC OP	
33B	Red Hill (CT056068)	
35	(CT049067)	CCF-held hill
35A	Kumgok (CT052064)	CCF-held
36	KMC OP	
37	COP-67/COP-37	KMC OP
37	(BS964983)	CCF OP
39	KMC OP	
40A	Ava/Hill48A (CT044059)	
40D	Tumae-Ri (CT045073)	CCF-held
41	Ronson (CT100102)	
41	Irene (CT097103)	USMC OP
44	(CT034057)	OP-4
45	(CT063085)	CCF-held
47	Elko	

Number	Name	Comments
48A	Stromboli/Ava/Hill40A (CT044059)	USMC OP
50A	Corrine	USMC OP, 21 men
51	KMC OP	Co. size
52	Dagmar (CT035050)	USMC OP, 1 off./27 men
56A	Samoa/Esther (CT029048)	USMC OP, 18 men
57A	(CT080085)	CCF-held
58A	Siberia (CT023048)	USMC squad OP
64	(CT007032)	CCF-held, vicinity Ingrid
64A	Ingrid (CT011030)	See Ingrid
66	Hill 123 (CT006040)	CCF OP, opposed Bunker
67	Arrowhead (CT063080)	CCF-held
70	Claw (BT995035)	CCF outpost
70A	Boot (997030)	CCF outpost
80	3 Fingers (BT983032)	CCF-held (vicinity OP-2)
82	CCF MG position (BT975035)	Vicinity 134
84	COP-2	USMC OP, Reinf. Co.
86	COP-1 (BT975012)	KMC OP, 27 men
87	(BS955930)	CCF-held
88	OP Blue (BT996026)	CCF-held
90	White (BT986024)	CCF-held
92	Marilyn (BT992015	USMC OP, 1 off./29 men
95	(BS964948)	Chinese gun position
98	(CT093097)	CCF-held
100	Ginger	USMC OP, 16 men
101	CCF-held	
104	CCF-held (CT044065)	850 yd. N of Stromboli
110	Felix	
111	MLR (CT098094)	Used in Berlin fighting
114	(CT029050)	CCF-held
116	(CT025052)	No-man's-land, N of Siberia
118	(CT17044)	CCF hill vicinity Hedy

Number	Name	Comments
119	Boulder City/MLR (CT084078)	Used in Berlin fighting
120	OP-4 (CT020050)	CCF-held
122	Bunker Hill (CT017046)	CCF until 11 Aug. 1952, USMC OP, 1 off./31 men
122A	New Bunker (CT016040)	Relocated Bunker Hill, same ridge
123	Hill 66 (CT006040)	CCF-held, opposed Bunker
124	Hedy (CT013036)	Extension of Bunker, USMC OP, 1 off./17 men
125	(CT081087)	CCF hill, N of Berlin
126	(CT089065)	High point, rear of MLR
128	Kate (BT998021)	USMC OP, 1 off./30 men
132	Star (BT986017)	Between OP-2 and Marilyn
133	(CT07091)	Chinese used (July 1952)
134	(BT978032)	CCF-held, between Three Fingers and Hill 67
139	CCF-held (CT080085)	Used in Berlin fighting
140	CCF-held	
146	USMC MLR	Right sector near the Hook
144	(CT029051)	CCF hill vicinity Dagmar
148	Bruce	
150	Same as 25A (CT069085)	CCF-held
153	(CT073082)	CCF-held, N of Vegas
155	Prominent hill on KMC MLR	
155	Same as 167 (CT071082)	CCF-held
157	Warsaw (CT105107)	USMC OP
159	Yoke/Hill 159 (BT001037)	Major CCF OP, 5 mi. N of Imjin
161	Omaha (CT090108)	CCF-held, about 1 May 1952
163	(CT090107)	CCF-held
167	Same as 155	

Number	Name	Comments
185	(CT098131)	CCF-held, near the Hook
190	Elmer (CT083093)	
190.5	Same as 191 (CT073088)	CCF-held in Aug. 1952
191	Same as 190.5	
201	MLR (CT020039)	High point S of Bunker Hill
225	Pork Chop Hill	U.S. Army–held
229	Paehok (CT014017)	USMC high ground behind MLR, tank & artillery CP
236	Taedok-san	CCF high ground opposing 229
266	Old Baldy	U.S. Army–held
355	Little Gibraltar	U.S. Army–held (2d Div. in 1952)

NOTES

INTRODUCTION
1. James, *Refighting the Last War,* 71.
2. Rees, *Korea,* 300.
3. Marshall, *World War I,* 137.

CHAPTER 1
1. Command Diary, 3d Battalion, 5th Marines, Mar. 1952, 11.
2. Trainor, "Fighting in Forgotten War," 65.
3. Meid and Yingling, *Marine Operations in Korea,* 508.
4. The Korean Marine Corps was trained and supplied by the U.S. Marines. A KMC regiment was assigned the left sector of the Jamestown Line.
5. Matthias, *Korean War,* 82.
6. Meid and Yingling, *Marine Operations in Korea,* 22.
7. Stan Rauh, Col., USMC (Ret.), letter to the author, 4 July 1997.
8. Command Diary, 3d Battalion, 5th Marines, Apr. 1952, 1.
9. Command Diary, Special Action Report, 3d Battalion, 5th Marines, 8 Apr. 1952, 5.
10. Command Diary, 3d Battalion, 1st Marines, Apr. 1952, 5.
11. Quoted in Meid and Yingling, *Marine Operations in Korea,* 20.
12. Quoted in Byrne and Pendas, *Bloody George,* 5.
13. Quoted in ibid, 6.

CHAPTER 2
1. Command Diary, 1st Marine Division Appendix, June 1952.
2. Quoted in Byrne and Pendas, *Bloody George,* 9.
3. Quoted in ibid, 7.
4. Quoted in ibid, 9.
5. Peterson, *Short Straw,* 241.
6. Hicks, "U.S. Marine Operations," 152.
7. Maj. Gilbert R. Hershey, USMC, 30 Oct. 1960, letter quoted in ibid.
8. Batterton, "Random Notes, 31.
9. Ibid.

10. Ibid.

11. John J. O'Hagan, letter to the author, 9 Dec. 1996.

12. Ibid.

13. Command Diary, 1st Battalion, 1st Marines, Psychological Warfare Summary, May 1952.

14. O'Hagan, letter to author.

15. Don McClure, letter to the author, 13 Nov. 1997.

16. Quoted in Matthias, *Korean War,* 57.

17. O'Hagan, letter to author.

18. Matthias, *Korean War,* 96.

19. Stan Rauh, letter to the author, 4 July 1997.

20. Lee Cook, letter to the author, 2 Apr. 1997.

CHAPTER 3

1. John R. Alexander, letter to the author, 14 Jan. 1998.

2. Ibid. Except for the narrative of Alexander, this section has been adapted from a taped letter to the author by Chris Sarno, 2 Feb. 1995.

3. Meid and Yingling, *Marine Operations in Korea,* 24.

4. See ibid., 77, for a comprehensive report of this action.

5. Command Diary, 1st Battalion, 5th Marines, May 1952, 12.

6. Nicholson, "Night Raid," 33.

7. Command Diary, 1st Battalion, 1st Marines, May 1952, Special Report, 5.

8. Ibid.

CHAPTER 4

1. Vincent Walsh, letter to the author, Dec. 1997.

2. Matthias, *Korean War,* 92.

3. Lee Cook, letter to the author, 2 Apr. 1997.

4. Command Diary, 2d Battalion, 5th Marines, June 1952, 13.

5. Meid and Yingling, *Marine Operations in Korea,* 89.

6. Command Diary, 5th Marines, June 1952, 15.

7. Berry, *Hey, Mac,* 278.

CHAPTER 5

1. Command Diary, 7th Marines, July 1952, 2.

2. Command Diary, 3d Battalion, 7th Marines, July 1952, 2.

3. Watson, "Imjin War," 105–16. This is an unpublished memoir.

4. Matthias, *Korean War,* 34.

5. Ibid, 36.

6. Stan Rauh, letter to the author.

CHAPTER 6

1. Command Diary, 1st Marines, August 1952, 1.

2. Fleming, "Liberty!" 139.

3. Keene, "Battles for Bunker Hill," 50.
4. This is an excellent example of the consequences of a thinly staffed James-town Line. The company designated to defend this particular sector, Easy Company, could only defend the MLR and its outposts. It did not have the strength to mount an offensive attack designed to retake a lost outpost. Reinforcements from reserve had to be used for this purpose and to replace the now decimated Easy Company. This movement, of course, drew from the reserve capability to stop a breakthrough. Typically, the entire outpost war was fought in this manner—robbing Peter to pay Paul and hoping that the bill never came due.
5. Command Diary, 2d Battalion, 1st Marines, Aug. 1952, 5.
6. Williamson, *Dearest Buckie,* 29.
7. Peterson, *Short Straw,* 259.
8. Hicks, "U.S. Marine Operations," 64.
9. Tanks are normally equipped with headlights to illuminate their way in the dark. Unfortunately they are bolted onto the exterior of the vehicle and are among the first items to be blown off or damaged in service. Few tanks in Korea had operational headlights.
10. "Personal interviews with Lt. Col. Gerard T. Armitage, USMC, August 15, 29, 1961." Armitage, interviews by, as quoted in Hicks, "U.S. Marine Operations," 66.
11. Frank Walden, telephone interview by author, 10 Aug. 1996.
12. Quoted in Meid and Yingling, *Marine Operations in Korea,* 117.
13. Peterson, *Short Straw,* 262.
14. A ripple is a cluster of 4.5-inch rockets arranged in four banks of six, total-ing twenty-four projectiles in all. In this case, nine ripples would equal 216 rockets. Each ripple, fired in less than a minute, creates a devastating series of impacts when it arrives on target.
15. Gus Mendez, letter to the author, Oct. 1997.
16. Watson, "Imjin War," 160–85.
17. Don McClure, letter to the author, 13 Nov. 1997.
18. Meid and Yingling, *Marine Operations in Korea,* 126.
19. Murphy, *Korean War Heroes,* 234.
20. Hicks, "U.S. Marine Operations," 76.
21. Williamson, *Dearest Buckie,* 32.
22. McClure letter to the author.
23. Hicks, "U.S. Marine Operations," 78.
24. Command Diary, 1st Marine Division, Aug. 1952, 5.
25. Condensed from Meid and Yingling, *Marine Operations in Korea,* 138.
26. Peterson, *Short Straw,* 292.

CHAPTER 7
1. Howard Matthias, letter to the author, 27 Sept. 1996.
2. Much of this section is adapted from Tom Lavin, letter to John Lee, Jr. (who

was investigating the death of his brother, Lawrence Lee, on Outpost Irene), 16 Feb. 1997. All quotations in this chapter come from Lavin's letter, unless noted otherwise. Used with permission.

3. The phenomenon of "seeing" a mortar round fall is not unusual. Many men in combat have reported similar sightings.

4. Quoted in Williamson, *Dearest Buckie,* 33.

5. Command Diary, 2d Battalion, 5th Marines, Aug. 1952, 14.

CHAPTER 8

1. Hicks, "U.S. Marine Operations," 100.

2. Adapted from Murphy, *Korean War Heroes,* 239, and from Lyons, "In the Highest Tradition." Readers of Marine Corps history will note the strong similarity between McLaughlin's actions in 1952 and those of Sgt. John Basilone on Guadalcanal in 1942.

3. Saluzzi, *Red Blood . . . Purple Heart,* 130.

4. Quoted in Byrne and Pendas, *Bloody George,* 13.

5. Watson, "Imjin War," 211.

6. Matthias, *Korean War,* 141.

7. Stan Rauh, letter to the author.

8. Glen ("Tom") Dye, audiotape to the author, n.d.

9. Watson, "Imjin War," 249.

10. Command Diary, 1st Tank Battalion, Sept. 1952, 2.

11. Chuck Burrill, interview with author, Oct. 1995.

12. Arthur Lipper, letter home, 16 Nov. 1952. Used with permission.

13. Table of Organization, K-1238 (War), Tank Battalion, Marine Division, Fleet Marine Force [FMF], 15 July 1949.

14. Command Diary, 1st Tank Battalion, Sept 1952, 4.

CHAPTER 9

1. Keith Yarnell, letter to Richard Suarez, Feb. 1993. Used with permission.

2. Watson, "Imjin War," 260.

3. Command Diary, 7th Marines, Oct. 1952, 4.

4. Harry Martucci, tape recording to the author, Nov. 1997.

5. Bob Thornton, letter to the author, 31 July 1998.

6. Don McClure, letter to the author, 13 Nov. 1997.

7. Watson, "Imjin War," 272.

8. Henry Conway, letter to William Watson, 1 Feb. 1993. Used with permission.

9. Howard Davenport, letter to the author, 3 Mar. 1997.

10. Williamson, *Dearest Buckie,* 59.

11. Lee Cook, letter to the author, 29 Jan. 1997.

12. Andy Frey, letter to the author, 20 May 1997.

13. Command Diary, 1st Marines, Oct. 1952, 2.

14. Geer, *Reckless Pride,* 126.

15. See Meid and Yingling, *Marine Operations in Korea*, 40, for a discussion of Operation Pronto and Leapfrog in Apr. 1952.
16. Command Diary, 1st Marine Division, Oct. 1952, 5.

CHAPTER 10

1. Quoted in Searls, "How It Was."
2. Quoted in Heinl, "Notes on 7th Marines Action," 1.
3. Meid and Yingling, *Marine Operations in Korea*, 187.
4. Fred McLaughlin, taped letter to the author, Oct. 1997.
5. Ibid.
6. Heinl, "Notes on 7th Marines Action," 2.
7. Mahoney, *Vignettes/Biographies*, V-29.
8. Quoted in Meid and Yingling, *Marine Operations in Korea*, 191.
9. Heinl, "Notes on 7th Marines Action," 2.
10. Command Diary, 7th Marines, Summary of Action Report, Oct. 1952, 1.
11. Hicks, "U.S. Marine Operations," 110.
12. Quoted in Searls, "How It Was," 1.
13. Quoted in ibid, 2.
14. Based on Saluzzi, *Red Blood . . . Purple Hearts*, 137.
15. Heinl, "Notes on 7th Marines Action," 4.
16. McLaughlin, taped letter to author.
17. Stan Rauh letter to the author, 4 July 1997.
18. Ibid.
19. Berry, *Hey, Mac*, 285.
20. McLaughlin, taped letter to author.
21. Heinl, "Notes on 7th Marines Action," 2.
22. Hermes, *Truce Tent*, 354.
23. Richard Stone, letter to the author, 17 July 1997.

CHAPTER 11

1. Command Diary, 1st Battalion, 5th Marines, Nov. 1952, 11.
2. Command Diary, 1st Tank Battalion, Special Report, "Operation Bunker," Nov. 1952.
3. A tank-dozer is an armored bulldozer, an M-46 gun tank equipped with a hydraulically operated blade. The blade mechanism, while exposed, is encased in armor to enable its use under fire.
4. See Command Diary, 1st Tank Battalion and 1st Battalion, 5th Marines, Nov. 1952. See also Fugate, "Operation Lady," 30.
5. This section adapted from Jordan, "Tank Patrol," 16.
6. Byrne and Pendas, *Bloody George*, 25.
7. Williamson, *Dearest Buckie*, 175.
8. Command Diary, 2d Battalion, 1st Marines, Nov. 1952, 16.

CHAPTER 12

1. Saluzzi, *Red Blood . . . Purple Hearts,* 143.
2. Grease gun refers to the .45–caliber M-3 submachine gun, a short-barreled weapon made largely of stamped metal parts. Its cylindrical body gave it the appearance of an automotive grease gun.
3. Howard Davenport, letter to the author, 19 Feb. 1994.
4. Lipper, letter home, 20 Dec. 1952.
5. Sherrod, "Something's Got to Give," 30.
6. Ibid.
7. Ibid.
8. Hunt Kerrigan was a most unusual Marine. Raised in a partrician family in the eastern United States, he rejected privilege to enlist in the Marine Corps at age seventeen. Nevertheless, he retained a strong sense of noblesse oblige and became an anonymous philanthropist to many enlisted Marines. Once, after being released from Yokosuka Naval Hospital in Japan (where wounded Marines were sent from Korea), Kerrigan, then a staff sergeant, left a number of signed blank checks with the Marine guard detachment. With the checks was a list of enlisted Marines from his platoon in Korea. A check was to be given to any Marine on the list if he became hospitalized, so that he could enjoy a free liberty in Japan. Another time, when he was the captain in charge of the Marine liaison detachment at Oakland Naval Hospital in California, Kerrigan secretly paid for most of the funeral expenses for a gunnery sergeant's daughter. Kerrigan was medically retired from the Marine Corps in 1962, but he tried unsuccessfully to return several times. He never adjusted well to civilian life. Kerrigan died in 1993.
9. Command Diary, 1st Battalion, 5th Marines, Dec. 1952.
10. Matthias, *Korean War,* 202.
11. Quoted in Byrne and Pendas, *Bloody George,* 18.
12. Quoted in ibid., 19.
13. Ibid.
14. Command Diary, 1st Tank Battalion, "Report of Use of Tank Fighting Light to Support an Infantry Raid," Dec. 1952.
15. Command Diary, 2d Battalion, 1st Marines, Dec. 1952, App. IV.
16. Ibid.

CHAPTER 13

1. Quoted in Joy, *How Communists Negotiate,* 156.
2. Command Diary, 1st Tank Battalion, Special Report, "Armored Personnel Carriers," Nov. 1952.
3. Command Diary, 2d Battalion, 5th Marines, Nov. 1952, 6.
4. Command Diary, 1st Battalion, 5th Marines, Nov. 1952, 20.

BIBLIOGRAPHY

Batterton, Lt. Col. R. J., Jr., USMC. "Random Notes on Korea," *Marine Corps Gazette,* November 1955, 28–34.

Berry, Henry. *Hey, Mac, Where Ya Been?* New York: St. Martin's Press, 1988.

Byrne, James, and G. Pendas, Jr., eds. *Bloody George,* vol. 4 of *Western Front Korea, 1952–53.* George 3/1 Association, 1991.

Command Diaries and Special Action Reports, U.S. Marine Corps, National Archives, viewing arranged by the Marine Corps Historical Center, Washington Navy Yard, Washington, D.C.:

> 1st Marine Division, Command Diaries, March 1952 to December 1952
>
> 1st Marine Regiment, Command Diaries, March 1952 to December 1952
>
> 5th Marine Regiment, Command Diaries, March 1952 to December 1952
>
> 7th Marine Regiment, Command Diaries, March 1952 to December 1952
>
> 1st Battalion, 1st Marines, Command Diaries, March 1952 to December 1952
>
> 2d Battalion, 1st Marines, Command Diaries, March 1952 to December 1952
>
> 3d Battalion, 1st Marines, Command Diaries, March 1952 to December 1952
>
> 1st Battalion, 5th Marines, Command Diaries, March 1952 to December 1952
>
> 2d Battalion, 5th Marines, Command Diaries, March 1952 to December 1952
>
> 3d Battalion, 5th Marines, Command Diaries, March 1952 to December 1952

1st Battalion, 7th Marines, Command Diaries, March 1952 to December 1952

2d Battalion, 7th Marines, Command Diaries, March 1952 to December 1952

3d Battalion, 7th Marines, Command Diaries, March 1952 to December 1952

1st Amphibian Tractor Battalion, Command Diaries, March 1952 to November 1952

1st Tank Battalion, Command Diaries, March 1952 to November 1952

Headquarters Battalion, 1st Marine Division, March 1952 to December 1952

Department of the Army. *Handbook on the Chinese Communist Army,* Pamphlet No. 30-51, September 1952. Washington, D.C.: Department of the Army.

Fleming, Thomas. *Liberty! The American Revolution.* New York: Viking, 1997.

Fugate, M/Sgt. Robert, USMC. "Operation Lady," *Leatherneck,* March 1953, 30–32.

Gannon, R. A. *The Laughter and the Tears.* Kearney, Nebr.: Morris Publishing, 1997.

Geer, Lt. Col. Andrew. *Reckless Pride of the Marines.* New York: E. P. Dutton & Co., 1955.

Heinl, Col. Robert Debs, Jr. *Dictionary of Military and Naval Quotations.* Annapolis, Md.: Naval Institute Press, 1966.

————. "Notes on 7th Marines Action ('The Hook'), 26–27 October 1952," memorandum to Director of Marine Corps History, 28 Oct. 1952.

Hermes, Walter G. *Truce Tent and Fighting Front,* Washington, D.C.: Office of the Chief of Military History, U.S. Army, 1966.

Hicks, Lt. Col. Norman W. "U.S Marine Operations in Korea 1952–1953 with Special Emphasis on Outpost Warfare." Master's thesis, University of Maryland, 1962.

James, D. Clayton, with Anne Sharp Wells. *Refighting the Last War, Command and Crisis in Korea 1950–1953.* New York: Free Press, 1993.

Jordan, S/Sgt. Curtis W. "Tank Patrol," *Leatherneck,* September 1952, 16.

Joy, C. Turner, VADM, USN. *How Communists Negotiate.* New York: MacMillan, 1955.

Keene, R. R. "The Battles for Bunker Hill," *Leatherneck,* August 1992, 49–53.

Knox, Donald. *The Korean War, Uncertain Victory.* New York: Harcourt, Brace, Jovanovich, 1988.

Lyons, R. D. "In the Highest Tradition . . . Alford Lee McLaughlin," *Leatherneck,* February 1954, 37–79.

Mahoney, Walter. Vignettes/Biographies. Release No. 2 (unpublished paper), 26 Dec. 1994.

Marshall, Brig. Gen. S. L. A. *World War I.* Boston: Houghton Mifflin, 1964.

Matthias, Howard, *The Korean War: Reflections of a Young Combat Platoon Leader.* Tallahassee, Fla.: Father and Son Publishing, 1995.

Meid, Lt. Col. Pat, USMCR, and Maj. James M. Yingling, USMC. *Operations in West Korea,* vol. V of *Marine Operations in Korea 1950–1953.* Washington, D.C.: Historical Division, Headquarters, U.S. Marine Corps, 1972.

Montross, Lynn, Maj. Hubard D. Kuokka, USMC, and Maj. Norman W. Hicks, USMC. *The East-Central Front,* vol. IV of *U.S. Marine Operations in Korea, 1950–1953.* Washington, D.C.: Historical Branch, Headquarters U.S. Marine Corps, 1962.

Murphy, Edward F. *Korean War Heroes,* Novato, Calif.: Presidio Press, 1992.

Nicholson, Maj. Dennis D., Jr. "Night Raid on Hill 67," *Marine Corps Gazette,* Sept. 1953, 28–35.

Peterson, Capt. Bernard W., USMCR (Ret.). *Short Straw, Memoirs of Korea.* Scottsdale, Ariz.: Chuckwalla Publishing, 1996.

Rees, David. *Korea: The Limited War.* New York: St. Martin's Press, 1964.

Saluzzi, Joseph A. *Red Blood . . . Purple Hearts, the Marines in the Korean War.* Owings Mills, Md.: Watermark Press, 1989.

Searls, Lt. Hebry, USN. "How It Was on the Hook." Public Information Office [PIO] news release, Headquarters, Commander, Naval Forces Far East [HQCOMNAVFE], December 3, 1952.

Sherrod, Robert. "Something's Got to Give in Korea," *Saturday Evening Post,* February 21, 1953.

Summers, Col. Harry G., Jr. *Korean War Almanac.* New York: Facts on File, 1990.

Trainor, Lt. Gen. Bernard E., USMC (Ret.). "On Fighting in a Forgotten War," *Marine Corps Gazette,* August 1998, 64–69.

Watson, William A. "The Imjin War," (unpublished memoir), 1989.

Williamson, Col. John I., USMC (Ret.). *Dearest Buckie, A Marine's Korean War Memoir.* Austin, Tex.: R. J. Speights, 1989.

INTERVIEWS AND LETTERS

Alexander, S/Sgt. John R., Ohio
Cook, Lt. Lee, Maryland
Conway, Lt. Henry, Maryland
Davenport, Pfc. Howard, Texas
Dye, Sgt. Glenn, Florida
Frey, Pfc. Andrew, Illinois
Hall, Cpl. Robert, New York
Lavin, Cpl. Tom, Tennessee
Lipper, Sgt. Arthur III, California
Martucci, Sgt. Harry, Connecticut
Matthias, Lt. Howard, Arizona
McClure, Pfc. Don, Washington
McLaughlin, Capt. Fred, North Carolina
Mendez, Pfc. Gus, California
O'Hagan, Sgt. John J., Illinois
Rauh, Lt. Stanly H., California
Sarno, Sgt. Chris, Massachusetts
Stone, Lt. Richard W., Connecticut
Thornton, Sgt. Robert J., New Mexico
Walden, Pfc. Frank, California
Walsh, 1st Lt. Vincent, California
Yarnell, Sgt. Keith, Indiana

ACKNOWLEDGMENTS

The first people to be acknowledged are all of the men who fought the Outpost War in Korea forty-seven years ago. I salute you.

Those representative few whom I contacted in my quest for material are owed a special thanks. Without them, the book could not have been written. These men were willing to share their memories, thoughts, and fears so that others can relate to those experiences and, in many cases, come to grips with their own feelings. War leaves us all scarred, some more severely than others. Veterans of the Korean War have done a better job of masking their scars.

Men who fought in Korea had a different attitude than veterans of later wars. More like those of the World War II generation, they were often proud of their service as they experienced a personal share of history. Yet, the Korean War was different from World War II—it had no clear-cut win or loss. No surrender. It just happened and then seemed to fade into obscurity, perhaps recorded on only half a page in a high school history book. It was forgotten or, worse yet, ignored—as were the men who fought there.

Researching this work has been a special privilege. In the process of gathering material, I have met literally hundreds of Marines. We have written letters, talked on the telephone, and visited in each other's homes. Our families have become acquainted, and I am proud to say we are friends.

Over my research period of nine years, many people have rendered extraordinary help and assistance: My wife Marj, who was always there with encouragement for my efforts and patience with the things that I ignored around the house; the staff at the Marine Corps Historical Center in Washington D.C., particularly Archivist Fred Graboske, and the active-duty Marines who shuttled records back and forth from the National Archives; Mrs. Christine Weiss, my daughter and research assistant, who helped with material at the UCLA Library, the National Archives, and the Marine Corps Historical Center; and Jim Byrne, historian of the George 3/1 Association, whose editing, advice, arguments, and support were so helpful in bringing this work to fruition.

Finally, among all contributors, there is one I think that readers will acknowledge stands out. Bill Watson (2d Lt. William A. Watson of Kentucky) wrote a truly outstanding memoir of his Marine Corps experience in the 10th Special Basic Class and Korea, from which I have liberally quoted. It is unfortunate that Bill has no intention of publishing his work. It would make a valuable contribution to the history of the period. As it stands I offer him special thanks for allowing me the privilege of using select excerpts.

ABOUT THE AUTHOR

Lee Ballenger enlisted in the Marine Corps in 1951 at age seventeen. In January 1953, he arrived in Korea, where he served with the 1st Division Reconnaissance Company and the 1st Tank Battalion. He was discharged in 1957 as a sergeant. A retired police officer, he lives in southern California. He is currently at work on a sequel to cover Marine Corps operations in 1953. This is his first book.

INDEX

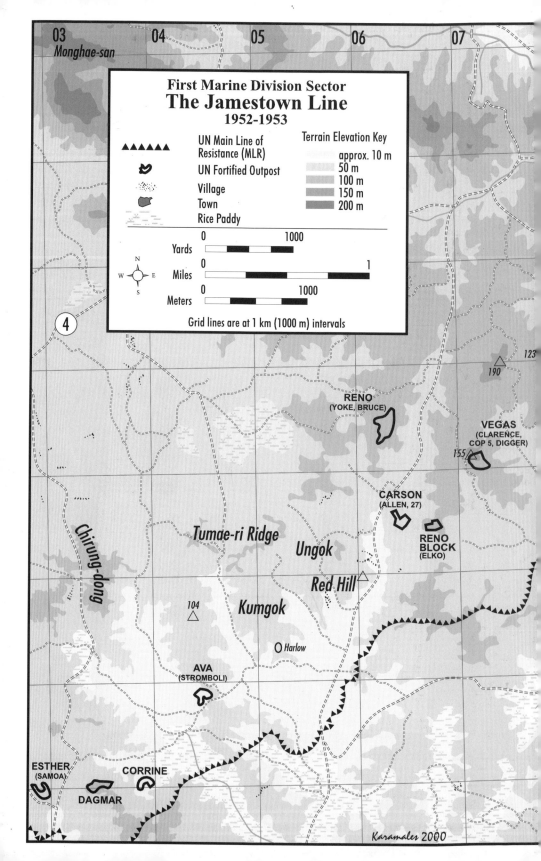

First Marine Division Sector
The Jamestown Line
1952-1953

▲▲▲▲▲▲▲ UN Main Line of
Resistance (MLR)

UN Fortified Outpost

Village

Town

Rice Paddy

Terrain Elevation Key

approx. 10 m
50 m
100 m
150 m
200 m

Yards   0 — 1000

Miles   0 — 1

Meters 0 — 1000

N W E S

Grid lines are at 1 km (1000 m) intervals

03 04 05 06 07

Monghae-san

④

Chirung-dong

Tumae-ri Ridge

Ungok

Red Hill △

104 △ Kumgok

○ Harlow

AVA
(STROMBOLI)

ESTHER
(SAMOA)

CORRINE

DAGMAR

RENO
(YOKE, BRUCE)

VEGAS
(CLARENCE,
COP 5, DIGGER)

155 △

CARSON
(ALLEN, 27)

RENO
BLOCK
(ELKO)

123 △
190

Karamales 2000